Legend of the Five Rings

The Way of the Wolf

"You call me a masterless man. You are wrong. I am my own master."
– Dairya

Credits

WRITTEN BY RICH WULF AND SHAWN CARMAN

ADDITIONAL MATERIAL BY REE SOESBEE

GAME SYSTEM BY DAVID WILLIAMS AND JOHN WICK

COVER ARTWORK: CARL FRANK

INTERIOR ARTWORK: CARL FRANK, EDWARD JAMES KRINGS AND DANIEL MOENSTER

MAP OF NANASHI MURA: DANIEL MOENSTER

ARTWORK PREPRESS: BRENDON GOODYEAR

ART DIRECTOR: JIM PINTO

LINE EDITOR: D.J. TRINDLE

EDITING: JANICE SELLARS, D.J. TRINDLE

INTERIOR LAYOUT: STEVE HOUGH

Rich would like to thank…

Ree and D.J. for giving me this chance, and all the other ronin who helped me get here – Mom, Dom, and all my friends at Rokugan 2000. Oh yeah, and Morito Tokei, the character who brought me to Rokugan. If not for him, I'd probably be an astronomer right now. Whew!

Ree would like to thank the Legion of the Wolf for the huge banner that graces her office wall.

Table of Contents

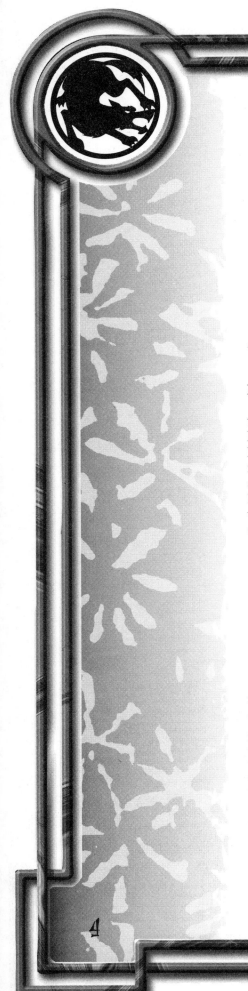

Prologue

This book takes place two years after the Scorpion Clan Coup...

It had been three days since life as he knew it had ended.

Tzurui turned back to look at the castle a final time. Though its walls were intact, Shiro Nanbu had fallen. Not a blow had been struck in anger. No arrow had been loosed. No war had been fought, but his family was no more. The holdings and lands of the Nanbu had been seized by the Emperor. The banners that once hung upon the walls had been removed. He turned toward the east road and began his journey.

Truthfully, the Nanbu had never been an important family. Never numbering more than a dozen samurai, they were insignificant in the greater political schemes of the Emerald Empire. Most samurai did not even know of their existence. Even their masters, the Soshi, considered them minor vassals. After the fall of the Scorpion the Imperial Legions had run rampant across the Empire hunting Scorpion traitors. Even then, it had taken quite some time for anyone to recall the Nanbu family's existence.

The Nanbu had nothing to do with Shoju's coup; they were so unimportant they had not been considered to participate. The Nanbu knew it made no difference. The Legions would come

one day, and they would bring the Emperor's justice with them. The Nanbu were living on borrowed time and when Tzurui looked upon the face of Tsuchiya, his uncle and daimyo, he could see the dead resignation that lay there.

When the Imperial Legions arrived, Tzurui's heart filled with fear. He had never seen real combat. The Nanbu bushi were few and the Legion were, well, a Legion. There was no chance for survival, only a chance to die with honor. All of Tzurui's life he had been told that an honorable death was the greatest fate a samurai could ask for, but to look into the eyes of little Kochohime, to know he would never live to see his daughter grow to become a woman, he was no longer certain. He steeled himself for the inevitable and promised that, if nothing else, they would not take his daughter.

It was then that Nanbu Tsuchiya stepped out of the gates to meet the Legion. Tzurui would never forget that moment. His uncle's clear, certain gaze would ever be pressed into his memory. It was the bravest thing he had seen in his life. Some of the other bushi attempted to step forth and join Tsuchiya, but the old samurai turned with a quiet smile and forbade them. Tzurui had not moved to join his master. It hurt his heart to remember.

The Imperial herald turned his horse about and fixed an angry gaze on the figure that had stepped out of the castle gates. An Imperial archer in the front ranks even drew his bow, preparing to slay the daimyo where he stood.

"I am Tsuchiya, daimyo of Shiro Nanbu," Tsuchiya said clearly, bowing his head.

"We come to determine your loyalties, Soshi," the legionnaire announced. Tsuchiya said nothing. He simply fell to his knees, pressing his face to the earth. "I am no Soshi. My people had no part in the Coup."

"Easy to say," the soldier retorted. "Perhaps you should have considered your love for peace before Otosan Uchi fell." The soldier's eyes gleamed with menace. Tzurui knew, they all knew, their fates hinged upon the next few moments.

"The fault is my own," Tsuchiya replied calmly. He sat back upon his heels, but kept his eyes downcast. "Punish not a man's family for his crimes. I am ready to prove my sincerity." Tsuchiya moved his arm slightly to reveal the sword he wore. He wore only the wakizashi, and his kimono was a stark white.

The color of death. The blade of seppuku.

The herald seemed to hesitate. "You shall have your chance, Tsuchiya-san," said a deep voice from the midst of the ranks. A soldier in brilliant golden armor rode forward. The commander of the Legion. "I am Matsu Chokoku," the soldier said, "and I would be your second."

Tsuchiya bowed his head again. The Lion was doing him a great honor to permit his request, much less to participate. Tsuchiya recognized his gesture gratefully. He rose as two soldiers and a shugenja approached to lead him away.

The ceremony had gone swiftly. Only a handful of family members and Chokoku's personal guard were allowed to observe the final moments. Tzurui was among them, though he did not wish to watch his uncle die. To his credit, Tsuchiya did not cry out as he drew the blade across his belly. His wife let no grief mar her face.

Chokoku drew his katana and held the blade high, pausing for the briefest moment to let his eyes flicker across the gathered family members. A final stroke, and the honor of the Nanbu was clean.

Tzurui now stood on the road outside what had once been Shiro Nanbu. Chokoku had spared the family and their retainers, but his orders were clear. The holdings of the family were to be seized, and the castle itself was to become a garrison. As for the remaining Nanbu, they were now ronin, samurai with no masters. What would become of them? It was no longer Chokoku's concern so long as they left the province as ordered. No doubt most would fall to petty crime. The life of a ronin was difficult and banditry came easily to trained bushi.

Tzurui gritted his teeth in disgust. It all seemed so pointless. Nanbu Tsuchiya was the finest man he had ever known. He could not have asked for a wiser and more honorable lord. And now he was dead. For what? For Bayushi Shoju's foolish ambitions. For a war that had ended before it began. For the Emperor's bloody vengeance.

"Where do we go now, father?" asked a small voice.

"We will visit your mother," he said, resting a hand on her shoulder. "Then we will find a new home." In his heart he knew it was a lie. The Emperor's hatred of Scorpions and all who served them was well known. It made no difference that Tzurui had lived all of his life in this valley, had never known a Bayushi besides the tax collector, and had only journeyed to Ryoko Owari once. To the Empire, he was a Scorpion. Few other daimyo would be willing to risk the Hantei's disfavor by taking him in.

He lifted Kochohime into his arms and walked. He hoped he could find a place for them quickly. Kochohime was a frail girl, much like her mother. She would not survive long on the road. Tzurui turned off on a small path that led to a single cherry tree and the Nanbu family shrine.

Long ago, the tree had been a gift from the daimyo of the Soshi, a symbol of the Scorpion's protection. The tree looked slightly twisted and withered, and Tzurui could not push away the omen. The tree was surrounded by square white stones, memorials to those that had passed into the next world. Tzurui set Kochohime down gently and took a dipper from a barrel of purified water, pouring it over the stone he knew so well. His eyes were red, but he did not cry. Samurai did not cry, not even ronin.

"*Konichiwa*, mother," Kochohime said brightly. The girl always spoke as if her mother was alive, and as if her mother spoke back. Though it disturbed him slightly, Tzurui never reprimanded her. He could not find it in his heart to deny the girl her only connection with her mother. Sometimes, he was jealous. He wished he could hear her now. She would know what to do. Tzurui said his final goodbyes, then turned to pray at the shrine, leaving Kochohime to continue whispering to her mother. He prayed to Jizo, Fortune of Mercy. He prayed to his ancestors. He called out to the spirit of Tsuchiya, begging forgiveness for his cowardice and promising that

his sacrifice would not be in vain. He prayed for a miracle to save his daughter from this life.

"Tzurui-sama," said a voice from behind.

Tzurui turned to see a broad shouldered man in shabby robes of deep brown. "Brother Hanoshi," he said, bowing as he rose and walked out to the road. "It is good to see you, friend."

"I heard what happened," the monk said grimly. "Tsuchiya was a good man. He will be remembered."

Tzurui frowned and shook his head. "Shiro Nanbu was seized. My family are outcasts. We have no home. My uncle died for nothing."

Hanoshi smiled. "Really?" he asked, and gestured toward the shrine, where the little girl still crouched whispering happily. "Tell me, something, Tzurui. Can you look into your daughter's eyes and tell me that? Do you honestly believe that her death would have been a better fate? The Fortunes have given you a second chance, my friend. Do not spurn it."

"A poor second chance," Tzurui said quietly. "She is a weak girl. She will not live long on the road."

"What of the monastery?" Hanoshi offered. "There is room for her there."

"I could not impose," Tzurui huffed. "She is my responsibility."

"And it is our responsibility to help those in need," Hanoshi replied kindly. "The Brotherhood will protect her."

Tzurui was quiet for a long time.

"We can protect you, as well," Hanoshi added. "There are many fates for masterless samurai. You could do worse than serving Shinsei. We could use a pious man like you."

Tzurui looked away. "Pious, perhaps, but not brave."

"Excuse me?"

"I was born a samurai," Tzurui said. "When my bravery was tested, I failed. I did not step forward to help my master when others would. I fear in my heart that it was my cowardice in that moment that brought this fate. I must prove my valor before my soul can be at rest. I cannot escape from my destiny."

Hanoshi nodded. "I understand. I do not think I agree, but I understand. You know the life that you resign yourself to?"

"Yes. I will become a soldier of fortune. There is a war brewing, to the east. There will be a market for mercenaries. I should be able to find work there."

"Tzurui, you have never been in a war," Hanoshi said.

Tzurui turned to the monk, his eyes intense. "War is where I belong. Will I find courage in a monastery?"

"You might be surprised," Hanoshi chuckled. "But suit yourself. If you ever change your mind, you will always have a place with us."

Tzurui nodded, then turned to look upon his daughter. She was seated cross-legged on the ground, completely engrossed in conversation with her mother's grave. He felt a lump grow in his throat. He knew he could not bring her, but could not bear to leave her behind. She was all he had left. She was his life.

"I will accept no charity," he said. "I insist on being kept abreast of her expenses and will repay every bit in full."

"Of course," Hanoshi nodded, not intending to force the matter.

"I will go now," Tzurui said. "You will explain this to Kochohime?"

"You do not wish to say good-bye?" Hanoshi asked, surprised.

Tzurui turned to his friend, and there were tears in his eyes now. "I cannot. If I did, I would be tempted not to leave her. I know that I am weak. Please help me in this, Hanoshi."

Hanoshi nodded, turning aside so that he would not see his friend's grief. When he looked back again, Tzurui had set off down the road.

Alone.

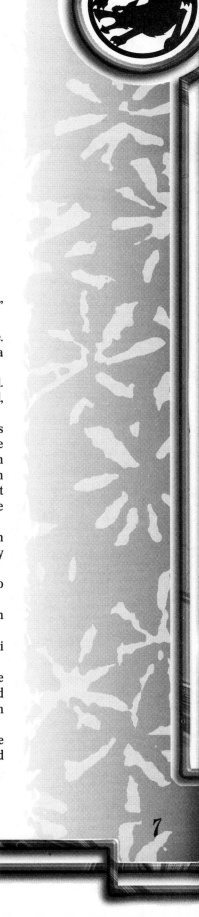

Chapter One:
The Unfettered
Ronin

The following are but a few of the indignities and discomforts that a ronin will have to look forward to:

1. *No Clan, No Family* – This may seem obvious, but think about it. No powerful relatives to turn to when things go awry. No clan magistrates to stand by your side when the law turns against you. No kinsmen to keep you abreast of what's happening in the court. No one to watch your back.

2. *No Holdings* – A samurai can walk into his lord's village in his territory and demand room and board, as it is his right. Not so the ronin. The ronin may be lucky if he's allowed to pay for rice.

3. *Guilty Until Proven Innocent* – Ronin are seldom given legal traveling papers. A wandering ronin with no papers will have difficulty. Most magistrates will assume wandering ronin to be bandits or worse. At best, the law will keep a sharp eye on the ronin, or insist that he leave the province immediately.

(*Continued on opposite page*)

Chapter One: The Unfettered Ronin

FROM THE JOURNAL OF IKOMA HIDEMASA

I am not an old man, but I have many tales. In my waning hours, when I know that death is upon me, let this be the one that is told. It is a tale of courage, of nobility, of sacrifice. It is a tale of how, in the end, a great hero was able to conquer the most cowardly and dishonorable of enemies.

That 'hero' was a farmer.

That 'enemy' was myself.

I am Ikoma Hidemasa. I am, and will ever consider myself, a Lion. Not even the Emperor can take that away. None can steal a man's honor but himself.

I had disgraced myself in the court. I made a foolish quip at the expense of my master's rival, a Crane I believed to be a weakling. When blades were drawn and the Crane's eyes met mine, I knew that I would die. I was afraid, I who knew no fear. I ran, leaving behind my name, my clan, everything that had been important, only to save my life, which only became more worthless for the lack of the rest.

I do not remember how long I ran. I became ronin, a lone wolf working for merchants to earn enough koku to survive. I loaded wagons. I killed men for rice. I dirtied my hands with the darkest labors. Arrogance of arrogance, I yet carried the daisho that was my birthright, and the great scroll, Leadership, that was my inheritance. In my initial flight, my first impulse had been to sell it. In time, as my memories of home began to fall away, I clung to it tenuously. I never opened it. I never dared. I knew I was not worthy. I simply carried it, and hoped... for what?

When the Otaku magistrate found me, truth to tell, I was relieved. I said, "This is the end. I can stop running and meet the death I deserve."

How surprised I was when she galloped past with a pack of bandits on her heels! I followed as best I could on foot. Luckily, the bandits did not notice me beside such a tempting quarry. Soon I arrived at a farmer's village, thickly barricaded and ready for war. The Otaku rode through the gates and the bandits turned aside, forced back by the pikes and arrows of the peasants.

I approached cautiously, wondering what could be transpiring. The peasants were few, and I counted only five true bushi besides the Otaku, all ronin. They had no hope against the horde that besieged them. What was the point of fighting? In my mind, they should have run. If it were me, I would have gathered all I could and run like the wind.

If it were me. But it was not.

Why were these simple folk, ronin, farmers, and a single true samurai any different from myself? I was a Lion!

Wasn't I?

Had I fallen so far?

In that instant, my decision was made. I could no longer hide in cowardice while "lesser" creatures sacrificed their lives. I approached the village, offering my services to their cause. They were suspicious, especially the Otaku, but when I claimed my heritage as an Ikoma and they saw the copy of *Leadership* that I carried, they decided that I could not be other than what I claimed.

Ironic. Using the fruits of my theft to prove the truth of my being. I promised this would be my final crime.

Over the next week, I saw fiercer battle than in my entire life combined. I saw peasants learn to wield a spear equal to the skill of any samurai in half the time. I saw the selfless bravery of ronin, warriors who have none to answer to but themselves. I know well what an unforgiving critic the self can be. I was shamed by such glorious company.

I saw that there was one weapon that these men and women had that all the bandit hordes in Rokugan could not steal away. It was a weapon I had cast away long ago. In the peasant village, I learned how to carry it once again, I learned to find hope.

To my surprise, that hope increased in my presence and was focused upon me. To the villagers, I was a Lion. A symbol of courage, honor, and leadership. To my horror, I realized that even the Otaku, not a ronin at all, was soon deferring to me in matters of the village's defense and the training. I had become more than just a mere observer. I had become their leader. Their hopes, the dreams, their survival depended upon me. If I was lax, the defenses would crumble. If I was cowardly, the village would fall. If I was weak, the village would die.

I was not lax.

I was not cowardly.

I was not weak.

The bandits came in force as the first winter snows fell. I had never before fought a battle in winter but I tell you that the hellish pits of Jigoku cannot be much different from what I saw on that day. The snow became a bitter pink sludge as the villagers and bandits fell dead in heaps all around me. I saw the five ronin fall. I saw the Otaku's horse fight on after its leader tumbled to the earth with a dozen arrows in her back. I saw peasants wearing the armor of fallen samurai, fighting with a ferocious bravery as they clung to their meager birthright. I remember the heat of the battle, standing back to back with one of the youngest of the ashigaru. He was a fiery young lad that I remembered from the peasant drills, bright and inquisitive. His manner and bearing were such that in other circumstances, in another life, I would have mistaken him for a noble Akodo.

Together we faced the bandit lord, a giant of a man with a fierce katana stained black with the blood of my new friends. I took the first step toward him. This was my destiny, I knew. I was meant for this combat.

But I was not meant to win, it seems. The bandit felled me with a single blow, opening my stomach from hip to hip.

As I fell, I saw the ashigaru boy strike down the bandit lord. I never even thought to ask his name. I wish I knew it now, but I do not wish to insult him. If I knew his name, I would scream his name through the halls of the ancestors when I go to meet them, scream it with all the power of my soul so that they would know who a true hero is.

What world is this, that allows such cowards as myself to be born samurai, but casts a brave soul like that boy's into poverty? As the village rebuilds, I see that the lad has taken command of the village. His spirit is strong, pure, and virtuous. Even the Otaku's horse seems to accept him and follows him about dutifully in the absence of her mistress. The boy carries the katana he stripped from the bandit lord, and wears it with pride. Another samurai might consider his adoption of the horse and the blade terrible offenses but I find that I cannot blame him. His crimes are meager in comparison with mine. If anyone deserves to be a samurai, it is that boy.

I do not have much time left. The winter snows grow thicker. Travel has become impossible and there are no healers here to tend my wound. I become more fevered by the moment and I know that soon I will sleep and not awaken. I have given my family's scroll, *Leadership*, to the boy, whom I have nicknamed "Toku." He has earned it, after the gift he has given me. A gift of which I was hardly deserving.

He has shown me true honor.

FROM THE LETTERS OF MIYA YOTO TO HIS NIECE, YUMI

What a strange and wonderful creature – the ronin. So misunderstood, even by themselves. I know that often my colleagues smirk behind my back for my fascination with the wave-men, but I pay them no mind. Every man has his vice, and I believe there are far worse evils than the study of these peculiar masterless warriors.

I have had many opportunities to interview ronin during my travels. My duties as a diplomat and herald often intersect with two of the ronin's most frequent occupations – the mercenary and the bandit. I can tell you from experience that ronin are ruthless men. They do what they must to survive, and the difference between a ronin and a mercenary is sometimes nothing more than economy.

Still, even the most cutthroat and vicious of these characters maintains a certain nobility and bearing that I find intriguing. No matter how foul their name has become, they bear their katana with pride. No matter what the world may consider them, in their mind they are samurai. Born to poverty, cast into exile, they cling bitterly to what they have left, even to the destruction of their own health, even to be hunted like criminals though they have done no wrong. If it were me, I would not be so brave. In many ways, I think a farmer is better off than a ronin. A farmer can always find a place, and is never a threat. But to become a downtrodden symbol of violence and nonconformity for no other reason than because your honor demands it? That is what it means to be a ronin.

I will write now not of the most skilled ronin I have met, nor the oldest, nor the wisest. I will

RONIN BENEFITS

Here is a brief list of some of the best parts of being ronin.

1. *No Clan, No Family* – You make your own destiny. You don't have to worry about some inbred relative you've never met popping out of the woodwork to make your life miserable with ludicrous demands.

2. *Freedom* – You aren't tied down to any particular place. You can uproot and move with very little effort. The only limitation is your natural reputation as a troublemaker, and for every samurai prejudiced against ronin, there is another who could use a hired hand.

3. *Connections* – Over the last several centuries, ronin have learned that the only people they can rely upon are each other. Though a random ronin is more often than not an untrustworthy sort, there is still a definite network of communication in ronin society. A ronin will always be willing to talk to another ronin. While you shouldn't trust strangers to watch your back, you might be able to draw out information that a clan samurai just wouldn't be party to.

(Continued on opposite page)

write simply of one of the most interesting. He was a small man with haunted eyes and a jagged, faded tattoo on one side of his weathered face. I first met him on a way-station along the Emperor's Road. He initiated a brawl with a much larger man, and came away the victor despite seemingly impossible odds. He carried no sword. He walked alone. He asked for no help and offered none. What a dark and solitary figure! The only item of any value that he possessed was a fine chestnut stallion, a steed in far better condition than its ronin master. Despite his lack of a daisho, he maintained that he was samurai and demanded to be treated appropriately. He had come upon hard times and was nearly starved. I found his character so intriguing that I hired him on as a yojimbo for a time, though I needed no additional bodyguards. During this time, I had opportunity to interview him at length. I hoped to learn just how he had come to this point on his life's road.

"What is your name?" I asked him.

He seemed to hesitate for a moment before he answered. "Sanzo," bluntly. No family, no clan. Merely 'Sanzo.' The same name as one of the legendary companions of Doji Hotei. An assumed name, or merely a coincidence? I did not press the matter. Many ronin prefer some degree of anonymity.

"If you do not mind my impudence, were you once of a clan?" I took care to frame my manner carefully. Though he bore no weapons, a ronin's past is nothing to be trifled with.

"I was," he replied with a faraway look in his eye. "I was a yoriki in a small village. I lived there with my family, until…" His eyes became even more glazed and he did not talk for several moments. He looked as though he had faced a severe crisis and lost a bit of his soul in the bargain. He gave no details, but I knew that he had met with great tragedy. His family, perhaps his entire village, were no doubt dead. I did not interrupt his reverie, but merely waited for him to return. The process took several minutes.

"I was a Dragon," this Sanzo said finally.

"A Dragon?" I said, surprised. Few Dragon become ronin. Despite their aura of mystery and inscrutability, the Dragon I had known are remarkably understanding of one another's flaws. A Dragon ronin seemed almost incomprehensible. "Had you no other relatives, perhaps a sensei? Would no one in your clan take you?" I realized at the last moment that perhaps the man was a

criminal or a renegade of some sort, and hoped that my question would not provoke him to violence.

"They would have taken me," Sanzo said. "But I would not let them. The Dragon Clan is no place for a coward."

"Again, excuse my temerity," I said with a polite smile. "But I have seen your valor. I have seen your eyes, and after a long life as a diplomat, I consider myself a good judge of character. You are no coward, Sanzo."

"No," Sanzo said with great resignation in his voice. "Now I am dead."

He seemed so dark and melancholy at this point that I turned the conversation to brighter matters. For the short time that I knew him, Sanzo was never cheerful, but he was dependable. He went about his work without complaint, and always had a certain dignity despite the quiet rage that always boiled just beneath his skin. Before he left my service, I took the liberty of offering him the gift of a new daisho to replace the one he had lost. He seemed surprised, for the cost of two swords was far more than the regular fee for a mere summer's work. Happily, he did not take the gesture as an insult but, for the first and only time during the period in which I knew him, he smiled. Without another word, Sanzo bowed deeply, tucked the swords into his tattered obi, and led his stallion away.

I often wonder where Sanzo's journey has led. I wonder what has made him as he is. What can change a man like that? What can twist his spirit and shatter his soul such that he becomes a shadow, that all he can do is move through the motions of his former life with a mechanical duty, searching, ever searching?

What, I wonder, are you searching for, Sanzo?

FROM THE JOURNAL OF KAIU SUMAN

I have worked forty years in my position as Master of the Wall. It is my duty to oversee the engineers, to make certain that every bit of the shield that bears our name and protects Rokugan from darkness is not vulnerable to attack. It is endless work. It is laborious work. It is grueling and thankless. It is necessary.

Ample workmen are always difficult to come by, especially for the occasional repairs required on the inside of the wall. Many samurai, even practical-minded Crab, are too proud to reduce themselves to such menial labor. Many of the ashigaru who fill our ranks have no skill in masonry or any aptitude to learn. The craftsmen we import often take a single look at the dark territories that lay beyond the Carpenter and turn away in terror. I cannot blame them. The Shadowlands are a rotten fruit and the Carpenter, as impressive as it is, is but a thin peel to protect us. Better that they look and turn away. We have no room for cowards or incompetents here.

Thus I turn this discussion to ronin. When I began my training under my father's guiding hand, I had thought him mad to suggest that ronin could be of any use in the care and maintenance of the Carpenter. Trust a man who serves no master? A mercenary who does not even have the good grace to put aside the daisho when the Fortunes demand it? Ludicrous! You might as well hire a mujina!

The day he became aware of my opinions, my father assigned me to a repair crew. At first, I was honored. The repair of the Carpenter is the most important task a Kaiu can ever be given. Then I realized, to my dismay, that my entire work crew was composed of ronin, including the foreman, who seemed to take a certain dark glee in assigning me the most grueling and backbreaking duties. The anger that burned in my heart was such that I would have cut him down right there, but there is no time for pointless feuding when repairs must be done. Leave that to the foolish Lions and their proud belly-slitting games. The Crab have work to do.

I watched these ronin. I watched them carefully. Many of them were not skilled masons but they seemed to take their lead from more experienced eta. Eta! I had not even bothered to notice the hinin workers, and why should I have? These ronin were wise. These eta had spent their entire lives working along the Carpenter, and knew how to repair the stonework swiftly and securely. The ronin were eager and versatile workers, and quickly mastered the art. Quicker, I admit with shame, than I did. The foreman, Kikkawa, was a master engineer. I assumed that he must have been a disgraced Kaiu, so great was his talent. I learned later to my surprise that he was not, but had learned all that he knew of stonework from experience.

As I continued awkwardly about my work, dressed in the light armor of my gempukku, one ronin laughed at me openly. "You'll get more stones laid if you loosen that armor and get to work, Kaiu!" she said. There was no venom in her tone, just a jovial familiarity that I found irritating. I could not contain my disgust. I turned away from mixing the mortar to address them.

"Armor is a necessity," I said, directing my voice to all the workers with a sweep of my hand. Here we were, technically within the Shadowlands, but many of them worked with only armored skirts or even simple loincloths. Only the sliver of jade each bore about their neck signified any awareness of the dangers we faced. "Don't you know that the enemy can strike at any moment? We must have our weapons ready if we are to triumph."

"We know, Kaiu-sama," Kikkawa said somberly, and the sincere note of respect jarred my temper. "But the best weapon against the Shadowlands is the Wall itself. Dressed as we are, we can complete it much more quickly and the Empire will be safe again."

I shook my head in irritation. "But what if an oni should appear?" I asked with a growl. "If a horde of goblins should crest the ridge, what will you do then?"

"We will die," Kikkawa said. "And while we die, the samurai above will rally to destroy them. Is that not the reason you hired us?"

I could say nothing. What I had taken for carelessness was bravery. What I had taken for dishonor in deferring to eta was nothing more than efficiency. These men were given a duty, my duty by birthright, but they were willing to risk their lives to see it done efficiently. Whatever these men had done to reach this state, whatever crimes they committed to become the outcasts that they were, no longer mattered. Those ronin rose high in my esteem. Higher than a few Crabs I know.

Forty years later, all of the ronin who I worked with on that day, including the noble Kikkawa, are dead. Within ten years, ten of the fourteen I met had perished from accidents related to their work on the Carpenter. Four moved on to safer exploits, each carrying my highest recommendations on their future endeavors.

FROM A GNAWED TREE LIMB FLOATING IN AKA-MIZU-UMI

To whoever read this, see the story of Mik'thik'thamatch, Rememberer of Blazing Gullet Tribe. Tribe gone-gone now. Gone-gone away and not much left now. But time tribe-tribe had was good one. Much food and many little ones and have Junkei to thank. Look on story and remember it good. Good-good-good.

RONIN BENEFITS (CONTINUED)

4. *No Expectations* – Rokugani expect the worst out of ronin. You're a bandit, a thief, a freak, merely for what you are. Whatever you do, whatever accomplishments you make, there's nowhere else to go but up. At times, your bad reputation can be used to frighten or intimidate others.

Ronin Heraldry

Ronin heraldry is a curious thing.

A ronin's reputation is crucial to his existence. It is upon the weight of reputation that a ronin might be granted fealty, or by which a bandit inspires fear. To this end, ronin emulate clan samurai by carrying mons and other banners of identification (see *Winter Court: Kyuden Kakita*). The mons of ronin are as numerous as the ronin themselves, and vary from the serenely beautiful to the bizarre. Many examples of these mons will be detailed and their origins explained throughout this book.

The complication in ronin heraldry comes from the fact that, technically, ronin do not exist. They are outcasts from society, and thus the Miya are forbidden to keep official records of ronin heraldry. As a result, many ronin steal one another's mons in order to try to capitalize on a rival's reputation or to sully another's name. The ronin have no legal recourse but to take direct personal action.

(Continued on opposite page)

Junkei was tall-tall pale skinned dayrunner, of the ones with the small teeth and the big eyes. The ones who let fly the bolts of steel that kill-kill. The ones who leave the rice in the fields so Nezumi feed and do no harm. The "humans." Junkei was be special human. Was be of the ones with the long claw and the short claw. The ones that make the war and kill-kill and bring the doom-doom. The ones that call they be the samurai.

We Blazing Gullet name Junkei Nezumi name. Give name Wild-Hair-Steel-Bringer-Eyes-of-Glory. He come to us without fear. He come to us with shiny-shiny things. He come to us with idea, and he come to give us sharp steel claws like the samurai. He teach us how to hunt the humans. He teach-teach us the holes in the samurai's shell. With him, we kill, we raid, we take what we want. We invite him into tribe with great happy-happy for he one who think like a Nezumi and treat us like Nezumi would treat Nezumi, not like humans who kill with scream and make Nezumi die. He laugh at this. He call us "bandits." Funny human-human word. Still, him want be chief all the same and we make him chief all the same.

Mik'thik'thamatch talk to Wild-Hair-Steel-Bringer-Eyes-of-Glory once and Mik'thik'thamatch ask-ask him this. This Mik'thik'thamatch ask: "Wild-Hair-Steel-Bringer-Eyes-of-Glory," Mik'thik'thamatch ask, "Why you no have tribe of humans?" Mik'thik'thamatch ask "Why smart-smart human like you come to nezumi to become great?" Mik'thik'thamatch ask. "Why you not stay among humans and become biggest chief-chief of all?" Mik'thik'thamatch ask. Mik'thik'thamatch ask all this, because man-man smart as Wild-Hair-Steel-Bringer-Eyes-of-Glory surely smart enough to become big-big-biggest chief if he can! Wild-Hair-Steel-Bringer-Eyes-of-Glory bring our tribe so much food and good-good things. More food than tribe can eat. More good-good things than tribe can carry.

Wild-Hair-Steel-Bringer-Eyes-of-Glory take a long time to answer that question. To Mik'thik'thamatch, it look like the question hurt him deep inside. Mik'thik'thamatch was sorry for asking question, but as much as Mik'thik'thamatch claw at the air he could not pull question back.

Wild-Hair-Steel-Bringer-Eyes-of-Glory never answer that question. The next time the bright rise up high in the sky, Blazing Gullet find that Wild-Hair-Steel-Bringer-Eyes-of-Glory is gone.

Not know where be go. Not know what be think. Why leave a tribe where you king? It hurt Mik'thik'thamatch to think about it. Did Blazing Gullet do something wrong? Did question hurt so much?

Then the samurai came, samurai in shells of red and black with sharp claws and long sticks and no-no mercy for Blazing Gullet tribe. They call us bandits, but they not as happy about word as Wild-Hair-Steel-Bringer-Eyes-of-Glory. Instead, they make war and kill-kill and bring the doom-doom to Blazing Gullet Tribe. Blazing Gullet die. Only Mik'thik'thamatch get away to make this stick and cast upon streams of history for all Nezumi to find and know.

Mik'thik'thamatch hope Wild-Hair-Steel-Bringer-Eyes-of-Glory become big chief-king samurai among the humans, because him give us good time, and him worth it.

Remember us.

From the Reports of Ide Ashijun, Emerald Magistrate

Ronin. Bah. Dogs! The only good ronin is a dead one.

I know this is a cliché, but when I speak it I feel that every word could not be more true. Every word rolls to my throat with ease; thus I speak it again and I speak it now.

Foul, barbaric, uncouth... my soul is in disarray. I must calm myself, lest the stomach ailment that has been my bane so much of late get the best of me. It bothers me most when I think of the ronin.

If ever there were a more lawless, dishonorable bunch, more deserving of complete and total annihilation...

Unfocused anger is a vice. Forgive me. I have had much trouble of late, many attacks upon my character and I fear that it has gotten the better of my normal good nature. Do not misinterpret me; I prize my position as magistrate more than any other and intend to bring my family name honor in the execution of my duties, but sometimes, sometimes I long for the times before I was given this mission.

The days before I was asked to find the man named Yugoro.

This maniac, this oni-spawn, this so called bandit-king has cut a bloody streak across the face of Rokugan and taken the jewels of its labor as well as its daughters for his own sadistic pleasures. No bold and dashing ronin of the kabuki he, no, this man is of the truer sort. A villain. A barbarian. A man who carries the daisho for no other reason than because of the effective instrument of death it makes.

You say that ronin are men of honor? I would laugh if the statement were not so pitiable. Men such as Yugoro know nothing of honor. They do not know their place. They rail against the structure of the Empire, the government we have created to protect the simple people from chaos and anarchy. They take everything that is sacred, all of the gifts that the kami have generously bestowed upon us, and cast it all aside as offal. What could such men know of honor?

I apologize if my outburst has caused you, dear reader, any discontent but by my passion I only mean to make my message clear. Forget what you have learned about these ronin. Forget about the romanticized notions with which they are often painted, the glorious and dreamy overtones often polished to a gleam in the courts. Courts, I might add, far from the terror of men like Yugoro. These men are nothing but dogs. Curs who kill without thought or reason. Men who think of bushido as nothing more than a constraint. Why, their very existence proves the sort of men they are!

Consider my words well. A samurai is a man who serves his lord for the glory of Rokugan, who seeks out honor for the benefit of his ancestors. If these men have no masters, then what purpose could they serve but their own? If they have no family name, what need could they have to carry the daisho but their own greed? These men are not to be trusted. Were they truly men of honor, they would retire to the monastery as justice demands.

Yugoro... One day, ronin. One day.

Alas, I must retire from writing for now. I have much to plan tomorrow, and my old ailment returns...

"Ronin", an Essay by Hamuko

I never knew what to think of the ronin. To tell the truth, the whole idea of them never really struck me as anything that important.

Until I became one. Amazing how your perspective can change.

My name is Hamuko. Once of the Soshi, I am now without family or clan. I was a shugenja, working as a minor courtier on assignment to Kyuden Isawa. My knowledge of the kami was nearly unrivaled among my family, and I soon became intimately familiar with many of the prominent Isawa. When the Coup came, I was caught unawares. I had never imagined Shoju capable of such a thing, to be quite honest. I had thought my master more subtle in his ambition.

When the Imperial Legions came, seeking the Emperor's bloody vengeance, the Elemental Masters were kind enough to intercede on my behalf in return for my loyal services and the friendships I had formed. My name was taken, my titles were stripped, but my life was spared. I wondered, at the time, if the sacrifice was worth it. I have heard stories of the poverty of the ronin and the eternal derision that is their lot. They are outcasts, often regarded to be criminals for no good reason. The thought of becoming one chilled my Soshi blood.

But now, I must say, I enjoy it quite a bit.

As a Scorpion, I was a skilled shugenja and courtier. Though my position brought my family great honor and esteem, three things always bothered me.

First, that those who knew me, respected me, but always from a distance.

Second, that while my words were known to have sway over both the kami and mortal man alike, my presence always drew suspicion. Ever would there be the fear of the Scorpion sting that might lie behind the pincers of sweet words.

Third, though my beauty was envied and many sought my hand in marriage, the Soshi ordered me ever to remain apart. A tantalizing dish, once tasted, grows cold. That was my uncle Bantaro's reasoning.

Now, however, everything has changed.

In the many months since the Coup, three clans have approached me, seeking to turn my skills to their service. First was the Isawa, who communicated his desire to place me at a high ranking position in his libraries. Next came the Kitsu, who have offered me a place among them as an honored advisor. Last were the Crab, more honest than the rest, who bluntly stated their desire for the secrets of my Soshi magic, and their willingness to grant me favors in return. I have accepted none of their offers, but have received

Ronin Heraldry (Continued)

This can be a bit of a headache, as many Lion and Dragon generals make use of ronin mercenaries during their campaigns. The inability to tell a reliable warrior apart from a charlatan causes great confusion. To avoid this, most generals who use mercenaries also frequently employ a ronin advisor to assist in ferreting out fakes. Those who could care less – indeed, the majority of Clan generals – assign their mercenaries to the front lines anyway, where it doesn't make a difference if the man being killed is a charlatan or the genuine article.

Opinions Regarding Ronin

Crab: "You say that the Ronin have something to prove? Come to the Wall, and you will have opportunity to prove yourself, or die like the honorless dogs you are."
– Hida Tampako

Crane: "What do I feel about ronin? Nothing. I do not waste time judging animals." – Kakita Yogoso

Dragon: "Although a fallen man does not mean a fallen heart, more often than not these ronin are no more than brigands. When I see a dead ronin, only then will I mourn them."
– Agasha Tamori

Lion: "You can depend upon ronin. If you pay him, you can depend on him to die in battle. If you turn your back, you can depend on his tanto in your kidneys."
– Matsu Goemon

Phoenix: "As water conforms to its vessel, so do these wave-men conform to their environment. You say that ronin are worthless vagabonds. Let us change ourselves, and this ronin plague will no more curse our lands." – Isawa Uona

(Continued on opposite page)

many gifts and favors as they vie for my service. I enjoy more attention as a lone wolf than I ever did as a presumed pawn of the Scorpion.

As for my status in the courts, many who feared me as a Scorpion now greet me warmly as a friend. They feel that my decision to abandon my name puts me apart somehow from the Scorpion stereotype. They are wrong, of course; I still have plans to put into action. The removal of my name is simply a means to an end. I keep this concealed, and thus I find that I am respected purely on the basis of my abilities. I am sought not because I am Bantaro's student. Not because I am Hametsu's liaison. Not because I am a representative of the Scorpion. I am respected because I am Hamuko. Ironically, now that I have lost my name, my name finally carries weight.

And as for the last, my prospects of marriage? Sadly, they are still remote. It seems that while those who would seek to manipulate me or use me for my "independent" status are great in number, those who would bring me close to their heart are nonexistent. It seems that some things are truly denied the ronin, just as they are in the tales.

Anonymous

(The following scroll was discovered tucked into a copy of Kakita's The Sword. Its writer has never been traced, and must therefore be presumed to still be alive as, were he to be found, he would certainly be killed.)

Courage and honor are like a bridge. You never know their true strength until they are tested, and then they either crumble or bear you across.

Samurai say that the honor of ronin is worthless, that they are creatures worse than eta, animals that can be trusted to do nothing but cause terrible violence. Villains to be cut down on sight.

I say that it is samurai who are weak. They hide behind their families and their alliances, living in their high-walled castles and feeding off the toil of the common folk. They do not understand the world that they rule. They do not know what it means to survive. They praise the virtues of bushido: honesty, compassion, courage, sincerity, duty, courtesy, honor, but do they understand them? Listen well to my words.

How can a man be honest when his words are not his own? When a samurai parrots the words of his lord, he is but a puppet, and honesty is impossible. To be honest with oneself, and true to your own desires, that is the honesty of a ronin.

Compassion? The samurai go out of their way to assist one another within their family or clan and call it compassion. Tell me when a Lion has stooped to help a Crane, or a Scorpion has gone out of his way to assist an impoverished Phoenix. To help one within your family is not compassion, it is simply looking out for yourself and cementing alliances. When a traveling ronin meets a stranger and shares his meal with no thought of reward, that is the compassion of a ronin.

What is courage? To the great armies of the clans, courage is easy. But what is courage when victory is assured? What does it mean to die for a cause when it is certain others will carry the tales of your glory? To deny the employment of a wicked master and face cold and starvation, to die in a shallow grave for a worthy cause no one will ever remember – that is the courage of a ronin.

And sincerity. A samurai's word is the same as his action? Prove this to me, for I have yet to see it. A man on his own must be as good as his word, or he will swiftly find that the world has no use for him. That is the sincerity of a ronin.

Duty? To be responsible for the consequences one is born into? The samurai live a life of wealth and privilege. The only consequences are those they throw upon themselves. A wave-man must live with the consequences of his actions every second, for at any moment his aberrant existence may be thrown into peril and only his past deeds will serve to prove him worthy. That is the duty of a ronin.

But what of courtesy? Are not ronin uncouth and discourteous? Do we not spurn the polite society that the samurai have built and laugh at the works of the clans? Perhaps. I know I have. But why should we not? The samurai do the same to us. Courtesy breeds courtesy, and respect can grow only in its own soil. That is the courtesy of a ronin.

Honor?

There are those who say that the ronin have no honor.

I have no argument.

Except to say that those who say such things are blind and ignorant fools.

Our actions speak for themselves.

Each wave-man is his own legend.

That is the honor of a ronin.

LIFE AS A LONE WOLF

What is a ronin? Directly translated, the term means "wave-man," an individual whose destiny has been cast into happenstance and uncertainty. By their nature, they defy all attempts to be defined, contained, or controlled. A ronin is more easily defined by what it is not then by what it is.

A ronin is a wandering warrior who, by chance or by birth, has no master. In Rokugan, where social interaction is rigidly defined, the ronin is an aberration. He is a warrior. Yet while it is a warrior's duty to rule the lands and hold titles, a ronin has no lands. He is a samurai, yet he must work to find income rather than live off of taxes. Many Rokugani are uncertain exactly where a ronin fits in their Celestial Order. As a result, many samurai prefer to ignore the existence of ronin.

A ronin is not a peasant. Though a ronin has no lands, he is still a samurai. Warriors are not farmers. The two are distinctly different levels of the Celestial Order. While a farmer may have some small hope, through great heroism and personal accomplishment, of one day becoming a samurai, a true samurai would never lower himself into the place of a farmer. This is not to say that it never happens, but it is certainly the height of dishonor.

A samurai working a rice paddy is a sad, defeated man.

The easiest method by which a samurai becomes a ronin is by birth. The son or daughter of a ronin is also ronin, if they choose not to denounce their status. It is nearly every born ronin's dream that they might one day prove themselves worthy to swear fealty to a clan, thus becoming a true, full-fledged samurai. Though this happens from time to time, it is infrequent even in the case of the very talented, as few daimyo are willing to set a precedent by allowing ronin into their clan. More often ronin are sent on quests with the promise of fealty, only to be denied on some technicality.

Even when ronin are granted fealty, they are seldom given the full rights and privileges to which clan samurai have access. Most ronin are admitted with probationary status, admitted to one of the clan's lesser vassal families. While the ronin is still technically a member of the clan and bears the family name, he is unlikely to be allowed such privileges as training at the clan academies or attending the daimyo's court. Such privileges are normally obtained after generations of service within the vassal families, though it is not unknown for a truly exemplary individual to speed the process considerably.

Other ronin begin their career aligned to a clan, but lose their status later in life. Skilled samurai who suddenly find themselves without a master can usually find a position working for a relative, but sometimes this is not an option. Many factors can lead to a samurai giving up his family name and striking out alone. Generally, the fact that a samurai can find no one to offer fealty implies failure, dishonor, or incompetence on his part. It is partially for this reason that many ronin are seen to be vagabonds, preying upon normal society.

Of course, the rest of the reason is that many ronin are vagabonds who prey upon normal society. The sad, simple fact is that ronin must support themselves somehow, and banditry is a viable option for a trained warrior.

Of course, other ronin struggle against this stereotype, working to prove themselves worthy in their own eyes as well as those of others. Without clan or family to urge them to greatness, a ronin hero must be his own example. He must succeed or fail on his own terms, and can only depend upon himself. Such rare heroes carry a special form of bushido in their heart. These men and women have a very personal code of honor that may not mesh completely with traditional Rokugani ethics, but is all the more powerful for its intensely personal nature.

In the end, no two ronin are alike. No two ronin have found their path by the same route. Their goals, their methods, their activities vary as much as the individuals themselves.

Chapter Two

The History of the Wave Men

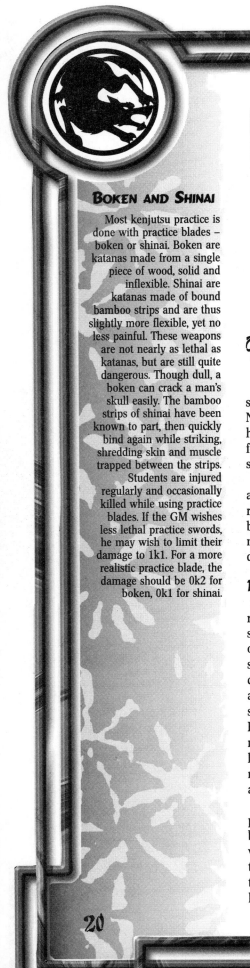

BOKEN AND SHINAI

Most kenjutsu practice is done with practice blades – boken or shinai. Boken are katanas made from a single piece of wood, solid and inflexible. Shinai are katanas made of bound bamboo strips and are thus slightly more flexible, yet no less painful. These weapons are not nearly as lethal as katanas, but are still quite dangerous. Though dull, a boken can crack a man's skull easily. The bamboo strips of shinai have been known to part, then quickly bind again while striking, shredding skin and muscle trapped between the strips.

Students are injured regularly and occasionally killed while using practice blades. If the GM wishes less lethal practice swords, he may wish to limit their damage to 1k1. For a more realistic practice blade, the damage should be 0k2 for boken, 0k1 for shinai.

History and Background

Types of Ronin

It seems that there are as many ways for a samurai to find himself ronin as there are ronin. No two tales have the same beginning. There are, however, several recurring patterns. The following are the most common causes for a samurai to find himself in such a position.

Note that each cause bears different stigma and carries different expectations. Again, no two ronin are alike. The details of a ronin's background are critical to his existence and can mean the difference between heroism end and a dishonorable death.

RONIN-BORN

As stated in the previous chapter, children of ronin are also ronin if they maintain their parent's samurai lifestyle. This is true even if the ronin's other parent was a heimin. The samurai parent's status overrides peasant status if the child chooses. This is the rarest method by which ronin are created. First of all, many ronin tend to be such loners that marriage is not an option. Rokugani marriages are political maneuvers more than anything else, and an unwashed ronin has very little to offer such an arrangement. As a result, legitimate marriages among ronin are rare, and ronin children more so.

Another barrier to continuing the tradition is poverty. A ronin, like a clan samurai, is identified by his katana. To the casual observer, a samurai without a sword is not a samurai and should be treated as such. A young ronin who has no sword to inherit has no way of proving his claim except his word.

Of course, there are always exceptions. There are wealthy ronin families in Rokugan. Some of them, like the Yotsu, maintain a family name despite their lack of clan affiliation. The majority of ronin-born belong to such families, or come from long lines of ronin. Ronin of this variety tend to be proud of their position. After generations, perhaps centuries, of self-reliance these ronin do not see the need to seek a master. They are doing quite fine, thank you. Many ronin families can trace their lineage to the days of the First War. Clan samurai tend to find these sort of ronin more reliable and less apt to cause banditry, vandalism, and other crimes, but their years of self reliance can also make them obnoxiously independent.

WEALTHY RETAINERS

Though a samurai's lord provides all of the wealth that his retainers require, this does not prevent some samurai from seeking outside income. Samurai can amass quite a bit of wealth independently, especially in wake of the Rokugan's developing economy and the growing power of the merchant class. At times, a canny samurai might amass more wealth than the lord he serves, a potentially embarrassing situation for both parties. This happens most often among the Daidoji, Ide, and Mantis, where mercantile behavior is common or encouraged. While one might expect this also to be prevalent among the Yasuki, it is not. Yasuki who gather great wealth are immediately promoted, and their former lords reprimanded for their inferior business acumen.

While an honorable samurai would turn over personal profit for the good of the clan, the simple reality is that not all men are honorable. The lure of power and riches can seduce even a noble samurai. Thus, many wealthy retainers pay their masters what they feel they owe, then "retire" from their duties to go into business for themselves. Having abandoned their master and clan, they are now ronin.

While these samurai are free to proclaim their former affiliations as much as they please, most do not. More than any other sort of ronin save the dishonored, these ronin are despised. At the very least, they are viewed with jealousy. At the worst, they are considered traitors. Of course, these brand of ronin are usually clever (or wealthy) enough to keep themselves well ahead of angry (and less prosperous) relatives. Since the new concept of "money-lending" has exploded on the

economic scene, ronin of this sort have little want for powerful allies.

DISCORDANT SAMURAI

Samurai who are guilty of minor infractions, such as an inappropriate display of emotion, a vocal outburst, or a minor lapse in etiquette, may find themselves cast out for "temporary discord." Although not technically ronin, samurai in this unfortunate position are formally cut off from assistance from their family or clan. This can also happen in situations where the samurai brought dishonor or embarrassment through no fault of his own (such as accidentally frightening his lord's horse into bolting). Such a punishment is also reserved for young samurai who have trouble controlling their temper, and can have a very sobering effect upon the unprepared.

Samurai of this type are free to proclaim their former clan affiliation, and may even wear their former colors and mon. However, if they do so, they are required to inform anyone they encounter of their current situation and are not allowed to rely upon kinsmen for support. These quasi-ronin are not given traveling papers and are exiled from their home.

Of all the types of non-clan samurai, this one has the greatest hope of redemption. His is assumed to be a temporary situation. Sometimes, the offender is given a certain amount of time (usually a year) in which he must survive, then return. Sometimes, he is required to prove himself in battle, perhaps to return with the head of an enemy. At any rate, once the pre-determined conditions are met, the discordant samurai is invited to return to his former position. Some go to such extreme lengths to be returned to their lord's good graces that they receive a promotion upon their return.

DISHONORED SAMURAI

The harshest of punishments is when a samurai is forbidden seppuku and cast into exile instead. This is no gesture of mercy. This is the height of cruelty, and never imposed lightly. To be made to continue existence as a living symbol of your own failure is a bitter fate. Many of this sort of ronin kill themselves for the unbearable shame, though this is an even greater dishonor, demonstrating that you were as unable to fulfill your duties in death as you were in life. Such a weak and cowardly person can hardly expect much better in the next life.

Dishonored ronin are forbidden to reveal their former family and clan affiliations. Their name is stricken from all records. They are less than dead. These are bitter, desperate men who have little hope of returning to the service of their former clan, or any other for that matter. When a clan samurai asks a ronin what master he served last, and that ronin does not answer, the samurai can guess the reason why. These sort of ronin are the most likely to end up criminals, tearing down everything they held sacred in their former life out of the absolute rage that consumes them.

"SIEGE"

Some believe Siege to be a former Crab, though he has made no effort to substantiate this claim. His actions speak for themselves. In his long and distinguished career, he has survived seven castle sieges, most of which successfully defended against a vastly superior attacking force. Siege is a master of supply, defense, and troop morale. A daimyo who expects to find his castle under siege will often go to any lengths or expense to obtain the venerable Siege's advice. If they can produce enough koku, they might even be able to entice him to come to the castle and witness the siege personally.

Siege is an elderly man, but still quite sprightly and able to use a sword. Occasionally, he can get wrapped up in his work and tends to ignore details such as etiquette and social niceties. He travels with his nine daughters, all ronin samurai-ko. These sisters are extremely protective of their father, and do their best to keep the absent-minded old siege master from getting into trouble.

Siege's personal mon is an anvil, representing one of his favorite Shintao quotes: "Be the anvil. Though a smith may use many hammers, he will only need one anvil."

In modern times, this was the fate met by the Akodo family and the Scorpion Clan. Those Akodo who did not commit *seppuku* or join the Deathseekers became dishonored ronin, as did Scorpions who fled their homes before the onslaught of the Imperial Legions or surrendered their name to save their lives. Scorpion and Akodo ronin are less fortunate than most. As their ejection was proclaimed by the Hantei, only he can rescind the order. Until that time, no Scorpion is allowed to swear fealty to any clan without special dispensation from the Emperor. The Akodo who chose not to swear fealty to other Lion families are free to do as they please, but most daimyos avoid granting these individuals fealty out of fear that to do so may displease the Emperor.

DEAD MASTER

This is the most tragic cause of ronin status, one of the least common, and the most romanticized. When a samurai dies without an heir, his retainers and yojimbo are cast to the waves. In such a situation, a samurai has the option of seeking employment with his lord's relatives, but sometimes this door is closed. If the daimyo died for an act of dishonor, then his retainers may be seen to carry a bit of that dishonor themselves and will be shunned. A lord's assassination, as well, reflects poorly on his personal guard, and may cause the clan to hesitate in finding them a new lord to protect. Occasionally, the dead samurai's relatives simply cannot afford the expense of new retainers and have no choice in the matter. Sometimes, a samurai who was intensely loyal to his lord will not wish to seek another master, but will endure the life of a ronin instead.

Ronin of this variety are allowed to divulge their former clan and wear their former mons and colors. Most choose not to do so as a sign of respect. A ronin must live by his sword; to wear your dead master's mon in hopes of attracting employment is to seek favor for his name rather than your own. While this is not illegal, it can be viewed as somewhat unscrupulous, and can cause a bit of resentment among members of the ronin's former clan.

MUSHA SHUGYO

While not a ronin, a samurai on a *musha shugyo* ("warrior pilgrimage") shares many of the ronin's benefits and stigma. The musha shugyo is a quest to better one's prowess by example. A warrior who chooses to undertake the pilgrimage must first ask permission from his daimyo. There is a pseudo-mystical sanctity to the musha shugyo, and permission is usually only denied in times of war. The musha shugyo is seen as the warrior's swiftest avenue to enlightenment and mastery of the blade. Most samurai only undertake one in their entire life.

To begin the quest, a samurai puts aside all symbols of his clan and family, setting forth alone. If he is accompanied, it is by other pilgrims. The pilgrim may divulge his affiliation, but most do not. This is a quest to be undertaken alone, and invoking one's family name is to rely upon them. The warrior's clan status is not revoked; it is merely irrelevant for the duration of the pilgrimage. Accepting assistance from the clan – from anyone – would violate the spirit of the musha shugyo. If a samurai tells another that he is on a musha shugyo, that should be sufficient to satisfy any curiosity. Few will question the pilgrim's honor by questioning further.

While on the musha shugyo, the samurai's goal is to learn as much as possible. Often, they follow a famous contemporary warrior in hopes of learning from them or mimic the journeys of some legendary hero of old. Along the way, they indulge in duels with bokken, shinai, or even katana in order to hone their skill. If, in their journeys, a pilgrim comes across a battle, they survey the conflict and then request permission to join the side that most suits them.

Those who would disguise their true nature behind the sanctity and anonymity of the musha shugyo should be warned – this is a warrior's pilgrimage. The pilgrim is expected to accept all challenges. A suspicious daimyo can easily deal with a spy claiming to be a pilgrim by sending forth skilled swordsmen with challenges until the musha is slain.

RONIN AGENT

Technically, a ronin operates without the benefit of protection or affiliation with any clan. Sometimes this is not the case. At times, politics or decorum can prevent a daimyo from acting in what he sees as an honorable fashion, forcing him to allow insults to go unpunished or enemies to run free. When a solution cannot be brought about without losing face, drastic measures are called for.

Extremely loyal or honorable samurai may be called upon to assume the role of ronin in order to gain vengeance, seek reprisal, or otherwise strike back against an enemy. Such ronin always act unofficially, of course, and if they are apprehended in the course of their duties they assume full responsibility. Only the extremely loyal are considered for such a mission, as to use ronin status in such a manner is highly illegal and dishonorable. These ronin operate as if they were dishonored or retired samurai, and refuse to expose their former affiliations. They will gladly plead guilty to nonexistent crimes in order to hide their true purpose and protect the honor of the lord whose interests they serve.

A samurai who undertakes such a mission does not expect to survive. Their missions are often nigh impossible. Even if they are successful, they commit seppuku upon the mission's completion to insure their lord's anonymity. When the Scorpion were a Great Clan, this sort of operation was standard procedure. Some would whisper that only the scale of their deception has changed.

Employment

The rigidly structured social system of Rokugan makes no place for lone wolves, yet somehow ronin manage to survive. Though the life is difficult, there are several options open for a ronin to support himself.

MERCENARIES

This is the most common position in which ronin will find employment. Depending on the political climate it can be easy to find work, especially if the ronin doesn't mind being thrown onto the front lines. Unfortunately, the prospects of advancement in this occupation are slim to none. One body is as good as another. If the ronin dies, that's one fewer mercenary to pay. If he lives, he'll be sent back to the front again next time. Even those mercenaries who do well in several campaigns find it difficult to gain glory for their exploits. They are hired hands. An adequate job is expected, not rewarded.

The Lion Clan makes consistent use of mercenaries. The Lion armies are arguably the finest in Rokugan; to maintain excellence on the field, the Lion employ quality disposable troops. Let other clans round up unschooled farmers and arm them with spears. The Lion would rather hire trained warriors for their heavy-casualty front lines, and if none of them return, so much the better – they're only ronin, after all. They especially favor disgruntled Crane ronin, who are acutely trained and know their enemy. Lion troops have ample opportunity to rest while the Crane kill their former kinsmen. The Crane do not regularly exercise this tactic in return; their public stance is that they have little use for ronin and that the Lion policy is dishonorable.

The Lion argue that their policy works. It saves lives and employs potentially dangerous ronin. The Lion feel it is more likely that Lion ronin do not wish to join the Crane. Those who have seen the power and glory of a Lion army from within would never be so foolish as to stand against them.

HONORED ADVISORS

These are those rare ronin who have distinguished themselves as specialists. Their skills and reputations – if not their social positions – demand respect as well as monetary compensation. Ronin of this type include courtiers, shugenja, former generals, experts on spirit lore, and duelists.

Ronin advisors can gain a special appointment as temporary hatamoto. Unlike a true hatamoto, they do not possess holdings or permanent titles. Subject to the daimyo's wishes, the ronin's advice is the final word on matters regarding his area of expertise. He was hired for a reason. Best to let such an individual fulfill his duties so that he can be on his way and stop taxing the daimyo's coffers.

Ronin specialists have little trouble finding a master, but they seldom swear fealty. Their skills are in such demand that they stand to gain more glory, fame, and profit by moving from one daimyo to the next. It is more likely that a ronin of this variety will attempt to work toward gaining enough status and recognition that he is granted a family name of his own.

PRIESTS

This is also another common occupation of ronin, for several reasons. First, many ronin blame themselves for their situation, and turn to the Tao for redemption. Second, it is an easy profession to adopt. Most samurai are literate and versed in the Tao, so adapting to the priesthood does not require much effort. For shugenja, it is

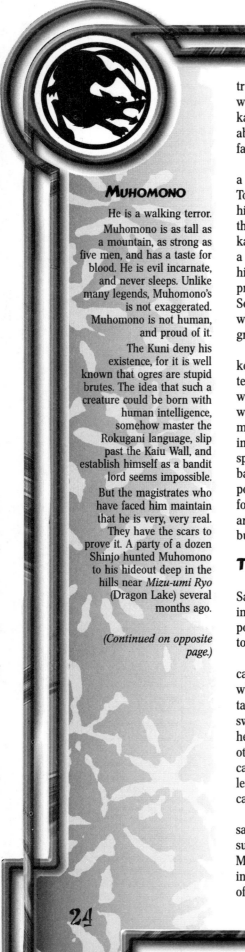

MUHOMONO

He is a walking terror. Muhomono is as tall as a mountain, as strong as five men, and has a taste for blood. He is evil incarnate, and never sleeps. Unlike many legends, Muhomono's is not exaggerated. Muhomono is not human, and proud of it.

The Kuni deny his existence, for it is well known that ogres are stupid brutes. The idea that such a creature could be born with human intelligence, somehow master the Rokugani language, slip past the Kaiu Wall, and establish himself as a bandit lord seems impossible.

But the magistrates who have faced him maintain that he is very, very real. They have the scars to prove it. A party of a dozen Shinjo hunted Muhomono to his hideout deep in the hills near *Mizu-umi Ryo* (Dragon Lake) several months ago.

(Continued on opposite page.)

truly no effort at all for they were priests to begin with. Priests need not have any power over the kami in order to preach the Tao, though such abilities are a plus. Anyone who is truly pious and familiar with the Tao is welcome.

The idea of a warrior taking on the position of a holy man may seem somewhat contradictory. To a Rokugani, this is not so. A samurai is the highest extension of the Celestial Order beneath the kami themselves, a step away from divinity. A katana is the symbol of this position. Ostensibly, a ronin priest carries his katana as a symbol of his former rank, nothing more. A true Shintao priest would never stoop to taking another's life. Some priests will not even defend themselves, but will only dirty their hands with violence if a greater injustice would ensue from their inaction.

A special variant of the ronin priest is the komuso. These itinerant priests have no home or temple, but wander the Empire preaching to whomever will listen. These men and women wear a special basket hat over their heads to maintain anonymity, so that their identity will not interfere with their message. They also carry a special flute, long enough to be played while the basket is worn. This flute is the symbol of their position, and they often play these instruments for the donations they need to survive. Komuso are almost invariably shugenja, though a few bushi are known to exist.

TEACHERS

The role of teacher comes easily to a ronin. Samurai are the most well-educated social group in Rokugan. Even the most thick-headed samurai possesses a variety of skills that are not available to common folk.

Of course, a ronin will be extraordinarily careful to whom he teaches his skills, especially when teaching heimin. Peasants are almost never taught kenjutsu, and are forbidden to touch any sword except for bokken and shinai. More often, heimin are taught archery, yarijutsu, jiujutsu, or other "lesser" combat arts. While most heimin cannot pay much (usually a zeni or two per lesson, if they're lucky), teaching several classes can earn a ronin a meager living.

High Skills are rarely taught to heimin. Most samurai do not feel that heimin are worthy of such knowledge and few heimin are interested. Merchants are an exception to this – they are very interested, make excellent students, and have lots of money.

Eta are never, ever taught by a samurai. Even ronin have standards.

If a teacher is skilled enough, he may attract samurai students. Such students may be taught whatever the teacher feels is appropriate. It is possible for a clan ronin teacher to teach secret techniques, but is also extraordinarily dishonorable, an insult to his former school and sensei. A ronin who enters into such an enterprise will find his former kinsmen unforgiving. The teacher and all his students can expect to be swiftly hunted down and executed by the sensei and alumni of the dishonored school.

Execution. Not seppuku.

Public. Humiliating. Immediate.

Examples must be made.

It is important to note that some schools (the Matsu, Kakita, and Otaku in particular) are protective of all of their teachings, not just the techniques. While teaching skills is seen as a milder offense, these schools consider any former student who teaches what he has learned (especially to peasants!) to be guilty of extreme dishonor. Such an individual will never find a place among his kinsmen again.

MERCHANT YOJIMBO

Samurai who are skilled bodyguards or duelists become yojimbo. When a yojimbo becomes ronin, it is quite difficult to continue this line of work. A yojimbo is trusted with another's life. Could any daimyo find it in his heart to put that sort of trust in a ronin? Hardly. It seems as if the professional yojimbo has little hope for survival in the ronin's world.

Unless, as usual, he is willing to sacrifice his honor.

As Rokugan's economy has grown, so has the power of its merchants. Merchants are only heimin, but many merchants wield enough economic power and influence to put minor daimyos to shame. In time, merchants have noticed the usefulness of yojimbo. If a powerful samurai can have a protector, why can't a powerful merchant? Of course, a true samurai would never sully his name by serving heimin, and even the most powerful merchant would not be suicidal enough to ask.

In ronin, the merchants found opportunity – a trained warrior without political ties, willing to sacrifice honor to survive. Many ronin are so down on their luck that they eagerly accept the opportunity to serve a new master. So perhaps

that new master is a heimin. Perhaps the motivation is money rather than duty. What of it? A yojimbo eats regularly, has all of his needs seen to, and is part of a larger organization. In a way, it's almost like being part of a clan.

Clan samurai don't see it that way. They look at a merchant's yojimbo and pity him. To be ronin is a terrible fate. But how much worse is it to surrender your sword to a lower creature, for so base a compensation as koku?

Incidentally, the merchants have discovered that Shiba, Daidoji, and Wasp ronin excel as yojimbo, and samurai from these families can always find profitable employment.

VILLAGE WARDENS

Many peasant villages are remote, and do not benefit from the protection of doshin or budoka, much less samurai. Solitary ronin often adopt such villages, turning their skills toward defense, maintenance, and the training of its inhabitants in return for a place to live. These ronin become fiercely protective of their new homes, and defend them with astounding steadfastness and courage. These are the peasant heroes and guardians that figure into many Rokugani dramas.

It is important to remember that though a ronin may protect and live in a village, that does not guarantee that his attitudes toward the lesser classes have changed. In fact, many wardens are extremely bitter about their current situation, and resentful about how far they have fallen. As a result, they become even more abusive of heimin and eta than they were as a clan samurai. Some of them become a greater threat to the village than the bandits they supposedly protect against. While others adopt their new village as their home and love the peasants as family, the simple truth is that most are entirely neutral toward their charges.

Why would ronin become village wardens if most care little for those they protect? Because to many ronin, a village is a means to an end. That end is fealty. A samurai who performs admirably in the protection of a village, builds good defenses, and trains the peasants well will be noticed by the daimyo of the province. The ronin may be invited to continue his work with official sanction and be made a yoriki or even a magistrate, swearing fealty to a lesser vassal family. Such ronin serve for years to prove their skill, sincerity, and sense of duty, but this is

considered the closest thing ronin have to a guarantee of fealty.

CRIMINALS

Then there are those who abandon bushido.

Bandits have plagued Rokugan since the beginning of its existence. With the recent explosion of the ronin population, this has only gotten worse. Many ronin are angry and unwilling to find a way to fit into the cracks of society. As a result, they turn to crime. Some form hordes of bandits that ravage the countryside and take what they please. More organized criminals operate in small groups, hiring themselves out as thieves, smugglers, spies, and assassins in large cities. As many as eighty percent of ronin turn to some sort of crime to supplement their existence within the first year of losing their clan status. Many of Rokugan's most notorious career criminals have been ronin. Therefore many ronin are naturally assumed to be criminals and vagrants. Although true samurai might wish to dissociate themselves from criminal ronin, such ronin are still samurai; only the Emperor can revoke samurai status.

For a ronin, crime is easy. Life as a trained warrior is only a short step away from life as a hired thug or a bandit. It's not a life of honor, but there is certainly great potential for wealth and power. The bandit lord Yugoro (described in more detail elsewhere in this book and in *Unexpected Allies*) is the most famous bandit currently operating in the Empire, followed shortly behind by the ronin known as Fade, who once plagued the area around Ryoko Owari.

Legends

THE FIRST RONIN

I would not have believed it unless I had seen it with my own eyes. Ten times one thousand men, marching to the north. The look of defeat I saw upon their faces was unlike anything I have seen throughout this war. Pity these men, whose lives have been tossed upon the waves. These ronin. – Suzume Masako

Ronin have existed for as long as there have been samurai. For as long as men have lived and died for the sake of honor, there were those who were left behind. However, for the first few centuries of Rokugan's history, ronin were few

MUHOMONO
(CONTINUED)

The three magistrates that survived have sworn not to underestimate the ogre again. Muhomono fled his hideout shortly after the Shinjo were defeated, and it is unknown where his current base of operations may be. The Unicorn are eager to bring him to justice, and have placed a bounty of fifty koku on his head. Shinjo Yokatsu has promised that this bounty will increase every time Muhomono takes another life: samurai, heimin, or even eta.

Muhomono's mon is bizarre and ever-evolving. He collects the mons of the samurai he has killed, and stitches them together in one ghastly bloodstained banner.

Muhomono is not a ronin, of course. That status is forever beyond him, as it is beyond heimin and eta. They, at least, have places in the Celestial Order, whereas he is an abomination of it. He may, however, provide an unpleasant surprise for those with no choice but to be on the road, and travelers speak in hushed tones when he is said to be near.

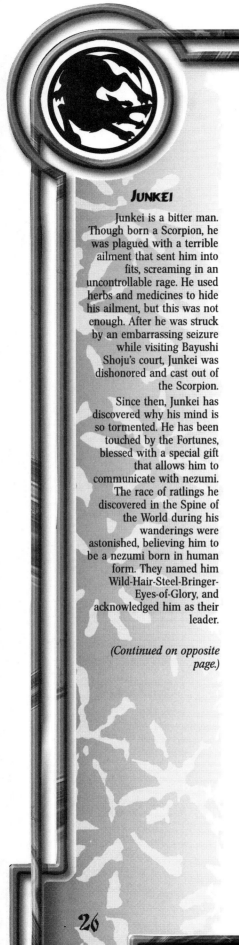

JUNKEI

Junkei is a bitter man. Though born a Scorpion, he was plagued with a terrible ailment that sent him into fits, screaming in an uncontrollable rage. He used herbs and medicines to hide his ailment, but this was not enough. After he was struck by an embarrassing seizure while visiting Bayushi Shoju's court, Junkei was dishonored and cast out of the Scorpion.

Since then, Junkei has discovered why his mind is so tormented. He has been touched by the Fortunes, blessed with a special gift that allows him to communicate with nezumi. The race of ratlings he discovered in the Spine of the World during his wanderings were astonished, believing him to be a nezumi born in human form. They named him Wild-Hair-Steel-Bringer-Eyes-of-Glory, and acknowledged him as their leader.

(Continued on opposite page.)

and far between. So many warriors died during the war with Fu Leng that able-bodied samurai became scarce. A trained warrior with no master did not have to search long to find another willing to accept his service. Samurai who somehow found themselves unable to find a master were the object of such shame and ridicule that seppuku or the abdication of warrior status were far more common fates. The word "ronin" was an academic term, used by the Isawa to describe these curious individuals, and did not come into common use until after the end of the First War, also known as the Crab-Crane War.

The First War was the first internal conflict in Rokugan's history. The Crane and Crab give conflicting histories as to how the war began, but Yasuki dissatisfaction and border disputes over the rich Kenkai Hanto Peninsula were clearly the chief motivating factors. An often overlooked factor in this war is the growing power of the *gozoku,* a political consortium of Crane, Scorpion, and Phoenix that exerted its power over the rule of two Hantei Emperors. (See *Winter Court: Kyuden Seppun,* page 38, and *Winter Court: Kyuden Kakita,* pages 82–84, for more information on the gozoku.)

The gozoku first began to grow in power during the reign of Hantei Fujiwa. Detecting a threat to his power, Fujiwa was determined to destroy them before they grew dangerous. Unfortunately, though Fujiwa was a skilled politician he had difficulty in finding allies. The Matsu were willing to assist, but Akodo Mitsuyuki, the Lion Clan daimyo, was weak and ineffectual. He forbade his samurai to offer anything more than token support out of fear of the gozoku's wrath. The Dragon had little political or military power to offer the Hantei, so he was forced to seek support from the Crab. Hantei Fujiwa had led his own personal troops in the defense of the Crab several years earlier during their struggle against Oni no Usu. Hida Ichido, Crab Champion, was thus fiercely loyal to Fujiwa. Ichido had grown resentful of the gozoku's growing influence and was ready to do whatever his Emperor requested.

Hantei Fujiwa decided that his first target would be the weak link in the gozoku triad – the Crane. The Crane Champion of the time, Doji Mizobu, was not affiliated with the gozoku. The true gozoku power in the Crane was Mizobu's son and heir, Raigu. Mizobu was a temperamental and often foolish man. Though Raigu tended

most of the clan's affairs, Mizobu was still the true leader. Fujiwa knew that Mizobu would present a weakness if he watched him carefully, a weakness that could cripple the Crane before Raigu rose to power and Fujiwa's true problems began.

In time, that weakness presented itself in the form of the Yasuki family. The Yasuki had grown in economic influence, but were kept out of the courts by the paranoid Mizobu, who feared any threat to his power. Fujiwa believed that by fanning the fires of jealousy in Mizobu's mind, he could encourage the Crane into a rash judgment. He could then drive a wedge between the Doji and Yasuki and stifle the gozoku's economic power before they became a serious threat.

Hantei Fujiwa hoped that such a coup would not only weaken the gozoku, but give Akodo Mitsuyuki enough courage to back the Emperor publicly. In the meantime, the Crab attempted to distract Mizobu from the Hantei's political maneuvers by threatening his borders, building fortresses ever closer to Kenkai Hanto Peninsula. As the Crane grew more nervous and distracted, the Lion became more bold. Mitsuyuki began to throw his support toward the Hantei, but only in word, not action. Still, it seemed as if Fujiwa's plan might work.

Sadly, the entire affair ended in tragedy. Tensions between the Crab and Crane exploded without warning. Open warfare began; for the first time Rokugani fought against Rokugani. Fujiwa dispatched Miya shisha to end the conflict, but the diplomats only made matters worse. The Emperor's efforts seemed to be stymied at every turn. Even the gozoku seemed baffled at Fujiwa's apparent incompetence. When Hida Ichido died under mysterious circumstances, the Crab completely lost faith in Fujiwa and withdrew their political support. The Crab turned their attention to the Crane, hoping to salvage something out of the war. The Emperor could not end the war. Due to his apparent incompetence, the power of his position had dwindled so much that he was no more than a figurehead. The gozoku offered to solve the entire affair, but Fujiwa spurned their assistance. In retribution, Doji Raigu kidnapped the Imperial Heir as a demonstration of Fujiwa's weakness. Defeated, the aged Fujiwa acceded to their demands for the sake of his son. Drawing upon the influence of three Great Clans, the gozoku brought the First

War to a close in short order. They even did so in the Emperor's name.

Hantei Fujiwa was a broken Emperor. He became little more than a pawn of the gozoku. At their demands, he ordered many samurai to be cast forth from their clans on the obviously spurious charge of "gross contravention of the tenets of bushido." These cutbacks were most severe in the Crab, for their defiance, the Crane, for their failure (and to weed out those loyal to Mizobu), and the Lion, to encourage Akodo Mitsuyuki to mind his own business. The names of the newly-created ronin were compiled by the Emperor's loyal scribe – gozoku leader Shiba Gaijushiko.

The gozoku had broadcast a powerful message: "Do not interfere."

Unfortunately, the imperial edict had drastic, unforeseen effects. Thousands of samurai were cast out. They had to go *somewhere*. Many felt that their dismissal had been unfair. Seppuku or retirement seemed unsavory prospects. Among the first to receive her dismissal was a fiery young samurai-ko named Matsu Mochihime. As legend has it, Mochihime strode into the Imperial Court, threw her haori to the floor, and turned to the Emperor and his court with a scowl.

"I am Mochihime," she spat. "I may no longer be Matsu. I may no longer be a Lion. But I am, and will always be, a samurai. When you wish to have my daisho you can pry it from my dead fingers." At that, she is said to have turned and marched from the Emperor's throne room, leaving Fujiwa and his gozoku masters gaping in indignation.

The tale is almost certainly apocryphal. The likelihood of a ronin being admitted to the Imperial presence, openly insulting the Hantei, and surviving to tell the tale seems utterly inconceivable. The Ikoma scoff at the tale's veracity at every opportunity. Still, the tale of Mochihime is very popular among the wave-men, and she is widely regarded to have been the first to embrace her status, proudly calling herself "ronin." It is said that she continued to serve the secret commands of Hantei Fujiwa for decades despite the power of the decadent gozoku. Stories persist of the heroic band of ronin that rode at Mochihime's side, fighting against the gozoku and paving the way for Fujiwa's daughter, Empress Yugozohime (Hantei VII), to throw off their shackles and restore Rokugan to its former glory.

The Ikoma reluctantly document a ronin named "Mochiko" who *did* exist in the time of Empress Yugozohime's reign; one of the Empress' first official acts was to command the Lion to grant her fealty. Matsu Mochiko won the Test of the Emerald Champion after Yugozohime's consort, Doji Usan, turned down the position.

Whatever the truth of Mochihime's tale may be, the concept of "wave-men" had been unleashed. With it came a dream-like image of the ronin as noble vagabond, mirrored by the darker image of the ronin as cutthroat bandit. The idea of the ronin as hero is very popular among farmers, merchants, and eta. Many kabuki plays are dedicated to the exploits of ronin heroes, and many legends dedicated to their adventures.

Among the samurai, the idea of a "ronin hero" is less romanticized. The loss of one's master is the most horrible fate a samurai can endure. The very idea of a samurai with no master is simply obscene. It is a situation that should not exist. It is a situation that should not be tolerated. Such a samurai is not an object of admiration, but an object of pity. Though clan samurai are well aware of ronin legends, such tales are often edited so that they end with the hero regaining fealty or being granted an honorable seppuku.

OISHI

In the waning days of Hantei XIII, the court of Otosan Uchi had become rife with corruption. This time it was not the fault of a political conspiracy, but rather the unrestrained urges of a generation of warriors that had known nothing but peace. Decades earlier, the Great Clans had allied together to bring down the menace of Iuchiban. Hantei XI had taken advantage of the alliance, forging a peace that would endure for half a century by drafting the Hitojichi (Hostage) Laws, which required every daimyo to spend at least a month of every year in Otosan Uchi. (See *Winter Court: Kyuden Kakita*, page 47, for more information on the Hitojichi.)

Unfortunately, there was a price for peace. Hantei XIII was hardly the enlightened statesman that his grandfather had been. He used the throne as an opportunity to flaunt his omnipotence. Otosan Uchi became a home to the Emperor's sycophants and toadies, ultra-rich samurai who cared nothing for bushido, but only for their own position. The rest of the Empire crumbled as the morals of the samurai class sagged. (The Ikoma hold that this part of the tale is spurious. The Son

JUNKEI
(CONTINUED)

Eager for revenge, Junkei trained the nezumi and used his remaining wealth to supply them with weapons. It is said that he taught them secret Bayushi bushi techniques, though this seems unlikely. He forged the tribe into a fighting force, striking against Scorpion trade routes and causing havoc.

Shortly before the Coup, a band of Scorpion magistrates were sent into Junkei's territory to deal with him. Though his tribe of nezumi was wiped out, Junkei escaped. He was last seen heading for Crab lands, hoping to find a new tribe of ratlings to obey his commands.

Junkei's personal mon is a pair of blazing white eyes on a black field, after the name the nezumi gave him.

27

MASATOYO

Masatoyo was a Shiba cast out from the Phoenix Clan for repeated questioning of his superiors' orders. He was a capable general, but not a great one. He was an able leader, but not spectacular. He had no experience, and was relatively low-born. The Shiba felt that they were losing little.

Since that day, Masatoyo has found work as a mercenary. He has learned to survive. He has become swift, clever, and deadly. He has embraced bushido as never before, for his honor is the only thing left that makes life worth living. He has become skilled at leading small crack groups of saboteurs, scouts, and archers. He strikes quickly, and is gone before the enemy can recover. His skills are in high demand. He is currently in employ of the Unicorn, and Yokatsu has considered offering Masatoyo fealty in reward for his consistent valor and courage. If this does not happen, Masatoyo has heard interesting rumors about an army in the Dragon mountains.

(Continued on opposite page.)

of Heaven would never be a party to such foolish behavior.)

Among Hantei XIII's servants was a courtier named Bayushi Kira. Though Kira was born of low rank, his wealth and connections had won him an important place as a liaison to the court. All visiting daimyos were required to report to Kira to be apprised of the ever-changing rules for etiquette and behavior. A minor breach of etiquette in the presence of the Emperor could bring swift and terrible reprisals for one's clan, and many daimyos required to visit due to the Hitojichi Laws knew little or nothing of courtly decorum. Kira became corrupted by his position, demanding exorbitant bribes from those he was to instruct, lest they be left unassisted in the court. His power swiftly grew.

So came the time for Hiruma Asano to pay his yearly visit. Asano was a minor provincial daimyo of the Crab, but a proud one. He despised the decadence to which Rokugan had fallen. Shiro Asano was impeccable. His men were warriors, true samurai, living examples of bushido. Their presence on the edge of the Shadowlands had not dulled their wits or their prowess. Asano was disgusted by the state of the capital, but he was a loyal subject of the Emperor and wished for nothing more than to serve his required time. Unfortunately this was not to be. Asano refused to meet the demands of Bayushi Kira. He would pay no bribes.

In retaliation, Kira used his weapons: rumor and innuendo. The "backwoods Crab" – never referred to by name – became that season's butt of jokes, a figure of mockery. Asano soon found himself utterly alone in the court, defeated by Kira's whispers. In desperation, convinced that he had permanently sullied his clan's reputation, Asano took his own life. So ashamed had he been, though, that he could not bring himself to face the Emperor and beg the permission of the Son of Heaven to end his own life. As a result of his gross flouting of protocol, Asano's lands and titles were confiscated. His wife was exiled to a monastery. The samurai who served him became ronin.

Among Asano's retainers was a grizzled bushi named Oishi. Oishi had served Asano for many years as hatamoto, commanding scouting missions into the Shadowlands and assuring that the bushi were well trained and equipped. Oishi, at his post in Asano province, was shattered when he heard the news. The former retainers of Asano

screamed for vengeance, but Oishi pleaded temperance. Safe in Otosan Uchi, Kira was unassailable. It seemed there was nothing they could do to seek justice. After closing his master's affairs, Oishi and the other ronin disbanded.

For a year, Bayushi Kira remained locked in his home in the heart of the capital. He commissioned spies to keep tabs on the Asano ronin, expecting them to attempt vengeance. His spies found nothing. One ronin had built a heimin archery academy. A second had joined the crusade of the mad Crane, Doji Hotei. A third had enrolled in a Kuni monastery to begin training as a Witch Hunter. After a time, Oishi surfaced in Ryoko Owari. He had divorced his wife, turned to sake and geisha, and had even started a drunken duel in a kabuki theater. It seemed that the ronin of Asano had given up.

After some time, Kira was no longer able to maintain his spies; the Emperor had distanced himself from the Bayushi to avoid controversy, and Kira's finances had dwindled. Kira dismissed his espionage network and contented himself with a contingent of sixty loyal bushi.

For a time, things were quiet. The ronin of Asano were called cowards and worse, examples of how far bushido had fallen. Samurai who would allow the killer of their lord to go unpunished while they reveled in sake and geisha were truly worthless. Some laughed, and said that the time of the samurai was dying.

They were wrong.

A year after the day of Hiruma Asano's death, thirty-one men in the hooded garb of firemen gathered on the streets around Bayushi Kira's home. Throwing aside their cloaks, they revealed armor and weapons carefully maintained for twelve months. Battering down the doors of Kira's home, they stormed the mansion and defeated the Scorpion's unprepared guards. Those who surrendered were allowed to live. Those who fought back were killed without mercy. All the while, a single, elderly ronin stood in the road before the gates of Kira's castle holding forth a placard for passersby, inscribed with the following:

"We are the ronin of Shiro Asano. This night we come to avenge our master with the death of Bayushi Kira. We intend you no harm."

At the head of the attack was Oishi, strangely sober and competent after his year of carousing. He hunted down Kira and challenged him. Kira drew his blade and attacked, but was no match for the Hiruma in either prowess or passion. Oishi wrapped the bloody head of Kira in a satchel and carried it to the heart of Otosan Uchi to present it before the tomb where his master's ashes lay.

When the Emperor's soldiers arrived to surround the men of Asano, the ronin surrendered peacefully. Their story had caught on like wildfire among the people: how they had plotted in secret despite the Scorpion Clan's best spies, how they had defied an unjust punishment in the name of honor, how they had fought against impossible odds and triumphed. They had demonstrated for all of Rokugan that bushido was alive and well.

Hantei XIII was perplexed. The men of Asano could not be excused for their criminal act, but to execute them would have been a political disaster. To satisfy both justice and the people, the Emperor granted the ronin the right of honorable seppuku. Kira's surviving retainers were given the same punishment. The ashes of Hiruma Oishi and his followers were buried beside their lord.

The Crab tell this story and accept every word of it as it is written here despite Ikoma claims that certain elements defame the character of the Hantei. Once a year, on the day of Kira's death, the Hiruma cast aside the dreary existence that is their lot and hold a festival in remembrance of the thirty-one ronin.

SUN TAO

No clan holds any records of the birth or death of a man named Sun Tao. Rosters of the great armies of Rokugan do not note his presence. Shugenja who attempt to contact his spirit have never met with anything other than silence. The name "Sun Tao" is clearly an alias, yet it is the only name that exists for this strange ronin. He seems to have never existed.

In legend, however, his tale is strong. In one version, he is a Lion, a direct descendant of Akodo. In another he is an Isawa, raised by the Akodo as a hostage. In a third, he is the youngest son of the Emperor, who journeyed out into the Empire once his brother's reign was secure. In a fourth, he is the son of barbarians. Whatever his origins may be, one detail is in agreement. Sun Tao began his career among the Lion, during the time of Hantei XVII. He was a clever student, and seemed to have a natural gift for strategy. Even the sensei of the Akodo School was impressed by the boy's superb mind, and all who knew Sun Tao knew that he would one day be a mighty general.

After five years of study with the Lion, Sun Tao was given the honor of being allowed to read the original copy of Akodo's Leadership. Sun Tao read the entire volume in a single evening, then stumbled to bed with the words burning in his mind. That night, he heard voices in his sleep, the voices of all the Lion Champions who put pen to paper on the great scroll. The voice of Akodo was louder then the others, and contained them all within its roar.

"You have begun your journey?" Akodo demanded.

"I have!" Sun Tao replied. "I have learned the art of leadership!"

"Leadership is only one of many virtues. You are incomplete."

"What must I do?" Sun Tao asked eagerly.

"Go into the Empire," Akodo commanded. "Each clan has its lesson. You must learn them all."

The next day, Sun Tao reported what had happened. His sensei was suspicious, but something in the young man's manner seemed to forbid argument. Sun Tao humbly requested permission to journey to the lands of the Crane, in order to learn from their generals.

"What can you learn from the Crane that the Lion cannot teach?" the sensei asked.

"I do not know," Sun Tao said. "That is why I must go."

"They will not accept you," the sensei said. "You are a Lion."

"Then I will be a Lion no more," Sun Tao replied.

"You would cast aside our name?" the sensei asked sharply.

"The message I seek is more important than the messenger," Sun Tao replied. "I will return, and share what I have learned."

The sensei had heard enough, and ejected Sun Tao from his presence. The young bushi soon came to the court of the Crane Champion, and requested permission to study under him. The Crane suspected that Sun Tao was a Lion spy, so he demanded a test. Sun Tao was given an army of fifty untrained men and sent to assault a ronin-occupied castle in the Crane's southern territories.

Sun Tao returned three months later, victorious. Once more, he requested permission to study with the Crane. Shocked but intrigued by Sun Tao's ability, the Crane agreed, hoping to divine the young ronin's secrets. Sun Tao learned much, adding the wiles of the Crane to the tactics

INAZUMA

Her name means "lightning."

She is a mighty shugenja, wielding the power of thunder and the gift of life. She never remains in one place, but travels where the Fortunes lead her, surviving through the sale of her medicines. She seems to be a master of magic so mighty that she travels deep into lands where other shugenja dare not go.

She is a fraud.

The Agasha told her she would never understand the kami, that she would never hear their voices. In anger, she stormed out of her home and determined to prove them wrong. She has not returned.

After that day, Inazuma determined to try to become what she was not – a shugenja. She has used her mastery of kagaku (see *Way of the Dragon*, Appendix III) to create impressive displays of thunder and lightning, and her knowledge of herbalism to create healing salves, but has no true magical power. She maintains her facade carefully, and always sticks to areas where she is unlikely to encounter true shugenja.

(Continued on opposite page.)

of the Lion. The Crane learned much from the brilliant young general, as well.

After five years passed, Sun Tao left the Crane. Their Champion offered him great wealth if he remained, but Sun Tao's quest was foremost in his mind. He promised to return, and share what he had learned. The Crane were saddened to lose such a great general, but they wished him well. The bushi the Crane had given him followed him with fanatic loyalty.

Next, Sun Tao came to the lands of the Phoenix. The Phoenix were happy to invite such an esteemed general to their lands, and offered to share their knowledge of warfare in return for his advisement. Sun Tao spent five years in the land of the Phoenix, and while he lived there, the Phoenix knew no war or strife.

As Sun Tao prepared to leave, the Phoenix Champion came to see him off. "I am sorry," the Phoenix said with a chuckle. "You came here to learn of war, but have known only peace. I hope you are not disappointed."

"Certainly not," Sun Tao replied. "These five years of peace have been a greater test than all my time with the Lion and Crane. I thank you."

With that, Sun Tao once again promised to share what he had learned with the Phoenix. He journeyed to the lands of the Dragon.

In those days, the Mirumoto served the purpose the Dragonfly Clan now fulfill, regulating travelers to the Togashi provinces. They would not admit Sun Tao to the high mountains. Sun Tao set up his camp in the foothills, waiting for the Dragon Clan daimyo to answer his request. The men and women who had come to follow him began to grow angry and resentful, for they had earned much prestige in the last decade. Surely they did not deserve to be treated so. Sun Tao simply waited. He learned to draw sustenance from the bare rock and scrub, and to keep up the spirits of his army when there seemed to be no purpose in waiting.

After five years, the Dragon Champion came down from his mountain.

"Thank you for your patience," the Dragon said.

"Thank you for yours," Sun Tao replied. "I will return to teach you what I have learned."

"I am pleased I could be of service," the Dragon replied.

And Sun Tao set off.

Sun Tao then journeyed to the lands of the Crab. For a time, he knew nothing but combat.

Three quarters of the bushi who followed him died for their ignorance on the Wall, ravaged by creatures they could not comprehend. After five years, the Crab Champion demanded that Sun Tao depart and pester his clan no more. He offered the general a suit of armor from the Kaiu Forge as a gesture of respect for the general's reputation, but begged him to leave his clan in peace.

Sun Tao apologized, and offered to return to teach the Crab what he had learned. The Crab told him not to bother.

The Champion of the Soshi came to Sun Tao next, and invited him to learn from the Scorpion. Sun Tao agreed, for despite his failure upon the Carpenter his quest was not yet done. For five years, he learned from the Scorpion and came away with a strange glint in his eyes. He promised the Scorpion that he would return when his quest was complete.

"Is it not complete?" the Soshi asked in confusion. The Scorpion had long planned to be the last to teach Sun Tao, and thus the first to learn his secrets.

"No," said Sun Tao. "There is one clan that I have not yet visited."

With that, the aged Sun Tao set off into the Burning Sands.

He never returned.

Sun Tao left his armor and writings to Terumuto, the most loyal of his followers. Terumuto dutifully crafted seven copies of Sun Tao's journal, intending to deliver one to each of the Great Clans, and one to the Emperor. Unfortunately, Terumuto was slain by bandits before he could deliver all of the scrolls. Only the copies intended for the Dragon, the Scorpion, and the Hantei reached their destination. The others, along with Sun Tao's armor, have been lost to the ages and are presumed to be destroyed.

FUYARI AND NANASHI

The tale of Nanashi, unlike many ronin legends, has a firm basis in reality. The ronin of Nanashi Mura have made certain that no exaggeration or omission has marred the tale. To Nanashi Mura, it is critical to remember their origins lest they forget their purpose.

As a rule, settlements populated largely by ronin do not last. These areas generally fall to disorder or are broken up by the army of a Great Clan out of fear of ronin organizing a revolt. Nanashi Mura, however, is a village that has

survived against all odds. Its story begins forty years ago, with a man named Shinjo Fuyari.

Shinjo Fuyari was a cunning man. Through skill and wit, he fought his way to a high-ranking position in the Unicorn army, but after he assumed his new rank he was corrupted by power. His unwarranted attacks against the Dragon and Crab were executed with such bloodlust that he brought shame to the Shinjo daimyo. He was dismissed from the clan.

Fuyari left peacefully, but peace was hardly his intent. He was charismatic, despite his wicked nature, and soon rallied a large army of ronin and ashigaru to strike against the Unicorn. His tactics were sound and his knowledge of Unicorn strategy was complete. He was certain his force could overwhelm the token presence at Mura Nisa Kawa Nemui (Village by the Sleeping River). Once he had fortified there, he believed that his knowledge of Unicorn defenses would enable him to conquer the unassailable castle at Toshi No Aida Ni Kawa (City Between the Rivers). From there, he would stifle the Unicorn's trade with the rest of Rokugan and wage war upon the entire clan. The plan seemed mad, but when his men heard the fire in his voice, it seemed possible.

It never happened. When Fuyari's army marched, they found themselves facing hundreds of ronin. Fuyari stepped forth to parley, not wishing to expend his army's energy unnecessarily. "Do you stand with the Unicorn?" he called out.

"No," answered a tall ronin in a deep hood, the apparent leader of this new army.

"Then stand out of our path!" Fuyari demanded. "We ronin strike against the confines of a society that laughs at us! We can defeat the Unicorn! Join us and share our triumph!"

The man laughed. His laughter carried across the morning air, floating to the ears of every man present. "And then what?" the man demanded. "Shall we destroy the Dragon? And then the Crab? And what of the Lion? Surely your impressive army can defeat the Lion! Shall we tear down all of Rokugan?"

"If I must," Fuyari growled.

"And what do you expect the Clans to do while you carry on your crusade?" the ronin asked. "Sit idly by? No. They will unite, and destroy not only you, but all wave-men out of fear for madness like yours rising again. You do not bring death to the Unicorn. You bring death to us all. You are no leader, Fuyari. You are a fool." With that, the hooded ronin strode forward and struck Fuyari across the face with his staff.

Fuyari staggered to his feet, opening his bloody mouth to issue the command to attack. He could not. For the first moment in a long time, the mad haze parted. He saw what he had become. He fell to his knees in shame, his rough fingers gouging the soil. Fuyari looked up wretchedly and asked a single question.

"Who are you?"

"I serve those who are yet to come," he said cryptically. "I am merely one more in an unending stream. *Nanashi.*"

No name.

"What must I do?" Fuyari asked.

"See to it that a thing like this never happens again," he replied. "I will be near."

With that the hooded ronin left, though his army remained to insure Fuyari's good behavior. Fuyari was true to his word, and led them away. He knew that his homeland would offer no succor, and so he journeyed across Rokugan, asking every daimyo who would meet with him for permission to establish a village. He was repeatedly denied.

After a year of failure, he found himself on Dragon lands. He set up camp in their foothills and submitted a request for an audience with the Dragon champion through the proper channels. The Dragonfly accepted his written supplication and never bothered to submit it to the Dragon, so they were quite surprised when a missive from Togashi arrived which instructed them to arrange a meeting for him with Fuyari.

As is so often the case with Togashi, no records remain of Fuyari's meeting with the Dragon daimyo. What is known is that Fuyari died shortly after the founding of Nanashi Mura on a southern parcel of Dragon land, having named his new city after the strange anonymous man who returned him to the path of honor. Still, Nanashi does not exist on any maps save those that ronin draw.

Ronin Organizations

Ronin can hardly be considered a unified group. Most belong to no family, attend no school, and acknowledge no leader. However, samurai thrive on order and authority, so it is only natural that organized groups should form. Sadly, most ronin groups are unstable. If they are weak, they crumble. If they are strong, a Great Clan may

INAZUMA (CONTINUED)

In many ways, she is a spoiled brat. Actually communicating with the kami is not important; she only wishes for others to believe that she can do so. For this reason, she always keeps moving, so that her presence in a village will be fresh and new and the heimin will stand in awe of her power.

Her mon is a stylized thunderbolt.

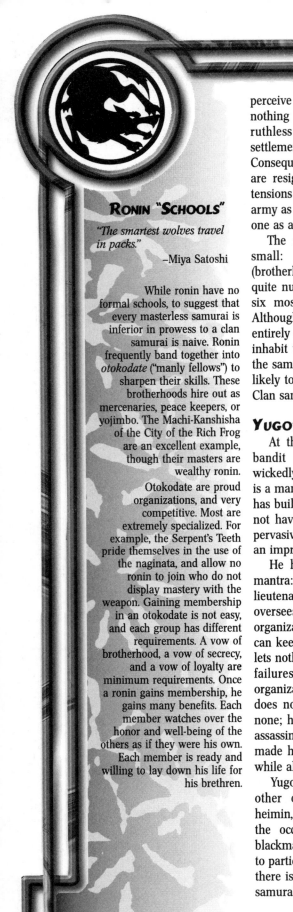

Ronin "Schools"

"The smartest wolves travel in packs."

–Miya Satoshi

While ronin have no formal schools, to suggest that every masterless samurai is inferior in prowess to a clan samurai is naive. Ronin frequently band together into *otokodate* ("manly fellows") to sharpen their skills. These brotherhoods hire out as mercenaries, peace keepers, or yojimbo. The Machi-Kanshisha of the City of the Rich Frog are an excellent example, though their masters are wealthy ronin.

Otokodate are proud organizations, and very competitive. Most are extremely specialized. For example, the Serpent's Teeth pride themselves in the use of the naginata, and allow no ronin to join who do not display mastery with the weapon. Gaining membership in an otokodate is not easy, and each group has different requirements. A vow of brotherhood, a vow of secrecy, and a vow of loyalty are minimum requirements. Once a ronin gains membership, he gains many benefits. Each member watches over the honor and well-being of the others as if they were his own. Each member is ready and willing to lay down his life for his brethren.

perceive them as a threat. The Hantei's laws have nothing to say regulating war on ronin; some ruthless generals consider crushing ronin settlements a good way to keep in practice. Consequently, the organizations which exist today are resigned to a future of strife as inter-Clan tensions grow; if they are not recruited by a Clan army as front-line troops, they will be targeted by one as a training exercise.

The most common ronin organizations are small: *juzimai* (gangs) and *otokodate* (brotherhoods) are the most common, and are quite numerous. The following are currently the six most powerful ronin-related organizations. Although the Kolat and Bloodspeakers are not entirely or even largely ronin groups, they tend to inhabit the fringes of Rokugani society in much the same way that ronin do, making ronin more likely to encounter their agents than the average Clan samurai.

Yugoro's Hordes

At the heart of a half dozen of the largest bandit juzimai in Rokugan is one man, a wickedly cunning bandit named Yugoro. Yugoro is a man of enterprise, and during his lifetime he has built a tremendous criminal empire. He does not have the experience of the Scorpion or the pervasive presence of the Kolat, but he has carved an impressive niche in a short time.

He has accomplished this by following one mantra: "Trust no one." While Yugoro has many lieutenants, he depends only upon himself. He oversees the most critical operations of his organizations personally. He knows that one man can keep a secret, and two men can break it. He lets nothing fall outside his notice, and allows no failures. Yugoro is his empire, and his organization will not survive his death. Yugoro does not care. He has no heirs and wishes for none; he is in business for himself. His bandits, assassins, smugglers, and opium dealers have made him a rich, powerful, and influential man while allowing him to operate from the shadows.

Yugoro's hordes, smuggling rings, spies, and other organizations are composed of ronin, heimin, and eta. He maintains connections with the occasional clan samurai (mostly through blackmail) but he does not allow such individuals to participate in his operations. In Yugoro's world, there is nothing more untrustworthy than a clan samurai. As Yugoro once said, "If a man is foolish

enough to throw his life away, how can he depended upon to guard my interests?"

Ronin who find their way into Yugoro's organization will find life difficult, but rewarding. Yugoro is bloodthirsty, merciless, and utterly heartless but he pays well. In addition, his experience and connections lead to less trouble with magistrates, higher discipline, and richer targets. If a ronin is willing to sacrifice everything noble about being a samurai, and can fight reasonably well, he may become quite wealthy.

Contact with other ronin organizations

Yugoro's hordes constantly gather information about other large ronin groups. He has heard legends of a group called the "Kolat" from the heimin he associates with, but considers them nothing more than superstition. His smugglers sometimes operate out of the City of the Rich Frog, but are entirely unwelcome in Nanashi. Yugoro is wary of the Bloodspeakers, but has found their magic quite useful and has worked (carefully) with maho-tsukai in the past. Yugoro has thus far avoided Toturi's Army, and is beginning to fear that the Black Lion's overdeveloped sense of honor may present a problem.

City of the Rich Frog

Toshi Sano Kanemochi Kaeru stands roughly equidistant between the edge of Unicorn territory and the never-changing borders of the Dragon. The two clans, historically, have been more indifferent to one another than any two Great Clan neighbors, sharing the least common ground in philosophical, technological, and military matters. They have rarely sought to intrude upon one another's territory, and the area surrounding the City of the Rich Frog has become an unofficial buffer zone between the two since the Unicorn's return. The Rich Frog has grown during this time, conducting trade between the two clans as they struggle to understand one another.

The ruling family of the city is a ronin family nicknamed *Kaeru* (Frog). The name is not officially acknowledged, but it is a familiar appellation that has stuck. The Kaeru claim to be the descendant of the founder of the city, a frog-spirit that tricked a greedy merchant and built the city with his wealth. If the story is true, the Kaeru have certainly inherited the mercantile skills of their ancestor. They are cunning – some would

say cutthroat – and conduct the city's affairs as if it were nothing more than a business. What profits the city, endures. What harms the city, leaves. Anything can be bought at a price, so long as the sale does not harm the city's future. For instance, under-the-table opium peddling is tolerated, but the Kaeru would never tempt the fates (or the Imperial Legions) by selling gaijin pepper.

The City of the Rich Frog has been appointed a single official magistrate (who is well-paid by the Kaeru to ignore their illegal activities). This magistrate has no yoriki, but is assisted by a band of "volunteers" called the Machi-Kanshisha. These individuals are actually an otokodate trained and funded by the Kaeru, but they do a fairly good job of keeping order as well as watching over their patron family's interests.

Contact with other ronin organizations

The city is open to communication with other ronin groups, but conducts itself cautiously. Yugoro's smugglers are tolerated, but bandits are not welcome. Ronin from Nanashi are welcome, but the Kaeru resent the heavy-handed sense of justice they wield.

The Kaeru are concerned about Toturi. The Black Lion's reputation and proximity to the city worries them, and they have sent several agents to answer his call to arms in hopes of determining Toturi's ultimate motives. The Kaeru are reserving their decision about Toturi until they determine whether becoming his ally or enemy would be more profitable.

As for the Kolat, several years ago the Kaeru attempted to determine whether such a phantom organization existed. They were approached soon afterward by an solitary individual. Whatever this person said during their meaning, the Kaeru have since abandoned all efforts at locating the Kolat.

NANASHI

Since the day the Dragon first sanctioned its construction, Nanashi Mura has been a haven to ronin. It can be at times a wild and lawless place, but as of yet there have been no serious problems. The Eyes of Nanashi, a local otokodate, regulate all local affairs under the direction of a village headman and appointed Dragon magistrate. With the assistance of a band of sohei (warrior-monks) of the Temple of Ebisu, they also police the village. Both groups have little tolerance for foolishness. So long as visitors obeys the laws of

Nanashi, they are welcome. Those who cause disorder are cast out.

Nanashi is not merely another stop on the road; the village is wholly dedicated to regulating, assisting, and policing the actions of ronin. If a dangerous ronin bandit is on the loose, Nanashi will send an agent of the Eyes to deal with it. If a ronin wishes to find employment, he can find it in Nanashi. If a ronin can not find acceptance, he can find a life in Nanashi. The village exists to make the ordeal of being a ronin a bit easier and has a standing "no questions asked" policy, so long as visitors obey the law.

This is not to say that Nanashi is perfect. The village's very existence is precarious. As it stands, Nanashi has the favor of the Dragon Clan, and stands as an example of relative order among chaos. Should the village falter in its values, its leaders succumb to corruption, or its alliance with the Dragon waver, however, it would be wiped out overnight.

Contact with other ronin organizations

Nanashi has posted a bounty of ten koku on the head of many notorious bandit lords, including all of Yugoro's various identities (the rulers of Nanashi are not yet aware that Yugoro is one man). This is an incredible sum for a village of ronin, but the Eyes are willing and able to pay it.

The Eyes of Nanashi look upon the City of the Rich Frog with quiet pity, regarding them as a missed opportunity. Nanashi has offered its assistance to the City on many occasions, but is always refused. The Kaeru, in turn, consider the Eyes of Nanashi a bunch of hypocritical zealots and Lion sycophants.

Toturi's army is an enigma. Recently, some members of the Eyes have begun to suspect that Toturi, like Shinjo Fuyari, plans a crusade against his former clan. Though the current headman disagrees, the Eyes have quietly begun to formulate a plan to halt the growth of Toturi's Army.

TOTURI

In the southern reaches of Dragon territory, an army gathers.

From the furthest reaches of the Empire, ronin journey to gather under a strange banner. It is no banner at all, for the wolf is no symbol save that of the ronin. It is an emblem of independence. To use it as a mon seems self-contradictory.

RONIN "SCHOOLS" (CONTINUED)

In most otokodate, asking another member about their previous life, especially the circumstances that led to becoming a ronin, is expressly forbidden. Any outsiders looking to discredit or harm one of their brothers by revealing past indiscretions can expect swift reprisals from the entire brotherhood. In an otokodate, ronin are never judged.

A somewhat less tight-knit but more common ronin group is the *juzimai.* Juzimai are, to put it gently, gangs. They band together to commit acts of crime or vengeance, and there is no guarantee of loyalty between members unless it helps the survival of the group. The most successful juzimai, large bandit hordes or smuggling rings, can last generations, and develop strict laws regulating members' behavior.

Ronin brotherhoods are as possessive of their secrets as any clan school. Some brotherhoods that are well established or old enough even possess a technique. Though these techniques are not as powerful as the techniques of a clan school, they are guarded with equal ferocity. A traitor who betrays these secrets can count on gaining a lot of enemies.

RYHODOTSU

The Koebi were a small but distinguished family. Vassals of the Crab, they had served the Hida with loyalty and honor for many centuries. Their village was so prosperous, and the quality of their work so impressive, that Kaiu Kenru recommended their name to Kisada for status as a Minor Clan. For a time, it was a subject of great interest in the court. Ryhodotsu, the eldest son of the aged head of the family, would certainly become the first daimyo of this new clan.

Two years ago, Ryhodotsu returned from tendering his annual taxes to the Crab to find the village of Koebi gone. A monsoon the likes of which had not been seen in over a century had ravaged the coastline. Not a single building still stood. Even the mighty castle of the Koebi had been destroyed. Ryhodotsu found only his the ancestral nemuranai jitte that would have been his inheritance. Alone and confused, he took up the arms and wandered off.

Ryhodotsu could have a place among the Crab, if he wished. He does not. The young ronin is torn with anger, bitterness, and despair. He wanders Rokugan, seeking a purpose.

But then no one has ever accused Toturi of being easy to understand.

If his objectives are unclear and his reasoning uncertain, Toturi's charisma cannot be denied. His call to arms has been answered by ronin who never dreamed of following another. So far, the force is small. Toturi makes his camp in Dragon territory, but the Dragon seem unconcerned. Kitsuki magistrates who came wishing to know Toturi's intentions left shortly afterward, apparently satisfied that he meant no harm. Another Dragon, an ise zumi named Mitsu, has been seen conferring with Toturi on several occasions. Rumors fly of a possible Dragon alliance, but a mere monk is hardly the sort of emissary to begin such an undertaking.

But then no one has ever accused the Dragon of being easy to understand, either.

Those who follow Toturi understand his mission. Justice. Honor. Courage. Brotherhood. Toturi's Army is all these things and more. As the Empire spirals deeper into civil war and borders fray, Toturi gathers bushi courageous enough to hold the center against impossible odds.

Contact with other ronin organizations

In truth, Toturi has no wish to lead. At first, he researched other ronin organizations, intending to join whichever faction aligned most closely to his objectives. He found none of them to his taste.

Yugoro is an enemy, pure and simple. The Black Lion has studied the Empire's criminal organizations and seen through Yugoro's facade. He knows that the bandit lord is one man. Once his army has reached a respectable size, Toturi plans to deal with Yugoro permanently, both to end the menace he poses and to serve as an example to other outlaws.

In the City of the Rich Frog, Toturi sees potential. He has purposefully placed his staging ground near the city, hoping to draw skilled ronin to his cause and establish trade with the Kaeru. An army marches on its stomach, and the Rich Frog is an excellent supply base.

Although Nanshi agrees with Toturi's stated objectives, the city needs only look to its founder's example to become nervous about large groups of ronin massing for possible action against the Clans. Although Toturi's messengers have denied any intention of striking against the Clans or the Emperor, Toturi's army and the settlement of Nanshi have a chilly releationship.

Toturi tolerates absolutely no dealings with maho-tsukai, and were he to discover a Bloodspeaker cell he would turn the full might of his small army upon it.

The Kolat, thus far, have escaped Toturi's notice. Kage has gone to great lengths to conceal the organization from his errant student, but with a man as perceptive as Toturi this is not easy. Toturi suspects that there is a movement in the underworld of which he is unaware, but believes that it must be small.

THE KOLAT

Oddly, the Kolat have more trouble concealing themselves from ronin than from any other group in Rokugan. Rumor travels like wildfire and the Kolat have been part of peasant legend since their activities during the First War. Ronin have closer contact with peasants, and their education, martial training and unique existence outside of the social structure makes them difficult to control. To the Kolat's irritation, the only ways to silence ronin is to kill them or recruit them. The former is hardly worth the risk of exposure, as ronin can do little harm alone. The latter is a far more attractive option.

Ronin are typically downcast, broken men looking for a place to belong. Many are disillusioned, and feel betrayed by bushido. Most ronin have few connections in society, and no one would miss them if they disappeared to be trained at the Hidden Temple. Thus, the recruitment of a ronin is a simple matter, and many are eager to join.

Some of the Masters feel that ronin may be the key to usurping the power of the Hantei. Ronin wield the skill of a samurai, but they control their own destiny. For this reason, the clans cast them out. To the Kolat, this idea symbolizes everything wrong about the society the Kami have built. Ronin are a sterling example of what a human can become; they should be rewarded, not punished. It is no accident that the initial explosion of the ronin population was the result of the First War, a war fomented by Kolat agents.

Contact with other ronin organizations

The Kolat keep themselves aware of ronin activity as they keep themselves aware of everything. They have agents in Yugoro's hordes, and know that Yugoro is one man with many guises. The Masters respect Yugoro for his ability but feel that his distrustful nature would make a poor recruit. The Masters have considered disposing of him, but fear that this would only cause chaos as his undirected hordes fought among themselves for the scraps of his empire.

The City of the Rich Frog is a means to an end. The Masters observed that the Kaeru were clever, but weak-spirited. Poor agents but excellent pawns. A bit of fear was all it took to make them fall into line.

At the other extreme, Nanashi has been declared off-limits. To the Kolat, Nanashi is a grand experiment, an example of free men bringing order to the world. The Kolat watch the village with interest, but do not interfere.

The Kolat hold a special hatred for the Bloodspeakers, gutless cowards that have failed their race even more profoundly than those that bend knee to the kami. Whenever the Kolat discover a Bloodspeaker cell they wipe them out personally or use their Yasuki contacts to turn them in to the Witch Hunters.

The Ten Masters, especially Toturi's former teacher, watch the Black Lion with a quiet patience. The Kolat have had agents near Toturi since the beginning, and wait for the day that their painstaking efforts will bear fruit.

BLOODSPEAKERS

The disciples of Iuchiban have a long history involving the lowly ronin. Ronin make excellent cultists, succumbing easily to the seductive power that maho offers. The majority of Bloodspeaker maho-tsukai are ronin shugenja. Ronin bushi who are loyal to the cause can always find a place as a temple guard or assassin. Ironically, for many of the same reasons that ronin make such excellent pawns for the Kolat, they are also very pliable tools for the Bloodspeakers.

Bloodspeakers operate in small cells, rarely interacting with or aware of one another. In the big picture, these cells are relatively harmless. Most of them are disorganized, have no long-term objectives, and do not seek to use their power for anything other than sowing chaos. However, this is certainly not to say that the Bloodspeakers are not dangerous. When these cells find organization and purpose, they can be incredibly deadly. Tragedies in the Ryoko Owari area and in Crab lands involving Bloodspeaker activity have led the Kuni Witch Hunters and Asako Inquisitors to step up their zealous hunt of these tsukai. When considering the Bloodspeakers, one must never forget the sinister mind that guides them, Iuchiban. Were he to return again, as he has in the past, the scattered and disorganized cells would unite instantly, led by a fierce, malevolent, and undying intelligence.

Contact with other ronin organizations

It depends entirely on the particular cell. A small Bloodspeaker Cell (six members or so) operates out of the hills near the City of the Rich Frog, but the Kaeru are unaware of its existence. Occasionally, Bloodspeaker cells have formed brief alliances with one or more of Yugoro's hordes. They have no contact with other major ronin groups. The Bloodspeakers are well aware of the hatred that the rest of Rokugan holds for them, and are careful about exposing themselves.

In the simplest terms, those samurai who have not sworn an oath to a lord or daimyo are considered to be ronin. The feudal system of Rokugan does not allow for 'fudging' those rules.

The Yotsu family were given the right to bear their father's name in order to distinguish them from other ronin – but they were not offered the right to swear fealty to the Emperor, the Seppun, or anyone else. In essence, they are still ronin – masterless men – and that's exactly how the Emerald Empire views them.

Any samurai who swears fealty to the Yotsu is still very much a ronin – their oath-line does not extend to the Emperor, nor to any true nobility. In effect, such an oath is no more than a bond between brothers, and not respected as part of Rokugan's feudal system. Other ronin might consider Yotsu-sworn samurai to be slightly 'better' (as they have a family name), but the noble houses of the Empire do not consider the Yotsu or their sworn samurai to be better than any other common wave-man.

Even an *honored* ronin is still a ronin.

Ronin Shugenja

Ronin shugenja are an object of much debate among the scholars of Rokugan. If a shugenja turns his back upon his family, do the kami turn their backs upon him? If a ronin is an aberration of the Celestial Order, then why do the spirits acknowledge his presence?

The matter has been a bone of contention among the Phoenix. Some strict-minded Isawa believe that the kami do hold ronin shugenja in lower regard. This is the reason why so many ronin shugenja seem to hold weaker power over the elements (i.e. no Free Raises). The fact that ronin can wield magic at all is simply a matter of force of will. The ronin, while undeserving of his samurai status, holds on to his station through willpower alone. In a similar manner, such an individual retains his power over the elements through force of will. The kami serve a ronin shugenja, but only reluctantly. The act of a ronin imposing his will upon the elements is a severe injustice and unnatural phenomenon, only a hair's breadth away from *maho*.

Another contingent among the Phoenix, spearheaded by more liberal-minded Asako, disagrees with this argument. The Asako point to such ronin shugenja as Fusaki, a gentle and earnest soul who studied with the Phoenix for many years. Could such an enlightened man enslave the kami? Hardly. The Asako argue that ronin shugenja are simply "souls in error." They are individuals who succeeded in their previous lives, but made some minor error. As they failed, they must endure life as ronin, but as they were somewhat successful, the kami ameliorate their suffering by giving them the gift of magic. This magic is not of the strength or quality of a true samurai, but then a ronin is not a true samurai.

Learning Magic

Ronin shugenja are extremely rare. Perhaps one in one hundred ronin possess any ability to command kami, and less than half ever realize their potential. Of this number, roughly one in three become shugenja of any note. Clan ronin shugenja are more common, as their schools are more adept at noticing those with talent.

As ronin shugenja are rare, it can be difficult to improve one's art. Many ronin shugenja seek out others of their kind to share spells, so the life of the komuso appeals to many. These itinerant priests are recognized wherever they go, and thus other shugenja in the area will know of a colleague's presence. Their position as anonymous holy men gives them a great degree of freedom. Most magistrates won't stop a komuso, so long as he doesn't seem to be causing trouble.

When two ronin shugenja meet, they usually journey together for a time. Opportunities to learn new magic are few and far between; only the most bitter rivals will pass up an opportunity. It is not unusual for two ronin shugenja to retire to a safe area where they can compare their ability. If one shugenja is superior, he may request that the other serve as his apprentice.

These requests are only made in cases where one shugenja's power is clearly superior. Otherwise the implication may be taken as a grave insult, and lead to a duel. If the potential apprentice accepts the offer, he is bound to the master's service for as long as the master sees fit, or until the apprentice can prove himself superior.

Ronin shugenja are therefore usually found in groups of two, apprentice and master. A few small groups are notable exceptions. The most common exception is, unfortunately, the Bloodspeakers, who are more than happy to attempt to seduce as many students as possible with the dark power of *maho*.

The Yotsu Family

"Give a man a name, and you give him a place in the Celestial Heavens.
Strip a man of his name, and you destroy all that he ever was, or his children will be.
Thus is the way of things... for now."
– The ronin Yotsu

Ten years ago, the Emperor's wife and children were killed by an assault coordinated by the bloodspeakers of Otosan Uchi. Their guards were slaughtered as they traveled from the Phoenix lands through Kiken na Roka, called Treacherous Pass, and the Imperial Palanquins were set on fire beneath the starry sky.

One hundred guards had been dispatched to escort the Empress to her home. They were the finest that the Seppun could offer, bolstered by an honor guard of Shiba yojimbo. No finer escort could have been offered; no less would have satisfied the request of Hantei XXXVIII. The tale of the ronin Yotsu begins amid their torn robes and shattered blades. It starts when one man picked up the fallen blade of a Seppun guardsman and walked boldly into the camp of the Bloodspeakers.

There, a tale of true courage was born.

Yotsu had been born a ronin, descended, some say, from a lost ise zumi of the Dragon clan who gave up his place on Togashi's mountain for the love of a woman. Their children, and their children's children, lived in the Mountains of Regret for three generations, meditating on the last lesson Togashi gave to Yotsu's grandfather before the ise zumi left the peak.

That lesson, and the will of the Kami, is what Yotsu believed gave him the courage and the ability to creep past more than twenty shugenja as they prepared to sacrifice the Emperor's children to the Dark God of the Shadowlands. Still, the stolen blade and Yotsu's own skill was not enough to do more than steal away with the Emperor's oldest son and heir, Sotorii. Yotsu had been in the mountains, hunting for food and lumber to keep his family warm. His eight children walked the land with him, keeping their father company and performing their chores. Their hut had been destroyed in an earthquake that had killed their mother, and so Yotsu and his eight children traveled through the Mountains of Regret, looking for a place of safety in which to pass the winter months.

When they saw the fires of the Bloodspeaker camp, Yotsu knew he had to see what was occurring. What he discovered was more horrific than he could have believed. A hundred men and more lay on the ground around the ritual fires. They had given their lives to protect the Empress – and they had failed.

The Bloodspeakers had heard the same prophecy that Shoju knew. The last of the Hantei would be the rise of Fu Leng. But they planned to create the last Hantei by murdering the children of the current Emperor – a plan that went awry as a stealthy mountain ronin slipped past their hastily erected barriers and guards, moving slowly beyond the ritual fires they placed to sacrifice the Empress and her child. His children remained in the rocky cliffs above the pass, hidden as they had been taught.

But Yotsu slipped past the guards as the ritual began, and knelt before the Empress' bound form. He uncovered her mouth and asked if he could die in her service, but the Empress Hochiahime only whispered, "No, ronin. Live. Take my son to his father. Tell them to mourn me, and to mourn the child I would have borne."

Knowing that the Bloodspeakers would follow him and destroy Sotorii if they knew what had occurred, Yotsu did the only thing he could. He returned to his children where they hid in the hills, and took his youngest son to the encampment. Leaving his toddler in the Empress's care, Yotsu took Sotorii to safety.

Yotsu's family had lived in the Mountains of Regret for three generations. Only rarely had they left the high peaks and twisting valleys, so Yotsu knew exactly how to hide the child and keep them safe from further Bloodspeaker attacks. Yotsu fed and cared for the five-year-old Sotorii as they journeyed through dangerous passes and treacherous lands. Any peasant might be a Bloodspeaker, hunting for the child – any samurai on horseback might be an agent of the cell. So Yotsu covered the boy in scraps of his clothing, and hid him among the seven children given to him by his wife.

The family traveled for seventeen days, taking long paths and covered terrain toward the palaces of the Seppun. By the time they had arrived, a grand Imperial Funeral was already being prepared – the boy's cousins, aunts, uncles and other relatives had been told of the found caravan, of the bodies that had been discovered.

Losing all hope, the Emperor declared a seven-day period of mourning for Hochiahime and her children. On the third day of that solemn occasion, a weary ronin and eight young boys and girls approached the Seppun palace and demanded to see the Emperor himself.

They were turned away.

Again, the next day, and the next, and always, they were turned away at the gate of the palace. Ronin were never to be accepted into the august presence of the Imperial Hantei, and to even suggest such a thing during the days of mourning was to insult the Celestial Heavens.

At last, Yotsu conceived a daring plan. When the Emperor and his palanquin marched from the Seppun palace, Yotsu stepped out of the crowd before the palanquin guards. Bearing the Seppun sword he had taken from the battlefield, and surrounded by his children, he stood quietly until the Emperor's guards came to take his head. Then, as Hantei XXXVIII opened his palanquin

THE BOOK OF SUN TAO

The writings of Sun Tao are, sadly, incomplete. Of the seven copies made, only three are known. All are difficult to read, as Sun Tao's assistant, Terumuto, had terrible handwriting and was a poor scholar. In addition, the journal is unfinished. The Unicorn have no recollection of meeting the wandering general, and thus Sun Tao's journey into the Burning Sands must have been a failure. What possible conclusions or observations the master might have made after studying the Unicorn, and how they might have altered his writings, will never be known.

What does exist of Sun Tao's book is extraordinary. Those who have had opportunity to read the volume deem it a master work on the subject of warfare, near or even surpassing Akodo's Leadership in insight. Like Akodo, Sun Tao preaches that the mastery of warfare is useful only to maintain peace, and much of the book seems more philosophy than strategy. There are several chapters detailing concrete strategic methods, most of which still hold true. The Crab argue that the sections on the use of siege are obsolete, but then the Crab disagreed with Sun Tao on a lot of things.

The following pages contain a few of the more frequently quoted excerpts from the Book of Sun Tao.

THE BOOK OF SUN TAO (CONTINUED)

"The three most valuable treasures I have found in my journey are compassion, economy, and humility. Compassion grants me bravery. Economy grants me influence. Humility allows me to survive. If a general gives up these three treasures, he will die."

"Only the ignorant fight to win. The enlightened win before they fight."

"True knowledge is in knowing, to observe heaven without stepping outside."

"Those who celebrate their triumph are bloodthirsty. The bloodthirsty will never triumph."

"The victorious general strikes while the enemy plans. The superior general attacks his enemy's alliances. The competent general attacks an enemy's army. The desperate general besieges an enemy's city."

"To succeed, a general must be unfathomable. Form must be concealed, and movements so unexpected that defense is impossible. Only the formless cannot be affected."

"If you are powerful, appear weak. If you are skilled, appear clumsy. One with great skill appears inept, both to confuse the enemy and to be aware of the path that has been traveled."

"If you can go no further, change. You will get through."

doors to see what the disturbance was, Yotsu let go of Sotorii's hands and watched as the five-year-old rushed tearfully toward his true father.

The Emperor recognized the boy at once, despite his foul clothing and travel-stained appearance, and swept the child into his arms. Calling out a command, he prevented the Seppun from killing Yotsu, and demanded that the ronin and his children be brought forward.

Upon hearing their story, Hantei charged the ronin with following the Imperial caravan to Otosan Uchi. When they arrived, Hantei held a formal ceremony, presenting the ronin with the sword borne by the Emperor's father, and charging Yotsu to pass his own name down to his children. "For a short time," Hantei said, "Your children were brothers and sisters to my son, and you, ronin, were his father. Now you are not only father to them, but to their line – the line of Yotsu. Rise, Yotsu Yatoshin, and bear my father's name, as well." The ronin was granted a small fiefdom in the Mountains of Regret, near the edge of the Centipede lands, and his children were invited to the Imperial court as playmates and companions to the boy they had saved.

Yotsu's escape is a tale told in legend, and sung by the Crane at Winter Courts. The Hantei line owes its future to his courage – and Sotorii owes his life to Yotsu's hand. Since then, Yotsu's eldest daughter (Urieko) has used her political leverage to become a minor governor in the Imperial City, ruling the lesser district of Yatoshin. Her younger sisters Seiki and Seou visit often, lending their talents to her cause. Ureiko served the Falcon, and gained training in their school, before returning to her father's side in Otosan Uchi and taking his place as district governor of the Yatoshin province.

The family's eldest brother (and second-born) is named Shoku. Together with the first convert to their school, a ronin woman named Sabieru, he quests throughout Rokugan to discover advantages and hidden treasures that could aid their family's growth and power. Their bloodthirsty ways complement one another, and their wedding was as much a matter of convenience as a formal acceptance for Sabieru to join the house of Yotsu. Together, Shoku and Sabieru use the strength of the sword to increase their family's influence and respect, gathering critical information and items for Urieko to use in her political crusade.

The next brother, Sumei, long ago went to the Scorpion lands to begin training there, and has not been heard from in some time. His last missive seemed full of hope – he had been accepted into a very exclusive school in the Shosuro lands, and although he would not be able to communicate with his brothers and sisters, he would soon be learning secrets beyond their dreams. Whispers in the night and shadows are all that the Yotsu have known of Sumei in nearly two years – and they fear that he has met with some danger.

The youngest brothers, Utai and Ukeru, still live with their sister in Otosan Uchi, and within the last two years have achieved their gempukku (they are just slightly older than Hantei Sotorii). It is expected that soon they will make their mark upon the world as well.

Yet still, the original lesson of the fallen ise zumi haunts the Yotsu line. "When a man falls," Togashi said, "he also rises. Remember this, and when ten thousand men have fallen to your name, you will join the stars in the Celestial Heavens, and your place will be among the Fortunes."

For three generations, the sons of that ise zumi have debated Togashi's meaning, uncertain how to understand the enigmatic command. On Yotsu's deathbed, he is said to have understood at last, and called together his seven children for one final command.

Ten thousand men must fall to Yotsu blades. Whether they fall on their knees in supplication, as Ureiko believes, or in death, as Shoku insists, their actions will pave the way for the immortality of the Yotsu line. The Yotsu truly believe that from their line will come the birth of a new Fortune, a new voice among the Celestial Heavens.

It has become their family quest, and their greatest secret.

Famous Battles of the Ronin

There is no place that is more a home to the bushi than battle. What greater service can be performed for one's lord than to kill his enemies and die in his name? The smell of blood, the sensation of cold steel biting through silken cords and flaps of metal into flesh, the sight of an enemy broken and driven before you…these are the things for which a heart filled with bushido longs.

Although the historians of Rokugan speak of a thousand years of peace, the truth remains that many significant battles have taken place during that length of time. In the majority of these battles, ronin found a role among the petty squabbling of the clans.

Ronin in Battle

Ronin have been present in virtually every battle that has been fought during the course of Rokugan's history. While samurai are eager to fight and die for their lord, a daimyo is seldom interested in losing men when it can be avoided. Even in the simplest engagement, there are duties that must be performed that have a very low rate of survival. This is the role fulfilled by the ronin in the armies of the clans.

Ronin hired by clan armies most frequently are assigned to the most hazardous front-line duty, or as scouts. Ronin are trained warriors to whom the clans have no obligation, making them ideal for initial assaults and heavy fighting. They have all the advantages of ashigaru troops with the added benefit of training. Creeping forward under the cover of darkness to ascertain the strength of an enemy's forces is hardly work worthy of a trained soldier, but it is nonetheless a necessary duty. Daimyos find ronin ideal for this type of work: if successful, the required information is obtained for a meager sum. If not, then precious little has been lost. In truth, this is all ronin are to the clans: a disposable resource.

When victory is achieved, a ronin lost in battle merely means one more living clan soldier who may continue to serve his daimyo.

The Official Record

The official accounts of the battles described below are kept in many libraries across Rokugan, including those in the lands of the Ikoma, the Asako, and the Kitsune. However, it is extremely rare to find mention of the contributions of ronin in any of these records. Regardless of how great their effort, the historians of the clans will not record that a battle was won or lost due to the efforts of an unwashed, deplorable ronin. The contributions of wave men to armed conflicts throughout Rokugan's history are known only through rumor, word of mouth, and the

occasional record written by an unorthodox author, so it is impossible to be certain of the accuracy of these records.

The Battle of Cherry Blossom Snow Lake

Early in Rokugan's history, what would eventually become the first of many battles was fought over the lands surrounding Beiden Pass, the so-called Crossroads of the Empire. The Empire was still young, and ronin were uncommon. Those few who did exist, however, were largely dishonorable men who valued only wealth. One such band of men had taken up refuge in the walls of Beiden Pass, hoping to prey upon the merchants from southern Rokugan traveling north through the pass. Realizing that they would be hunted into oblivion if the Lion won the day, the ronin threw their meager lot in with the Scorpion, desperately hoping that the devious Bayushi would permit them to continue their predations.

Suddenly assaulted by arrows and landslides from the walls of the pass itself, the Lion general was certain that he had been trapped, that the Scorpions had concealed troops around the pass to ambush and sabotage the efforts of the Lion army to advance and seize the lands south of the pass. Not aware of the insignificance of the bandit force, the Lion general was preparing to pull his samurai back from Beiden Pass rather than risk losing ground when word came that a Dragon army was advancing toward the battle from a hidden camp. The general vowed that though he might be defeated, the Scorpions would suffer greatly for their deception. The Lion army surged forward to engage their enemies, hoping to achieve a victory before the arrival of the Dragon, whose allegiance was unknown.

For reasons still unknown, the Dragon arrived and flanked the Lion army, forcing them to retreat. The Lion general found his forces attacked from the front by the Scorpions, flanked to one side by the Dragon, and assaulted on the other side by an unknown force. Although the damage caused by the ronin bandits in the hills was minimal, the landslides they forced into the pass made it difficult for the Lion units to maneuver successfully. Knowing that it would take long hours of deadly battle to stop either one of the clan armies facing them, and possibly even longer to ferret out and destroy their mysterious assailants from the mountains, the Lion

The Book of Sun Tao (Continued)

"An operation may be clumsy, yet swift, and therefore successful. An operation can never be skillful, yet prolonged. Prolonged warfare is a bane to all."

"Take the enemy's equipment. Every pound of your enemy's food equals twenty carried from your home."

"Those who render their enemy helpless without combat are triumphant."

"Victory is never repetitious."

"Always leave an avenue of escape. Never press a desperate enemy."

"A general who is too eager to die, will be killed."

"A general who is too eager to live, will be captured."

"A general who is easily angered, will be shamed."

"A general who is self-righteous, will be disgraced."

"A general who allows himself to love, will be troubled."

"Those who seek peace yet bear no treaty, are schemers."

"Only brambles will grow where a battle has been fought. The only crop sowed by conflict is suffering."

"To prepare for death is not to die, but to ready your mind to react without stopping to ponder."

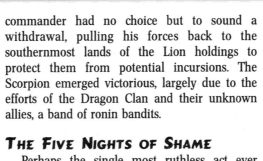

commander had no choice but to sound a withdrawal, pulling his forces back to the southernmost lands of the Lion holdings to protect them from potential incursions. The Scorpion emerged victorious, largely due to the efforts of the Dragon Clan and their unknown allies, a band of ronin bandits.

THE FIVE NIGHTS OF SHAME

Perhaps the single most ruthless act ever committed by any of the Great Clans, the Five Nights of Shame shocked the entire Empire, even more so because the normally pacifistic Phoenix Clan was the perpetrator. When the Council of Elemental Masters learned that the people of the tiny Snake Clan had been corrupted by the evil of a Shuten Doji, their course of action was clear. Mobilizing their forces to move on the lands of

the Snake in Dragon Heart Plain, the Masters recognized that the unknown power of the Shuten Doji represented a serious threat to their army. With the plain surrounded, the Masters sent in an exploratory force of ronin to test the defenses of the Snake. The Masters remained behind with the army, using powerful magic to discreetly observe the ronin's progress.

The ronin scouts were utterly destroyed by the foul maho of the Snake shugenja. The Masters learned of the deadly abilities bestowed upon the Snake by the Shuten Doji, and although the subsequent battles between the Phoenix and Snake claimed the lives of many brave Phoenix warriors, many lives were saved by the sacrifice of the wave-men. In five nights' time, no living thing existed within the lands formerly held by the Snake Clan.

Since that day, the Phoenix Clan has been notable in its relatively open support of ronin. Although still treated as less than true samurai, ronin in the lands of the Phoenix generally find life slightly easier than elsewhere in the Empire as the clan is more open to hiring ronin as yojimbo or yoriki. In this way, the Phoenix remember the spirits of the ronin who were sacrificed to save the lives of their kinsmen.

THE BATTLE AT WHITE STAG

In the fifth century of Rokugan, a gaijin naval force laid siege to the Imperial City itself, Otosan Uchi. The strange and powerful weapons of the foreigners caught the forces of Otosan Uchi completely off guard, and a hasty retreat was conducted in order to ensure the future of the Hantei line.

For two full weeks, the gaijin occupied the city and the lands surrounding it, including the hub villages that lie on the outskirts of Otosan Uchi. These villages see a great deal of ronin traffic, and at the time of the invasion there were a large number present. Many fled when the gaijin appeared, while others assisted in the successful retreat of the Imperial Court. Some remained within the city itself, either in hiding or in seeming compliance with the invaders. A few embittered ronin even sided with the gaijin in hopes of bettering their lot in life.

A small group of ronin still within the city concealed themselves from the gaijin for the duration of the invasion. The leader of this group, a shugenja, was in magical communication with members of the Phoenix in the assembled forces

preparing to retake the city. Short hours before the counter-offensive was to be launched, this band of ronin stole into the bay in a tiny stolen fishing craft. As the first rays of dawn greeted Otosan Uchi, the ronin began setting fire to the gaijin ships.

Distracted as they were by the events unfolding in the harbor, the foreign invaders were not prepared to deal with the massive attack launched by the combined clans of Rokugan. As the waves of samurai rushed through the streets, driving the gaijin toward the harbor, the ronin overpowered the crew of a smaller gaijin vessel. Unable to decipher the workings of the flame-belching gaijin weapons, the ronin used their captured vessel as a sea-borne battering ram. With magically summoned winds driving the sails, the small vessel slammed into the gaijin flagship at full speed, sinking both vessels.

Their flagship gone, the spirit of the gaijin captains was broken, and the balance shifted in favor of the massive Rokugan army. Although victory would surely have gone to the Rokugani in any event, the noble efforts of the ronin saboteurs unquestionably saved many lives among the forces of the Emperor.

Interestingly, the majority of ronin who remained within the city were executed for supposedly cooperating with the gaijin invaders. These ronin were said to have spread false rumors that gaijin ambassadors had been invited into the Imperial City by the Hantei prior to the invasion; the Emerald Champion had them killed for their treasonous accusations.

The Battle of Kenson Gakka

One of the most brutal and shocking conflicts in Rokugan's history, the Battle of Kenson Gakka is notable not for ronin involvement during the battle, but rather afterward. In retaliation for a failed coup at Kyuden Ikoma in the southern reaches of Lion territory, the Matsu descended like a storm upon Shiro no Meiyo, the northernmost holding of the Scorpion Clan. Every man, woman and child within the walls of the city were killed.

Except for one.

A single Scorpion, Shosuro Butei, escaped the destruction. He returned to the lands of his clan while the Lion rebuilt the city, renaming it Kenson Gakka, "Humility's Lesson." Eager to participate in the retaking of the castle to avenge the death of his sister, the Shosuro was dismayed

to find that the Scorpions planned to use the network of tunnels beneath the city to take their revenge after the Lion had sufficient time to grow complacent. Several hundred years worth of complacency.

In disgust, the Shosuro left behind his family and clan and became ronin. For years he traveled the Empire, learning the ways of the sword and honing his deceptive abilities. Five years to the day after the Battle of Kenson Gakka, he returned to the lands of the Lion.

Using his acting abilities to evade detection, the ronin became the single most hunted assassin in the history of the Lion Clan. In three years' time, he murdered nearly four dozen prominent Lion officials throughout the Lion holdings, the majority of whom had been soldiers at the Battle of Kenson Gakka.

The ronin Butei was finally executed after being arrested for a crime he had not committed. While it was the tendency of samurai to overlook the bedraggled, unwashed ronin that permitted him to enact his vengeance for so long, it was likewise the clans' use of ronin as scapegoats that proved his ultimate undoing.

The Battle of the Cresting Wave

In the year 716, an army emerged from the Shadowlands unlike any seen since the days of the first war with the Dark One at the dawn of Rokugan's history. Led by the Maw, an oni of incredible power and cunning, this dark army pushed the Crab Clan back from their southernmost lands north to the Saigo River, where the sacrifice of a single Kuni shugenja held the army at bay for over two months while defenses were readied.

During the feverish seventy-three days of backbreaking labor necessary to build the great Kaiu Wall, the Crab Clan recruited ronin by the dozen to help fill in the gaps in their forces. As Crab samurai were recalled from their duties throughout the lands of the clan, ronin replaced them and kept the clan functioning as best they could during such difficult times.

Ronin were also drawn to the Kaiu Wall in huge numbers. For room, board, and a sense of self-respect, wave-men stood side by side with Crab samurai and peasant laborer in the construction of one of the Empire's greatest engineering feats. As the project neared completion, the Crab bushi prepared for war

while the ronin mercenaries directed the work crews. When at last the wall was complete, the ronin took their place alongside the Crab in the defense of the wall.

The Maw's forces hurled themselves against the newly constructed wall for days on end. Ronin and Crab fought together to protect the Empire from the predations of the Shadowlands. When at long last the Maw's forces began to recede, the daimyo of the Crab, Hida Banuken, launched a ruthless counter-attack. Samurai of the Hiruma family, augmented by ronin troops to make up for their lost numbers, emerged from hidden tunnels throughout the outer edge of the Shadowlands. These fanatical troops hurled themselves against the remnants of the Maw's forces with reckless abandon. Already weakened from the battle at the Wall, the Shadowlands army was shattered in short order.

Simultaneously considered one of the Crab Clan's greatest defeats and victories, the Battle of the Cresting Wave resulted in the adoption of numerous surviving ronin into the Crab Clan to replenish their flagging numbers. It also began a tradition among the Crabs of recruiting ronin for scouting and security details, allowing a greater number of true bushi to serve their duty on the wall rather than be relegated to less prestigious tasks.

THE BATTLE OF SLEEPING RIVER

The Battle at White Stag threatened the existence of the Imperial line, but the Battle of Sleeping River threatened all of Rokugan. Left unchecked, the Bloodspeaker and his forces would have overrun the Emerald Empire, destroying a society 800 years in the making.

Alerted to Iuchiban's presence by the *ise zumi* Togashi Yamatsu, magistrates of every clan scoured the countryside of Rokugan for the Bloodspeaker. Every suspicious activity or rumor was investigated, no matter how outlandish or obscure. Ronin were drafted in large numbers to serve as doshin or yoriki to magistrates in need of extra hands. Many ronin earned the enmity of the peasants during this period, for their strong-armed inquires were neither gentle nor forgiving.

When the magistrates investigating Iuchiban's reappearance first heard word of his forces massing at Sleeping River plain, they sent word to all clan daimyos to send troops to the area. They also conscripted ronin to scout the area and investigate the claims. Bands of ronin prowled the area surrounding the Sleeping River plain for

days before the clans arrived. Bloodspeakers entering or leaving the area were mercilessly slaughtered by the ronin, but at heavy cost to the wave men.

When the assembled armies of the clans finally reached the plains, they were met by the tattered remnants of the ronin scout teams. Quickly describing the size and organization of the Bloodspeaker's troops to the army generals, the exhausted ronin were placed among the vanguard of the forces to lead the armies into the plain. It was they who first faced Iuchiban's hordes, and they were the first to feel the horrible power of the Bloodspeaker's powerful *maho* spells.

For seven long days, the battle raged. Of the more than two dozen ronin dispatched to Sleeping River ahead of the armies of the clans, only one is known to have survived to see the battle's conclusion. Grievously wounded, the ronin Chiroru was offered a place within the Fox Clan, whose daimyo was present representing the children of Shinjo at the battle.

Chiroru simply replied, "My brothers died without a clan, Kitsune-sama. If I arrive in Jigoku wearing your mon, they will not know me." He succumbed to his wounds a short time after. His remains were cremated and spread across the Sleeping River Plain by the Fox Clan so that he might watch over it in death as he had in life.

THE BATTLE OF WHITE SHORE PLAIN

The battle that took place between the Unicorn and the Scorpion following the former's return to Rokugan claimed the lives of many ronin. As the renowned Scorpion general Bayushi Tozasu was organizing his troops, he covertly added hundreds of ronin to his already sizable army in order to increase their ranks. Although this development went unnoticed by the other clans in Rokugan, the ronin in question were taken aback by the acceptance they received among the Scorpion forces. Many became convinced that if they were valiant enough in battle, they could be adopted into the clan.

However, there were other ronin in the lands of the Scorpion who saw that Tozasu was hiring ronin when there were elite troops who were remaining safe at home in barracks. These perceptive few quickly found pressing business elsewhere in the Empire, leaving the Scorpion holdings lest they suddenly find themselves hunted by magistrates.

During the time in which the Scorpions were amassing their forces, the Unicorns were desperately attempting to acclimate to their new surroundings. Entreaties to the clans were met with reluctance, as the Emperor had yet to either recognize or denounce the newcomers as the true children of Shinjo. Ide diplomats returned from the courts of the clans empty-handed, but Otaku scouts returned from unaligned peasant villages with ronin in tow. The ronin, although wary of the Unicorns' strange ways, were eager to prove themselves to the newcomers by providing information on terrain, sources of food and water, and the customs of the samurai clans throughout Rokugan.

A month after the formation of the Scorpion army by Tozasu, the ronin-augmented forces met the Unicorns on the field of battle in southern Rokugan. The Scorpions were completely routed by the Lion-supported Unicorns. Despite the knowledge of the interlopers' formidable cavalry, Tozasu failed to take the necessary precautions to counter their advantage. The hundreds of ronin among the Scorpions were devastated by the charging Shinjo cavalry and Otaku battle maidens. Tozasu himself committed seppuku on the battlefield after his troops' defeat was certain. Tacticians throughout the Empire chided the carelessness of the Scorpion forces.

Once settled into the lands that once belonged to the clan of the Ki-Rin, the Unicorn Clan retained the services of the ronin, using their knowledge to ease the clan's transition into Rokugan. Many of the wave-men served alongside the Shinjo and Moto families for years, and were even offered fealty for their service, a practice adopted by the Unicorn during their journeys outside the Empire.

And in the far reaches of the Rokugan, a few perceptive ronin learned a valuable lesson: to the Scorpion, expendability is a virtue.

THE NIGHT OF FALLING STARS

Frustrated from years of subtle manipulations by the courtiers of the Crane Clan, the forces of the Lion marched upon the city of Shiro no Yogin in the western reaches of the Crane holdings. The Crane, alerted at the last moment to the advancing Lions, barricaded themselves within the city's walls and prepared for the inevitable. When the Lion did arrive at the gates they were greeted with a barrage of refuse and filth, a horrible insult for a samurai to endure.

The Lion army laid siege to Shiro no Yogin, allowing no one to enter or to leave. Matsu Aiguto, the general of the Lion army, knew that the Cranes must somehow be getting supplies past the blockade, for they had not had time to stockpile food before the Lion's arrival. Aiguto could not wait until the Crane reinforcements arrived to lift the siege, but he knew that anyone responsible for aiding the Cranes would flee at the first sight of a Lion samurai. The shrewd Matsu chose instead to dispatch a group of ronin mercenaries to locate the source of the Crane's supplies.

Within three days, the ronin reported to Aiguto that they had located a network of tunnels in a local village that extended under the walls of Shiro no Yogin. Not wanting to remove any more troops that necessary from the siege, Aiguto responded with a simple order: destroy the tunnels by any means necessary. He implied that he did not wish to know the methods by which the ronin would accomplish their task.

With no shugenja among their ranks and no knowledge of how many tunnel exits existed, the ronin devised a plan. They waited until they believed that Crane samurai had left the city, then entered the single tunnel exit they had discovered, lit a large fire, and sealed it. Smoke began to escape from five more exits in and around the village. Then, the ronin waited. Eventually, Crane samurai emerged, coughing and choking from the smoke. The ronin mercenaries quickly defeated their teary-eyed adversaries.

Their supply lines severed, the Cranes began to feel the effects of the siege. Within a few days, they were out of food and water completely. The Lions stormed the walls of the city behind their ronin shock troops, in an effort to seize and fortify the lands before the arrival of Crane reinforcements. In a final act of defiance, many of the Cranes hurled themselves from the walls of the city. The torches they clutched as they fell toward the river below gave the name "Night of the Falling Stars" to the battle.

The Lion clan holds Shiro no Yogin to this day, despite the political machinations of the Crane and the haunting presence of Daidoji Yurei's spirit. Without the quick thinking of the ronin mercenaries who served Matsu Aiguto, the siege could have been drawn out for much longer, allowing the Crane army to arrive and preventing the occupation of the city by the Lion forces.

THE BOOK OF SUN TAO (CONTINUED)

Many samurai eagerly hunt these lost copies, for Terumuto did not record the same information in every version. The Dragon manuscript, for example, has much more information about terrain than either the Scorpion or Imperial manuscript. The Imperial manuscript seems to be much shorter than either of the other two. The most telling hint of variation is suggested in the Book of Sun Tao's closing lines.

"From the Lion,
I learned tactics.

From the Crane,
I learned excellence.

From the Phoenix,
I learned patience.

From the Dragon,
I learned humility.

From the Crab,
I learned loss.

From the Scorpion,
I learned the rest.

I shall endeavor to return these gifts."

–Sun Tao

The Battle of Kyuden Kitsune and the Night of a Hundred Deaths

One of the more recent battles in Rokugan's history, the Battle of Kyuden Kitsune is also one of the most ronin-intensive battles ever fought. The Kitsune family of the Fox Clan has relatively few bushi, and the Usagi family of the Hare Clan has ever been one of Rokugan's smallest families. With both sides eager to conserve their numbers, many ronin were hired on either side of the conflict.

Prior to the intervention of the Emperor, ronin mercenaries led by small numbers of clan samurai participated in a number of vicious armed conflicts. Even after the arrival of the appointed mediator Kakita Toshimoko, both sides retained large numbers of ronin in the event that a peaceful solution could not be reached. This arrangement, while very profitable for the wave men involved, lasted only a short time. The harsh violence of the Night of a Hundred Deaths saw dozens of ronin on both sides of the conflict brutally slain.

In the months that followed this grisly conclusion, there were rumors that the misunderstanding between the two clans had been arranged by a particularly crafty ronin in order to generate employment for his band of warriors. Furthermore, there were whispers that the skirmishes between the two clans had including many ronin staging their own deaths on the battlefield only to be unknowingly hired by the opposing side afterwards. Whether these rumors hold any truth, no one can say, for the ronin in question were all slain during the Night of a Hundred Deaths.

The Battle of the Rolling Waves

Several centuries ago, a Mantis bushi named Nakano was placed in charge of an illicit trade arrangement between his clan and the Yasuki traders of the Crab Clan. Discretion was of the utmost importance, for the trade involved a number of artifacts of Ivory Kingdoms origin. An honorable man, Nakano felt distaste at disobeying the edict from the Emperor strictly regulating the traffic of such items, but his duty to his daimyo and clan demanded complete obedience. The profits from this trade would greatly improve his daimyo's ability to negotiate more legitimate status among the other Great Clans.

Unfortunately, the Yasuki merchant was a shrewd and conniving trading partner. When the two met to make the final exchange, the Crab demanded more than was originally agreed upon. Indignant, Nakano refused. A heated exchange followed, and in the end Nakano left the meeting, stalwartly refusing to accede to any arrangement beyond the original.

Returning to his vessel a short time later, Nakano found it occupied by the local magistrates, apparently alerted to the contents of the ship by the disgruntled Yasuki. Trapped, Nakano quickly confessed to the trafficking of illegal goods in order to prevent the loss of honor from reaching his lord. Stripped of his clan and honor, he was denied the opportunity for seppuku and imprisoned to await a public execution. Furious that the devious Yasuki could have so entrapped him, Nakano managed to overpower his guards and escape from the prison. Freeing his crewmen, Nakano stole aboard his vessel and sailed into the night.

For years on end, there was no sight of Nakano or his ship. Many suspected the Mantis daimyo of hiding the ronin, but Imperial Magistrates sent to the Islands of Silk and Spice could find no trace of the ship. In time, they were forgotten, assumed to have died from the hazards of the sea.

Seven years after his disappearance, Nakano reappeared with a small force of crudely constructed kobune and launched an attack against a caravan of Yasuki sea vessels sailing north along Rokugan's coast. Although rare in the Empire, naval combat was not unfamiliar to the Crab as they had faced many of the Dark One's aquatic minions over the years. However, this was far north of the Earthquake Fish Bay, and the Yasuki were caught completely off guard and totally unprepared. Volleys of flaming arrows set fire to numerous trade ships, consigning the crew to certain death in the strong currents along the coast. Ronin bushi leapt from ship to ship, engaging the merchant's yojimbo in brutal combat. Despite superior numbers, the Yasuki forces were quickly overwhelmed.

Nakano and his men took nothing from the battle, knowing that returning the goods to the Mantis lands would only incriminate the clan. They sank every vessel in the caravan save the lead vessel, aboard which the Yasuki merchant who had betrayed Nakano had been captured. The devious merchant was strapped to the mast of the kobune and left alive while the vessel was

44

The Quiet Battles

Uninterested as they are in the comings and goings of ronin, many historians overlook what to them seem tiny, insignificant skirmishes that occur across Rokugan from time to time. Although these "battles" are usually of little or no importance whatsoever to the clans, they are often life and death events for the peasantry of the Empire. Wandering ronin find themselves drawn into these conflicts, although upon whose side they will fight is often unknown even to themselves until the last possible moment.

For examples of these battles, see the entries for "The Battle of the Rolling Waves," "The Battle for the City of the Rich Frog," and "Battle at Nightingale Village."

sent drifting into the maw of the Great Water Spider. Some say his screams are still heard by those who are drawn into its wake.

No certain sightings of Nakano and his men were ever recorded following the Battle of the Rolling Waves. From time to time, Mantis merchants would report that pirate attacks against their ships had been thwarted by the arrival of mysterious vessels bearing no identification. These nameless ships mercilessly assaulted the pirate forces, allowing the merchants time to escape. Although his name is recorded among the vilest of pirates and no Mantis would admit it to a person not of the Clan, Nakano is secretly considered a sacred ancestor among the Mantis Clan even today.

THE BATTLE FOR THE CITY OF THE RICH FROG

Three decades ago, the attention of the Empire was focused on the conflict occurring between the Fox and the Hare near the Three Man Alliance Plain. Few were paying attention to the events unfolding within the City of the Rich Frog. Nestled between the lands of the Lion and the Unicorn, the city was protected by neither clan, only an Imperial Magistrate. To complicate matters, the magistrate had succumbed to a strange fever and died, and his replacement had yet to arrive from Otosan Uchi. When the citizens heard of a massive bandit force moving toward the city, they panicked. They sent word to the nearby Unicorn Clan, but they knew that help could not arrive in time. Locking themselves within their homes or fleeing outright, they prepared for the worse.

When the bandit force, which numbered over four dozen warriors, finally arrived, they advanced toward the city only to be greeted by the sight of a single ronin coming forward to greet them. Curious, the bandit leader stopped his men and demanded to know what the ronin wanted.

The unarmored ronin responded, "When one of you has defeated me in single combat, only then may you take this city."

Smiling at an opportunity to demoralize the city's inhabitants, the bandit leader sent forth one of his finest warriors to fight the presumptuous ronin. Within seconds, the warrior was dead, his head neatly severed.

Snarling in agitation, the bandit warlord sent forth another warrior. And another. And yet another. In an hour, nearly two dozen bandits lay dead at the ronin's feet. The ronin, exhausted and bleeding from a dozen wounds, stood and looked toward the warlord expectantly.

Enraged, the warlord ordered the remainder of his men to kill the ronin where he stood. The bandits fell upon the wounded ronin as would a pack of wild dogs. Though he fought bravely, he could not stand against so many opponents, and he died beneath their relentless assault.

Eager for more blood, the bandits moved to sack the city. They were interrupted by the sound of hooves and the battle cry of samurai warriors.

The Unicorn had arrived.

The bandits stood no chance against trained samurai. They were slain to a man, and the city was saved from a pillaging that would have cost dozens of lives. Since that day, ronin have been welcome within the City of the Rich Frog, which often lays claim to one of the largest ronin populations of a city its size anywhere in the Empire. A shrine commemorating the event still stands near the outskirts of the city.

BATTLE AT NIGHTINGALE VILLAGE

Although more of a skirmish than a battle, this recent small-scale combat is fresh in the minds of many Rokugani, and serves to confirm for most the view of ronin as thieves with no honor. During a recent Winter Court of the Asako, the Hantei's niece Otomo Yorishiko was kidnapped by a merciless band of ronin bandits. This unthinkable affront to the Imperial line was only compounded by the fact that Yorishiko had, immediately before the festival, announced her eligibility for marriage. Hearing of this, the ronin leader Niban kidnapped the princess, apparently under the delusion that he could marry her and become a true samurai again.

Fortunately, there was a band of samurai present at court who were familiar with Niban, having encountered him shortly before the festival began. While the Phoenix mobilized their forces, these valiant warriors rode forward to the Village of the Nightingale, a village founded by Niban presumably to give a home to his followers.

In a bold and dangerous maneuver, the samurai struck the village at dawn from the beneath the surface of the river which protected the village from the northwestern side. The samurai successfully extracted the princess and moved her to safety shortly before the Phoenix forces arrived to crush the ronin, destroying the Village of the Nightingale in the process.

Chapter Three

Character

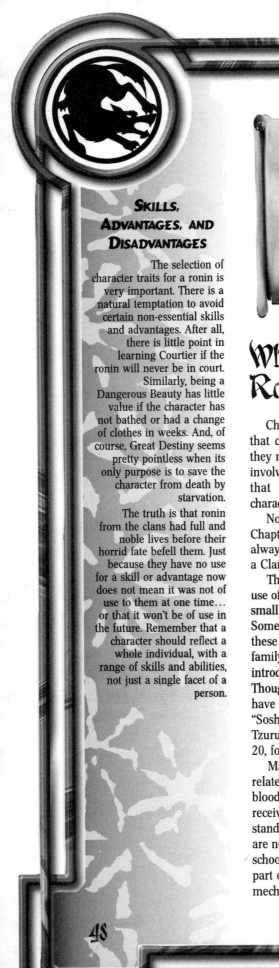

SKILLS, ADVANTAGES, AND DISADVANTAGES

The selection of character traits for a ronin is very important. There is a natural temptation to avoid certain non-essential skills and advantages. After all, there is little point in learning Courtier if the ronin will never be in court. Similarly, being a Dangerous Beauty has little value if the character has not bathed or had a change of clothes in weeks. And, of course, Great Destiny seems pretty pointless when its only purpose is to save the character from death by starvation.

The truth is that ronin from the clans had full and noble lives before their horrid fate befell them. Just because they have no use for a skill or advantage now does not mean it was not of use to them at one time… or that it won't be of use in the future. Remember that a character should reflect a whole individual, with a range of skills and abilities, not just a single facet of a person.

Character

What is a True Ronin?

Chapter Two describes many different paths that can lead to becoming a ronin. So what do they mean? Except for the ronin-born, almost all involve being cast out of a clan. Does this mean that the only ronin-born are True Ronin characters?

No. Each one of the types of ronin described in Chapter Two (except for the ronin-born, which are always True Ronin) can be either a True Ronin or a Clan Ronin.

The easiest way to explain this is through the use of vassal families. Every clan has a number of small families of ji-samurai that serve beneath it. Some of these families have family names, but these names are subordinate to the name of the family they serve. The Nanbu family, in the introduction story, are a good example of this. Though the rest of Rokugan considers Tzurui to have been a Scorpion, and referred to him as "Soshi Tzurui," his family would call him "Nanbu Tzurui." (See *Winter Court: Kyuden Seppun*, page 20, for details on vassal families.)

Many of these families are only distantly related to the family they serve. In most cases, the bloodlines are so thin that these ji-samurai do not receive the family's Trait bonus. Their political standing and wealth are pitiful enough that youth are not admitted into the clan's bushi or shugenja school. Though vassal families are considered part of their clan, many ji-samurai characters are mechanically no different from True Ronin. Thus,

a ji-samurai who becomes masterless is created as a True Ronin.

A Clan Ronin character can also originate from one of these vassal families. In such a case, the character was more closely related to the original bloodline and received the family Trait bonus, and had enough political ties to be admitted to the family school, at least for a short while.

Clan Ronin and Traits

When should a ronin character keep his family trait bonus and when should he lose it? Considering each type of ronin individually:

Wealthy retainers – Invariably these sorts of ronin should not maintain their family trait bonus. They have turned their back upon the family for mere koku. The ancestors are only too happy to return the favor.

Discordant – As this sort of samurai is not a proper ronin at all, the family Trait bonus is maintained. The GM can feel free to make an exception in the case of a particularly incorrigible individual who doesn't intend on returning or mending his ways.

Dishonored – This can be sticky. If the samurai was dishonored for a crime that was not his fault, or sincerely intends to fix the harm he has done, he will maintain his bonus despite the fact that the clan will never accept him. If he couldn't care less, or committed the act that dishonored him with malice and forethought, then the bonus is lost.

Dead master – This depends upon the nature of the master's death. If the samurai died violently, and the ronin intends to avenge his master's death, then he keeps the bonus. If he is too cowardly or callous to care about his dead master, the bonus is lost. If the master's death was not violent, then the bonus is kept.

Musha Shugyo – As they are still in the clan, the bonus is kept.

Ronin Agent – These ronin still serve the clan's interests, albeit illegally, so they always maintain their family bonus.

New Skills

KUENAI (AWARENESS)

Kuenai is the skill used in the place of Etiquette for interactions with the baser, cruder elements of Rokugani society. The environment inside a seedy sake house in Ryoko Owari is an environment as different from the courts of the Great Clans as it is from the Burning Sands. This skill reflects a character's knowledge of what to say and to whom to say it in the darker underbelly of Rokugan's society. Any attempt by a ronin to locate employment or information of a questionable nature uses this skill. This is a Low Skill, and it is dishonorable for non-ronin samurai to demonstrate knowledge of such unworthy interactions.

HISOMU (AWARENESS)

There comes a time in the life of every waveman when he must avoid the detection of those who seek him. This is not the ability to move stealthily; that falls under the auspices of the Stealth skill. This is the learned ability to move through an urban environment without leaving evidence or clues that others can use to follow them. Hisomu is a measure of a ronin's ability to remain hidden from the public eye, to move about without others taking notice of him. If the ronin is being sought by a magistrate, bounty hunter, or other unfriendly party, he may roll a contested Hisomu + Awareness versus the hunter's Investigation + Awareness. This skill is only usable in urban environments, and is considered a Low Skill.

INSTRUCTION (AWARENESS)

Any man can teach another man a skill, providing that the teacher has that skill at a higher level than the student. However, the teaching of a Technique is another matter altogether. Techniques are complex combinations of multiple skills, physical prowess, and mental discipline. To teach such a thing to another is a difficult task indeed. After a length of time equal to a minimum of one month of study per Rank of the Technique, a sensei must roll Awareness + Instruction against a TN of 40 – (the student's Intelligence x5). The TN of this task may never drop below 15. The sensei of all clan schools possess this skill at high levels, and there are even certain ronin who possess it. It should be noted that the penalty for teaching a Clan Technique to another without the permission of the master of the school is death.

New Advantages

MUSHA SHUGYO (4 POINTS)

The "ronin" is actually a bushi on a musha shugyo, a warrior pilgrimage. The bushi has, for a time, left behind the ways of his clan to seek wisdom through experiencing the fighting styles of samurai throughout the Empire. Everyone the bushi encounters during his journey will treat him as a clan ronin. Although not frequently practiced, most Great Clans respect the tradition of the musha shugyo and believe that it can only strengthen the resolve of a young warrior. Most pilgrimages last a minimum of one year and can only be ended with the completion of an act of incredible skill and prowess set by the ronin's former sensei. The character is treated as a Clan Ronin, and suffers all the social disadvantages and prejudices that accompany such a position. When the character feels that he has learned all he can from his wandering, he may return to his clan and resume his study. This advantage may only be taken by Clan Ronin.

PATRON (VARIES)

A samurai in a position of authority (most likely a city governor, but possibly a provincial daimyo) has noticed the ronin and appreciates his skill and discretion. From time to time, when a suitable duty arises, this individual contacts the ronin regarding employment. Although the task in question will be difficult and possibly even life-threatening, the ronin will be well compensated for his work. A ronin who successfully completes such a duty also gains Glory points equal to his Patron's Glory Rank. The GM is the final authority on whether or not a given task performed for the Patron is sufficient to warrant the reward of Glory. The cost of this advantage is equal to the Glory Rank of the Patron, rounding up. Any Glory Rank exceeding 6.0 rounds down to 6 points; the ronin can not receive more than 6 Glory points per successful assignment. This advantage is only available to ronin, since samurai of the clans gain Glory from their lords without the need for such an advantage.

Example: The ronin Jubei has caught the eye of minor Unicorn lord Ide Nabeth. Nabeth's Glory

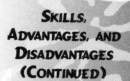
Clan ronin who possessed the following Advantages prior to being exiled from their clan can no longer benefit from them due to their loss of station: Ear of the Emperor, Gentry, Imperial Spouse, Noble Birth, Sensei, Social Position. Although it is theoretically possible that these Advantages could be gained by ronin after their fall from grace, it is extremely unlikely and should be carefully considered by both the player and GM. True Ronin taking any of the above mentioned Advantages must have GM approval and an exceptional reason for such a thing.

With that in mind, being a ronin is still the single most defining aspect of a clanless character's life. Despite what they have known in the past or may know again in the future, there are certain abilities that reflect their current status in life. In addition to the basic skills outlined in the ronin packaged in the main rulebook, here are some new skills, advantages and disadvantages of particular interest to ronin characters.

FEALTY

Gaining fealty can be difficult business. A character who wishes to earn the right to swear fealty can only do so through clever role-playing, usually as the reward for an important quest or invaluable service. Only when a daimyo feels that the ronin is worthy is such an offer made. If the offer is accepted, there is a ceremony of some kind. Some clans are more formal than others – a Crane daimyo will hold days of festivals to celebrate the loyalty of his new retainer (as Cranes rarely grant fealty, they can afford the odd festival), while a Crab will simply hand the new samurai his tetsubo and show him where to stand on the Wall. In any case, it is customary for the new samurai to receive a katana as a symbol of the bond he now shares with his lord.

After the oath is given, the character usually becomes a member of a vassal family rather than a direct member of the great families. For example, consider Musubi, a ronin who swears fealty to the Asako family. Musubi is far more likely to be sworn to an Asako vassal family. In his relations with those outside his family and clan, he will be referred to as Asako Musubi, and will be recorded on the Imperial records thusly, but the Phoenix will yet refer to him as Nani Musubi until such a time as his family shows enough worth to be inducted into the "true" Asako.

Rank is 4.6. For 5 points, Jubei may take Nabeth as a Patron. Every successful assignment that Jubei completes for Nabeth-sama results in the awarding of 5 Glory points to Jubei.

PERSONAL MON (1 POINT)

Any ronin may choose to adopt a mon to represent himself, although many ronin are too preoccupied with matters of survival to bother doing so. Of the mons worn by ronin, the vast majority go totally unnoticed by the samurai of the clans. This ronin's mon, however, is different. Its design is eye-catching and has a quiet symbolism that appeals to the sensibilities of the samurai soul. There is no immediate mechanical benefit for the ronin, but upon the completion of every ten successful assignments undertaken by the ronin, he gains a permanent Free Raise to use in every social situation with a potential employer.

PROVINCIAL HERO (4 POINTS)

"You lead heimin well, ronin. Are you ready to lead men?"–Hida Yakamo

Through years of hard work and devotion, the ronin has achieved a degree of acceptance in one particular region of Rokugan. The peasantry there looks to the ronin as a hero and friend for his actions, and the local magistrates choose to ignore him so long as his behavior is not outlandish or extreme. While in this region (which may be a single large city or a sprawling rural area with half a dozen tiny villages), the ronin will always find some degree of employment, no matter how meager. Protecting a caravan, serving as a bouncer at a sake house, or enforcing the rulings of a village headman all fall in this category. Note that this does not mean the ronin is paid for his labor, but rather receives free room and board. For many ronin, that is a far greater reward than koku. Ronin who are Provincial Heroes are among those most likely to be offered the opportunity to swear fealty to a clan or family.

SILENT (3 POINTS)

Although unpleasant, the harsh realities of a ronin's life sometimes result in beneficial side effects. The unfortunate necessities of hunting for food and evading the grasp of magistrates often trains a ronin to move very quietly when the need arises. The character rolls one extra die on all Stealth tests.

New Disadvantages

BOUNTY (VARIABLE; SEE TABLE)

A price has been placed upon the head of the ronin for a crime, although whether or not he is guilty is between the player and the Game Master. The level of the disadvantage depends upon the nature of the crime, which also

CP Value	Offense	Bounty	TN*
2 points	Minor	1–5 koku	25
4 points	Serious	10 koku	15
6 points	Violent	20 koku	10

*The TN is the target number needed on a perception test for a Magistrate to recognize the Ronin.

determines the amount of the bounty and the nature of those who hunt the ronin in order to collect it. A ronin accused of a minor offense will likely only be hunted by magistrates from the province where the offense took place or other ronin who simply want the bounty. A violent offense, however, means that magistrates in the lands of all the Great Clans have heard of the offense and are watching for the ronin, who will likely be executed in very short order if captured. It is even possible that a Wasp Bounty Hunter may pursue a character responsible for such a heinous act.

BROKEN DAISHO (3 OR 5 POINTS)

A ronin's daisho is all he has to validate his claim to his samurai heritage. If his daisho is lost, he is no more than a common peasant. The katana is also the primary means by which a ronin plies his trade. Whether as a yojimbo, a doshin, or the guardian of a simple village, a ronin needs his blade to execute his duty. A ronin whose wakizashi has been broken still has his katana to support himself, but he suffers from the stigma of having his honor broken. A ronin with a broken wakizashi (3 points) rolls one fewer die during social interactions with those of the samurai caste. A broken wakizashi may be reforged into a tanto or aiguchi. A broken katana is of significantly more import. The katana is the soul of a samurai. Without it, his place in the Celestial Order is questioned. A ronin with a broken katana (5 points) keeps one fewer die in social interactions with other samurai. A broken katana can be reforged into a wakizashi, but unless it is it does 1k2 damage and leaves a very characteristic, jagged edge when it cuts. Obviously, this disadvantage can be removed by acquiring a new sword, but unless the ronin is singularly dishonorable, he will keep the broken sword of his ancestors, thereby keeping the penalties as well.

DARK FATE (3 POINTS)

This is the opposite of Great Destiny. Your character can achieve great things in his day, but his death will be spoken of in hushed whispers, if at all. Some enormous failure will mark the end of his days: he may be the one whose mistake results in the Shadowlands overrunning the wall, or his misstatement may result in a costly war against another clan, or perhaps he will simply become Tainted and turn against the people of Rokugan. Only a premature death via battle or seppuku can stop this fate. Once per story, when the character takes damage that will kill him, he is reduced to 1 Wound instead. Sounds advantageous, doesn't it? In truth, he is only being kept alive to meet his dark fate, one which will damn him, his family, perhaps even the entire Empire. Death might be preferable.

FORGOTTEN TRAINING (7 POINTS)

There are some among Rokugan's population of wave-men who have been without a clan for years or even decades. A young samurai cast out from his clan can survive for many years in the Emerald Empire, eventually becoming an aged ronin warrior. These older ronin have been absent from the dojo of their clans for the majority of their lives, and some have great difficulty remembering their training. This is rarely the case for a first-level Technique, as this is the basic style of fighting that the ronin practices his entire life. Higher level Techniques are much more difficult to recall. When entering a combat situation, the ronin must roll his Willpower versus a TN of 10 to recall his Rank 1 Technique. Higher level Techniques require Willpower rolls at +5 to the TN per Rank of the Technique.

HEIMIN (8 POINTS)

The ronin hides the greatest secret of all: while some true ronin can claim genuine samurai ancestry, he cannot. The ronin is the son of a farmer, merchant, craftsman, or another member of the non-samurai caste. If any samurai were to discover the truth, the ronin would be quickly and mercilessly executed for violating the Celestial Order. In addition, the ronin's complete unfamiliarity with the details of Rokugan's culture makes it very difficult for him to adapt to new situations. The cost of advancing all High Skills is doubled for the ronin, and any roll involving social interaction with samurai has its target number increased by a minimum of 5 (GM's discretion). The character's beginning Glory Rank is zero and may not be raised above zero during character creation. A character with the Heimin Disadvantage does not have to take Social Disadvantage: Ronin. This advantage may only be taken by True Ronin.

UNHYGIENIC (2 POINTS)

In addition to the considerable social stigma that comes from being cast out from a clan (or never having been accepted into a clan in the first place), there are other stigmas attached to being a ronin. Many wave-men become so distraught over their lot in life that simple matters of hygiene become trivial and unimportant to them. They go weeks and months without bathing, a practice incredibly offensive to other samurai, who often bathe multiple times per day. A ronin with this disadvantage bathes very infrequently, and often has a very unpleasant odor as well as a filthy appearance. He will be denied entrance to the court of virtually any clan, and keeps one fewer die in social interactions with other samurai. Also, the incessant itching caused by this condition prevents the ronin from benefiting from any Technique or Advantage that offers Free Raises on a Willpower roll. This disadvantage may be bought off with experience points.

Ronin Bands

"Prosperity shall not divide us. Tragedy shall not divide us. The past does not exist. It is the present that binds us, and carries us into the future as brothers." – the oath of the Nanashi Mura otokodate

FEALTY (CONTINUED)

Vassal samurai are rarely invited to attend the clan academies, though it does happen from time to time for truly exemplary individuals (like PCs). Invitation to the school should not be assumed, as some clan samurai are never invited to these prestigious schools. If the bushi possesses techniques from another school, then he must purchase the Multiple Schools advantage, and must possess sufficient Insight to gain his next Rank. If the ronin knows no techniques, then learning the techniques of the new school requires nothing but time.

True Ronin shugenja who swear fealty and are allowed to train at a clan shugenja school may attempt to learn that school's secrets. To do so, they must learn all of the skills that are part of their school's starting curriculum, then spend at least a year in uninterrupted study. At the end of this time, the shugenja must spend 5 XP (the equivalent of the Multiple Schools advantage). The shugenja is now a Rank 1 shugenja, and permanently gains all of the attendant benefits of his new school (free Raises, etc). If the shugenja has enough Insight to rise higher than Rank 1, he may receive additional training to meet his full potential. Shugenja who swear fealty can gain invitation to clan academies with greater ease than their bushi brethren, as a trained and loyal shugenja is a powerful resource for the entire clan.

A True Ronin bushi who swears fealty and knows no techniques may apply to join other types of schools (courtier, witch hunters, *ise zumi*, etc.) if he is so inclined. If permission is granted, then the character begins training. The character must learn all of the curriculum skills of his new school, spend a minimum of one year in study, then spend 5 experience points in order to gain his Rank 1 technique (or first tattoo). Additional Ranks can be learned as normal, if the character's Insight is high enough. The character is no longer a bushi and will be expected to behave accordingly (courtiers do not stomp about in full armor, etc.)

Ronin who swear fealty to a family do not gain the family Trait bonus. Though the ancestors of the family may accept the ronin as a member of the clan in spirit, the bloodlines are too thin for the character to gain any advantage. However, a ronin who has never received a school Trait bonus may attempt to do so after gaining Rank 1 at his new school. This bonus is not free, but only costs the ronin three times the number he wishes to raise the Trait to instead of five. In addition, he must learn all skills that are part of the skill's normal curriculum before the bonus can be gained. This bonus can only be gained once, ever.

Ronin bands form for a variety of reasons. Some seek the power that lies in numbers to bring wealth. Some band together as a protest against injustice. Others are simply thrown together by circumstance.

Many ronin bands have existed for so long that they have begun to develop the rudiments of techniques, and guard these secrets as fiercely as any clan school. Those who wish to join the band must first prove themselves. If they are found worthy, they are taught the technique. If not, they are ignored. Several examples of these ronin bands follow, ranging from the ruthless juzimai to the more respected and lawful otokodate.

A True Ronin character may elect to become a member of one of these organizations. Each band lists certain requirements that all members must meet before they are allowed membership, and so long as the starting character meets these requirements he can begin as a member. The ronin technique that each band provides can be obtained at character creation, if the character is willing to pay the character point cost listed by that technique. A ronin need not learn the secret technique in order to be a member of a band, but if the ronin elects to learn his technique later, the cost is three times the character point cost in experience.

A ronin can be a member of only one ronin band, for these brotherhoods are jealously competitive. The secret techniques of these tiny bands are the foundations upon which future schools may be built, and the members of these bands know it well. Only true members are privy to their secrets.

A Clan Ronin can begin play as a member of one of these groups, but he cannot begin with the band's technique. He can, however, wait until he has enough Insight to gain Rank 2 and then purchase the technique as usual (with GM approval).

Likewise, a member of a ronin band who swears fealty to a clan cannot immediately begin learning his new clan's techniques. The ronin must purchase the Different School advantage and gain sufficient Insight to reach Rank 2 before he can learn the Rank 1 Clan Technique. Invitation is not automatic; the character is left to his own to obtain permission from his new sensei, a rare instance indeed for a first generation ronin, although such extraordinary individuals as player characters are often the exception to the rule. Depending upon the circumstances in which the character left his brotherhood, his former brothers may accept his decision to swear fealty or look upon him as a traitor. In either case, he is no longer considered a member of the brotherhood and can no longer rely upon their aid.

Although the following ronin abilities are referred to as "techniques", they are not proper techniques like the ones taught in Clan dojos, but are more like advantages. A ronin who has learned one of these techniques is still considered Rank 1. Other abilities which affect opponents' techniques are still effective against ronin techniques.

Along with the techniques that are granted by membership in a ronin band, the character also gains other advantages. All members of a ronin band gain a 2-point Minor Ally: Ronin Band Advantage. This can be very useful, as most bands are extremely loyal, willing to sacrifice their lives and honor for a comrade. The ronin character also receives a 2 point Obligation Disadvantage toward his ronin band, as he is expected to show loyalty in return. No extra Character Points are gained for this Disadvantage, and it does not count toward the character's maximum 10 CPs of Disadvantages.

Note that the skills and traits listed with each of these bands are *not* bonuses: they are *requirements*. Any prospective member must possess all of these requirements at the listed ranks, or they may not join the brotherhood or learn their technique.

THE EYES OF NANASHI

The Eyes of Nanashi have existed for the thirty years since the establishment of the ronin city. Their technique is impressive considering their short history, but this is largely due to the presence of the mysterious sohei monks that have adopted the city as their home. The sohei are harsh masters, but are willing to train anyone to whom the Eyes grant membership.

Membership in the Eyes guarantees staunch allies, for the Eyes are more loyal to one another than any other band. Unfortunately, membership carries great expectations. First, the ronin is forbidden to offer his services to any enemies of the Lion, and must offer his services to all Lion samurai at a discount. In addition, the Eyes are sent forth to bring ronin bandits and fugitives to justice, often requiring them to endure long, difficult, and thankless quests alone or in small groups.

The Eyes are supported via a special fund collected weekly from the major businesses in Nanashi Mura. The pay is not much, enough to cover room and board in Nanashi and access to the private level of the Nanashi Dojo. Membership in the Eyes is more a matter of pride and duty than a path to easy wealth.

Type: Otokodate
Required Traits: Water 3
Required Skills: Law 2, Kuenai 1, Kenjutsu 2, Jiujutsu 1
Other Requirements: Honor of 2.5 or higher, 2 point Obligation to Lion Clan
Location: Nanashi Mura
Technique: *Righteous Fury* – (7 points) The ronin carries the true message and objectives of Nanashi in his heart. He may add his Honor to his Initiative and TN to be Hit.

THE MACHI-KANSHISHA

The Machi-Kanshisha of the City of the Rich Frog are the enforcers of the Kaeru family, but also serve as peace keepers. The magistrate has offered to appoint some of these men as official yoriki, but the Machi-Kanshisha always refuse. They serve the interests of the Kaeru first. A merchant who defies the Kaeru can expect a visit from the Machi-Kanshisha. Though the Machi-Kanshisha are a corrupt lot, they are not easily bribed. The Kaeru pay them very well.

To maintain the illusion of peace in the City of the Rich Frog, the Machi-Kanshisha seldom draw their katana. Instead, they carry out most of their duties using a simple bo, saving their katana for true combat. Many of the Machi-Kanshisha have taken to carrying a long, iron smoking pipe slung over one shoulder, which they use to beat foes into submission and then relax afterward. These pipes are as long as a bo, can be wielded using Bojutsu, inflict 2k2 damage, and can be purchased for 3 bu.

Type: Otokodate
Required Traits: Agility 3, Perception 3
Required Skills: Bojutsu 2, Commerce 1, Kuenai 1
Other Requirements: Patron (Kaeru family)
Location: City of the Rich Frog
Technique: *Smoke and Mirrors* – (5 points) The simplest weapons are never to be underestimated. The ronin receives a free Raise when using a bo or pipe (*see above*). The ronin can knock a foe prone or disarm him by making three Raises (including the free Raise).
Special: The character receives a free bo or iron smoking pipe (*see above*).

THE FOREST-KILLERS

This juzimai is the oldest and largest of Yugoro's many bandit hordes. In fact, the band pre-dates Yugoro. Early in his career Yugoro joined the juzimai, killed the band's masked leader, and replaced him. The technique is not Yugoro's. In fact, he has not even learned it, out of fear he may accidentally use it while in one of his other guises and jeopardize his identity.

The Forest-Killers are cutthroat, ruthless bandits. They live in a ruined castle deep in the Shinomen and prey upon those foolish enough to travel through its depths. Outside the Falcon Clan, the Forest-Killers are the most experienced woodsmen in the Shinomen, and have explored areas deep within it that no other mortal has seen. Of course, they typically don't offer their services as guides. Recently, several former members of the Hare Clan have joined the Forest-Killers, greatly adding to their lethal mastery of the forest.

Type: Juzimai
Required Traits: Strength 3, Agility 3
Required Skills: Kenjutsu 2 or Archery 2, Hunting 3, Stealth 1

BROTHERHOODS

Three types of ronin brotherhoods are described in this chapter and elsewhere in this book. For your convenience, they are also defined here.

Otokodate – ("Manly fellows") Bands of ronin that gather for mutual protection. These groups tend to be organized and seldom stray outside the boundaries of the law. Members swear vows of loyalty, secrecy, and never question one another about their past lives.

Juzimai – Gangs of ronin banded together for no other reason than the power that lies in numbers. These groups wreak havoc upon the law, finding work as bandits, smugglers, assassins, and other unsavory sorts.

Apprenticeship – The only sorts of ronin bands composed entirely of shugenja. These are nothing more than the wandering students of a particular ronin shugenja teacher.

CREATING TECHNIQUES

Inevitably, a player is going to want to design custom techniques. Players of ronin tend to be especially eager to do so, after spending much time looking at the techniques of their clan samurai comrades with quiet envy. So is there a standard way for a ronin (or any samurai) to create new techniques?

In a word, no.

Yes, it's true that there are characters in the game that have created their own techniques. (Notably, Kitsuki Jotomon in *City of Lies* and Yoritomo in *Way of the Minor Clans*.) Yes it's true that all those Rank Techniques have to come from somewhere. However, both Jotomon and Yoritomo are extraordinary individuals, one-in-a-million sort of heroes that one simply does not come across very often. It's one thing to be an extraordinary fighter. It's quite another to develop a whole new method of combat.

So what if a player still insists on his character creating techniques and becoming one of these legendary heroes? This should be treated on a case by case basis, but the following sidebar gives some general guidelines

Other Requirements: Honor no greater than 2, Bad Reputation (bandit), Way of the Land: Shinomen Forest

Location: The Shinomen Forest

Technique: *Fool's Harvest* – (7 points) The Forest-Killer is swift, deadly, and efficient while wreathed in shadows. Receive a free Raise on all Stealth rolls. If the ronin manages a successful attack on an unaware target, he automatically gains initiative next round if attacking that same target. Both effects can only be used in a natural (not urban) environment.

THE WEAVERS

The Weavers are ronin assassins, traveling from place to place in the humble disguise of basket merchants. Their knowledge of Rokugan's underworld allows them to know when and where to reveal themselves to gain employment, as do their rather high-placed connections.

The Weavers, although they do not know it, are agents of the Kolat.

The Weavers are swift, efficient, and professional. They always complete a contract, and never report the names of their clientele, not even when tortured. (Of course, every detail of the Weavers' operations and clients trickles back to the Hidden Temple, but no one has to know that.)

Why would the Kolat risk themselves this way? Why sell the services of their pawns to outsiders? Simple. Through the Weavers, the Masters have obtained a long list of disreputable individuals whom they can blackmail when the time is right. Through the Weavers, the Kolat gain an additional source of income to add to their already impressive resources, for the Weavers do not sell their services cheaply. And, through the Weavers, the Kolat assassins can keep themselves in practice.

The best hiding place is often in plain sight.

Type: Juzimai

Required Traits: Perception 3, Willpower 3, Awareness 3

Required Skills: Stealth 3, Poison 1, Acting 3, Knife 2, Kuenai 1, Hisomu 1

Other Requirements: Clear Thinker, Dark Secret (Kolat),

Location: Mobile

Technique: *Twist the Weave* – (6 points) The ronin has embraced the arts of stealth, subtlety, and assassination. For every Raise he makes on

Stealth, Acting, and Poison rolls, he receives the effects of two.

THE TESSEN (IRON FANS)

The Lion and Crane continue their bitter conflict. Violence Behind Courtliness City and the surrounding villages are increasingly plagued by crime and violence perpetrated by desperate heimin refugees and angry ronin, victims of Imperial edicts. The Crane (who currently control the city) are harsh and unforgiving, often sending large groups of armed magistrates through problem neighborhoods to bring those responsible to justice. In addition, they have issued a mandate throughout the city, forbidding any non-Crane from bearing weapons. Ronin are allowed to carry their daisho as symbol of their station, but drawing a blade in public is a serious offense.

The Tessen are a brotherhood of ronin who attempt to keep the crime in the city to a minimum, as much for the sake of self-preservation as justice. They wield paired iron fans, as these are not bound by the technicalities of the Crane mandate and can be easily concealed. The Tessen patrol the cities in pairs to keep the peace. They serve as bodyguards and escorts, more often to heimin than to samurai due to the Crane's disdainful opinion of ronin. The Tessen are seen as a nuisance by Crane magistrates, and are often treated just as severely as common criminals when they are discovered. As such, they keep a low profile.

Ironically, the Tessen are composed mostly of dismissed Lions and Cranes. These individuals get along no better than they did before becoming ronin, causing deep factionalism within the otokodate except in periods of extreme crisis.

Type: Otokodate, though the Crane consider them Juzimai
Required Traits: Reflexes 4
Required Skills: War Fan 3, Athletics 1
Location: Toshi Ranbo wo Shien Shite Reigasho (Violence Behind Courtliness City)
Technique: *The Iron Fan* – (5 points) The ronin has learned to transform the simple tessen into a blur of motion, creating a defense that even skilled swordsmen find quite remarkable. The ronin may use his War Fan skill in place of Defense while using a fan, and may add his War Fan skill to his TN to be hit while wielding a fan in his off hand.
Special: The character begins with paired tessen.

THE BROKEN GUARD

The Broken Guard are a band of mercenaries led by the ronin Saigorei, a former member of the Imperial family and master of the pike. Many members of the brotherhood were former retainers of the Akodo, and their name is as much a reference to what they have become as to their specialty – anti-cavalry combat. The Broken Guard have a strict code – each member donates a part of their income to a communal fund for the group's support during lean times. Under no conditions are any ronin of the Broken Guard allowed to engage in banditry or other crimes. Saigorei may be Imperial no longer, but he's not about to be associated with outlaws.

The Broken Guard have amassed a reputation for their skill in a short time, helping the Fox Clan to repel a large horde of mounted bandits that have plagued their forest in the past year. They are also quite popular with the common people, as one of the few otokodate to allow ashigaru into their ranks. Hida Tsuru has expressed interest in hiring Saigorei and his Broken Guard to train his own soldiers, a fact that Shinjo Hanari would find quite troubling.

Type: Otokodate
Required Traits: Strength 3, Agility 3
Required Skills: Any polearm 3, Battle 1, Defense 1
Other Requirements: Honor 1 or greater
Location: Mobile
Technique: *Tiger's Teeth* – (4 points) The ronin has learned the strength that lies in leverage, and the weakness that lies in speed. While using a polearm, the ronin may make two free Raises and keep an extra dice of damage. Both of these advantages are only gained against opponents at least three feet higher than the ronin (i.e. mounted opponents).
Special: The character begins with a polearm of his choice.

SCALES OF THE CARP

The Yasuki Family have a richly deserved reputation as skilled merchants and traders, a reputation that can sometimes be their undoing. Many cities (especially in Crane territory) are suspicious of Yasuki merchants, often forbidding them entry at all.

The Scales of the Carp are the Yasuki's answer to this situation. The Scales are a secret society of ronin traders, smugglers, and gamblers funded and trained by the Yasuki. The Yasuki family provides the Scales with equipment, weapons, information, and (mostly) quality merchandise in return for seventy percent of the profit. In addition, the Scales can depend upon Yasuki assistance when they have trouble with the law, and can always find a cheap inn or hostel willing to house them within Crab lands.

Type: Juzimai
Required Traits: Perception 3, Willpower 3, Awareness 3
Required Skills: Commerce 3, Sincerity 2, Gambling 1, Kuenai 2
Other Requirements: Major Ally in Yasuki family, Patron – Yasuki Family,
Location: Yasuki Provinces, frequently mobile
Technique: *The Carp Smiles* – (4 points) The ronin has become adept in reading and manipulating the emotions of potential customers. When making opposed skill rolls involving Commerce, Sincerity, or Gambling the ronin's target must drop all dice that roll lower than the ronin's skill Rank + Trait. Anything higher than an 8 is never dropped. (For example, if a ronin who has a Commerce of 4 and Awareness of 3 is trying to sell a basket to an uncertain Mirumuto samurai, then the samurai

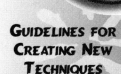

GUIDELINES FOR CREATING NEW TECHNIQUES

• The character should have enough Insight to obtain the Rank of the Technique to be created, and 50 additional Insight besides.

• The character should have at least Rank 5 in the primary skill that the technique will use (Kenjutsu, Courtier, etc.).

• The character must have the Great Destiny Advantage. This sort of thing doesn't happen everyday.

• The character must spend a minimum of one year perfecting the technique. No adventuring. Just practice and study.

• The character must be finished with his current school, or must purchase the Multiple Schools advantage.

If these requirements are all satisfied, then the GM and player should come up with a technique together. In the end, the GM is the final arbiter of whether or not the technique will be allowed. No matter what, no ronin can create Rank 4 or Rank 5 Techniques.

Pikes are extremely inexpensive weapons compared to katanas and yumi, allowing large groups of soldiers to be armed for a relatively little expense. They are also devastatingly effective against cavalry, as the long reach of the spear allows the pikeman to bury his weapon deep into a steed or its rider before it can get close enough for an effective attack.

Against a charging opponent without a polearm, a character set for charge with his own polearm always gains initiative. Against a mounted opponent, the pikeman may attempt an "unhorsing maneuver." First, this requires a successful attack roll against the TN of the horse. Second, the pikeman makes an opposed roll with the rider, rolling his Water against the rider's Earth. If the pikeman succeeds, the rider is unhorsed. If the pikeman makes three Raises on his opposed roll, he may cause the horse to fall on its rider, doing 2k2 damage. If the rider succeeds, the rider takes damage from the pikeman as normal but continues his charge, requiring a TN of a mere 5 to strike the unmoving pikeman and shattering his polearm.

must drop all dice that roll a 6 or less in his efforts to resist.) Targets that do not have enough money or those that have absolutely no interest in the merchant's wares are immune to this effect, unless the merchant can somehow convince him he has what they're looking for.

THE SWORD OF YOTSU

The Sword of Yotsu is a small, select group of true ronin (no clan ronin are accepted into the unit) who swear loyalty to the Yotsu family and take the name. They live in Otosan Uchi and serve Yotsu Urieko as their house daimyo, following her orders and defending her province. They also follow the rest of the Yotsu family on various quests, and are given quests of their own as they prove their loyalty and dedication to the family.

They have existed for only 10 years, but their band is one of the strongest and most respected ronin bands, and possibly the only ronin with any access to the Imperial Court (through the Yotsu family head). Membership requires tests of honor and courage, but most importantly, it requires the samurai to be inducted to fall upon his knees before the Yotsu family, swearing his fealty upon the sword given to them by Hantei XXXVIII.

They are supported by the district wages of the Yatoshin province, and while in that province are expected to uphold the laws of the Empire and see to the running of the district. They serve both as bodyguards and adventurers for the Yotsu line, and as magistrates of the Yatoshin province – heavy responsibilities for any ronin to bear. But because the Yotsu may be the only ronin who are making progress forging their place in the Empire, there are many who wish to serve. Of these, only 35 have sworn the oath to the Yotsu family, and been granted the name as their own.

Type: Otokodate
Required Traits: Intelligence 3, Perception 3
Required Skills: Etiquette 2, Law 2, Kenjutsu or Iaijutsu 2
Other Requirements: True Ronin, no Bad Reputation flaw
Location: Otosan Uchi
Technique: *Shelter of the Blameless* - (4 Points) – The ronin is dedicated to the protection of the Yatoshin province, but more to the protection of those who are too weak to defend themselves. The Yotsu believe firmly that they serve the best interests of the Empire and the Fortunes. They may add their Intelligence to all of

their initiative rolls, and if they are genuinely acting to protect an innocent who is unable to defend themselves, they receive a free raise to all their attack rolls.

Special: The character is always considered an Imperial Magistrate when in the city of Otosan Uchi, and may receive special privileges because of the family's position and influence there. Yotsu equipment always includes a katana and one fine kimono (for use when they are representing the Yotsu in formal occasions).

Ronin Shugenja

Ronin shugenja have far fewer options than bushi. Most improve their art by hiring on as a scribe or librarian for one of the established clan libraries, eventually gaining enough prestige and respect that they are allowed to copy a few of the clan's less important spells. Spells that are specific to particular clans, or that are very rare (such as the spells in *Walking the Way*), are never shared with ronin shugenja. On the other hand, if the shugenja is allowed to swear fealty, he could potentially gain access to whatever spells the master of the school deems fit. Note that ronin librarians are *never* assigned to any sections of the library containing magical scrolls or clan ciphers. Trust only goes so far.

Another option for gaining new spells is to begin play as a member of one of the following shugenja brotherhoods. These brotherhoods tend to have only a dozen or so members at any time. While not as militant as otokodate and juzimai, shugenja brotherhoods are nonetheless protective of their members. A shugenja who joins one of these brotherhoods gains a 2 point Minor Ally Advantage but also gains a 2 point Obligation toward their school, in the same manner as otokodate and juzimai. Membership also gives the character knowledge of the brotherhood's cipher, codes in which each brotherhood transcribes their spells. These brotherhoods allow their members to copy new magics as reward for loyal service, or for delivering a heretofore unknown spell to the brotherhood's library.

THE ORDER OF ISASHI

Little is known of the ronin shugenja who first called himself Isashi, only that he appeared near the end of the second war against Iuchiban. Without thought of reward or any regard for his own safety, he traveled in the wake of the demonic armies, healing the wounded and brining the dying to their final rest. He was perhaps Rokugan's first combat medic, offering healing to anyone who needed it regardless of clan or station. When he was slain by Iuchiban's demonic hordes near the end of the war, a dozen more ronin shugenja formed an order of healers in his name and continued his work. To this day, the Order of Isashi travels throughout Rokugan, visiting the most war-torn and savaged areas of the Empire and offering their aid as healers. Primarily they are found near the Carpenter Wall (as the war there never ends) though in recent years they have appeared more often in Lion and Crane lands as well.

Type: Brotherhood
Required Traits: Water 3
Required Skills: Calligraphy 1, Herbalism 2, Medicine 2, Meditation 1
Other Requirements: Higher Purpose (heal the sick), Soft Hearted; at least two of the shugenja's starting spells must have a healing function.
Location: Carpenter Wall, mobile
Special: *Isashi's Gift* – (6 points) Whenever the shugenja casts a spell that heals or negates damage, poison, or illness he receives two free Raises.

THE FORTUNE'S GRACE

Among the common people shugenja serve most frequently as mediums, go-betweens with the spirit world. Foremost among these is an order of ronin shugenja known as the Fortune's Grace, who specialize in communicating with household spirits and calming angry ghosts for the peasantry. The shugenja of the Fortune's Grace are exclusively women, who begin their training from an early age and take strict vows of celibacy in order to maintain their purity from the physical plane's corruption. (A shugenja character who takes this school and violates her vow of celibacy loses the school advantage listed here, but retains all of her other abilities as a shugenja.)

The Fortune's Grace are mobile throughout Rokugan but their main temple is a small monastery a day's travel from the Shrine of the Ki-Rin.

Type: Sisterhood
Required Traits: Air 3
Required Skills: Lore (Ghosts & Spirits) 3, Meditation 2, Theology 2
Other Requirements: Obligation (4 points, vow of celibacy), Innate Ability (Commune)
Location: Phoenix territories, mobile
Special: *To Touch the Kami* – (4 points) So long as the medium maintains her vows she holds a close connection to the spirit world, even closer than most shugenja. She may cast Commune a number of times a day equal to her highest Ring without affecting the number of spells she may cast that day.

CULT OF THE BLOOD-RED MOON

The Cult of the Blood-Red Moon is one of the largest and most successful Bloodspeaker cells. Its current leader is a mysterious individual who claims to be the reincarnation of Jama Suru. Whether or not this is true is anyone's guess, but the results of the dark shugenja's research are astounding. Suru's Bloodspeakers are less vulnerable to madness and corruption than most tsukai, making them capable of casting more black magic and rendering them more difficult to track by tsukai-sugasu. The Cult of the Blood-Red Moon is composed of heimin and ronin seeking a quick avenue to power, power which Suru gladly bestows upon them. The Cult is designed as an NPC-only brotherhood, and its point values are included for informational purposes only.

Type: Bloodspeaker Cell
Required Traits: Earth 4,
Required Skills: Lore: Maho 3, Meditation: 2, Cipher 1, Calligraphy 1
Other Requirements: Shadowlands Taint (at least 4 points), Dark Secret (tsukai), Shugenja
Location: Phoenix provinces
Special: *Bleeding the Elements* – (8 points) The maho-tsukai has mastered the art of turning the dark power of his magic away from himself, dispersing it to the elements. Each time the tsukai casts maho, he may make an Willpower roll vs the same TN as the spell. If this roll is successful, then the amount of Taint the character accumulates is lowered to one fourth (round down). Unfortunately, the use of this technique is not subtle. The immediate area immediately begins to show symptoms of Taint: plants wither and die, statuary takes on a fiendish look, animals move away, etc. The cultist may also choose two *maho* spells as part of his starting repertoire.

Ronin Heritage Tables

Ronin heritage may seem somewhat of an oxymoron. After all, what sort of heritage could a samurai with no master bear? What sort of noble ancestors could such an ignoble warrior possibly have? Get those ideas out of your head. Remember, a born ronin is rare. Such an individual is the offspring of a successful parent, a ronin of such prowess and repute that they could afford to pass their station on to their children. As a result, born ronin have as many stories to tell as a samurai of the Great Clans. This heritage table is for born ronin characters. True ronin characters from vassal families may choose to roll on this table, or roll on the table of the clan which their family once served. Clan ronin do not roll on these tables.

Heimin characters may not roll on this heritage table, as they do not yet have any heroic ancestors. Their history is just beginning.

In any case, a character may roll on the following tables up to three times, but each roll costs one Character Point. Begin with Heritage Table 1 and proceed as instructed. No extra Character Points are gained for any Disadvantages given by this table.

At the GM's option, the following tables are generic enough that a Minor Clan character could also use them. The only exception to this is the Great Battles, which should be replaced with battles appropriate to the specific clan or re-rolled.

Heritage Table 1: The Unfettered Ronin

Roll	Result
1-2:	Undistinguished Past. No benefits or penalties.
3-5:	Dishonorable Past, see Table 2.
6-7:	Honorable Past, see Table 3.
8-9:	Mixed Blessings, see Table 4.
0:	Great Clan Heritage, see Table 5. (*This result may only be rolled once.*)

Heritage Table 2: Dishonorable Past

Honorless dog! This result will reveal the origin of your family's ronin status. If you roll on this table multiple times, then you must have had one pretty foul ancestor. If you value your life, keep your distance from your ancestor's former clan. Roll on table 5 to determine the clan your ancestor came from, but gain no other benefits from that table.

Roll	Result
1:	*Murderer!* Your ancestor was a villain of the worst sort, slaying his daimyo and fleeing justice! The clan still hunts your family's blood with a terrible vengeance. You begin the game with a bounty on your head of 20 koku.
2:	*Illegitimate!* You are the shameful result of an unholy affair between a samurai and an eta! Lose one rank of Honor, begin the game with the Dark Secret Disadvantage and pray to every Fortune that you can name that no one finds out.
3–4:	*Coward!* Your ancestor abandoned his clan in the heat of battle, heaping disgrace upon your line. Gain a Sworn Enemy in your ancestor's former clan.
5–6:	*Dishonored!* Your ancestor was cast out of the clan for shameful behavior. His kinsmen expect no better from his spawn. Roll two fewer dice on all social interactions with the former clan.
7–8:	*Disloyal!* Your ancestor left the clan to seek his own fortune, and lost it instead. Begin the game with no koku. All of your starting equipment is Poor Quality, except one item.
9–0:	*Oath-breaker!* Your ancestor left to spare the clan from any stigma as he undertook a potentially dishonorable vendetta. Unfortunately, he failed. Now, you must fulfill his vow or bear the dishonor. Gain the Driven Disadvantage. Your ancestor will not allow you to swear fealty to any clan, no matter the circumstances, until your vow is fulfilled.

HERITAGE TABLE 3: HONORABLE PAST

Your ancestor is the sort of ronin after whom legends are crafted!

ROLL	RESULT
1–3:	Significant Death, see Table 3A
4–7:	Prestigious Duty, see Table 3B
8–0:	Heroic Deed, see Table 3C

HERITAGE TABLE 3A: SIGNIFICANT DEATH

ROLL	RESULT

1–3: *Killed in a duel.* Gain 3 boxes of Honor and 1 rank in either Iaijutsu or Kenjutsu.

4–8: *Killed in a battle.* Unfortunately, this is rarely a positive thing, as ronin are usually the scapegoats of the Great Clans. Roll again to determinte the battle:

1–2: *Battle of White Stag* – Your ancestor was one of the saboteurs who destroyed the gaijin ships in Golden Sun Bay. Add one piece of Gaijin Gear to your starting outfit, but add Dark Secret as well. Your family knows that the gaijin of White Stag were invited to Otosan Uchi at the Emperor's request, and the Ikoma would go to great lengths to silence such knowledge.

3–4: *Battle of the Rolling Waves* – Your ancestor was one of Nakano's famous pirates. Though these men were generally considered villains, they are heroes among the Mantis. Gain one rank of Sailing and a Minor Ally in the Mantis. Lose one rank of Honor.

5–6: *Battle of White Shore Plain* – Your ancestor fought on the side of the Scorpion, dying an ignominious death in part of their great game. In an uncharacteristic gesture of kindness, the Scorpion made minor restitution toward your family. Gain a Minor Ally among the Scorpion, but gain a 2 point Obligation toward that same Scorpion.

7–8: *Battle of Sleeping River* – Your ancestor died in combat against the dark forces of Iuchiban. However, before he died, he returned with… something. Begin with a nemuranai of the GM's choice – but keep in mind that this is a Bloodspeaker artifact. Be careful.

9–0: *Five Nights of Shame* – The battle against the Snake Clan was a dark time in Rokugan's

history, but it forged a special bond between Phoenix and ronin. Gain a Fine Quality item of Phoenix make, or an extra spell if you are a shugenja. On the down side, all maho that targets your character receives a free Raise.

9–0: *Seppuku.* Roll again to determine the circumstances:

1–6: After cleansing himself of the shame that cast him from the clan, your ancestor committed seppuku to preserve the honor of the line. The clan approved, and has kept close tabs upon your ancestor's descendants. Some day you may be invited to return to the clan, if you set a good example. Their eyes are upon you. Do not fail. Roll on Table 5 to determine the clan, but gain no other benefits from that table.

7–0: After undertaking a secret mission for the benefit of the clan, your ancestor took his own life to hide the secret. You will never be allowed to swear fealty in that clan, but you gain a Major Ally within the clan who gives you help, support, and advice. Begin with the starting outfit of a bushi of that clan.

HERITAGE TABLE 3B: PRESTIGIOUS DUTY

ROLL	RESULT
1–2	*Yoriki.* Your ancestor served as an assistant to an Emerald Magistrate. Gain 5 boxes of Glory and one Rank of Law.
3–4	*Skilled Teacher.* Your ancestor shared his knowledge with the world, and passed it on to you as well. Gain 5 Character Points which must be used to purchase five new skills at Rank 1.
5–7	*Village Ward.* Your ancestor made his name by protecting and fortifying a heimin village. You gain Way of the Land for that area for free, and may purchase a True Friend or Ally from that area for 2 points less.
8–9	*Advisor.* Your ancestor's skills placed him in high demand throughout Rokugan, and the family prospered. You gain one rank in Battle, Iaijutsu, or Siege (whichever was your ancestor's specialty). If you roll on the Random Starting Outfit Table (in the Appendix) add 2 to your result.
0	*Temple Guard.* Your ancestor humbly lent his sword to the defense of a group of pacifist monks. As a result of his generosity, your line has been blessed by the Fortunes. Gain 1 Void.

HERITAGE TABLE 3C: HEROIC DEED

ROLL	RESULT
1–2:	*Rescue!* Your ancestor recovered the lost heir of a powerful daimyo. Gain 1 rank of Honor and a Major Ally in that clan. Someday, you may be allowed to swear fealty if you prove the heroic deed was not merely a fluke.
3–4:	*Hero!* Your ancestor defeated a powerful ronin bandit lord. Gain 3 koku and roll an extra dice on all interactions with magistrates.
5–6:	*Artist!* Your ancestor created a great poem, painting, story, or other work of profound and lasting beauty. Select any one artisan skill and receive two free Raises whenever you use it.
7–8:	*Sage!* Your ancestor was a great and wise shugenja, who created many strange and powerful spells. If you are a shugenja, gain an extra spell of your choice (including rare or clan-specific spells). If you are a bushi, gain one level of Magic Resistance.
9–0:	*Explorer!* Your ancestor mapped out a previously unexplored area of the Empire. Gain Absolute Direction, one rank of Navigation or Sailing, and begin with a map of that area.

HERITAGE TABLE 5: GREAT CLAN HERITAGE

Some bloodlines run stronger than others. Though you no longer bear the name of your former clan, your ancestors still consider you one of their own. They constantly watch over you, encouraging you to greater things. You may purchase any ancestor from the clan you roll on this table, and may begin the game with the family Trait bonus of one of that clan's families by paying an additional 4 CP. (Actually 5 CP total, counting the Heritage Table roll.)

Note: Though many ronin in Rokugan are Scorpion, most of these are Clan ronin. This table reflects this.

ROLL   RESULT

1:	Crab
2–3:	Crane
4:	Dragon
5–6:	Lion
7:	Phoenix
8:	Scorpion
9:	Unicorn
0:	Minor Clan
	1: Badger
	2: Centipede
	3: Dragonfly
	4: Falcon
	5: Fox
	6: Hare
	7: Mantis
	8: Sparrow
	9: Tortoise
	0: Wasp

HERITAGE TABLE 4: MIXED BLESSINGS

ROLL   RESULT

1–2:   *Hunted!* Your ancestor learned some disturbing truths about his former clan. Gain Lore: Kolat at Rank 1 and a Major Enemy in the former Clan.

3–4:   *Bounty!* Your ancestor defeated a powerful bandit horde by joining their ranks and betraying them from within. Gain 5 koku of bounty money, but lose one rank of Honor. Other ronin may know your family's reputation, and will be wary of trusting your word.

5–6:   *Demon-slayer!* Your ancestor fought and defeated a terrible oni at the side of the Kuni Witch Hunters. Gain a Major Ally in the Kuni, but also gain 1 die of Shadowlands Taint for the retributive strike the dying oni leveled against your family's bloodline.

7–8:   *Treasure!* Your ancestor discovered a weapon of Excellent Quality. Perhaps it is even magical. Unfortunately, it is also stolen. You'd return it to the proper owners, but you're afraid that your ancestor may have been the thief.

9–0:   *Tragic Hero!* Your ancestor faced a powerful daimyo in a duel. The daimyo was quite elderly, and stubbornly refused to let anyone duel in his place. Your ancestor allowed himself to be defeated in order to let the clan save face. Gain a Rank 3 Favor from that clan as a gesture of their gratitude. On the down side, your ancestor is now widely regarded to be a weakling, a coward, and a fool. Your Glory is considered 2 Ranks lower until the day you swear fealty. (You could use the favor to negate this effect, but then you've gained nothing.)

Chapter Four

Who's Who
Among the Ronin

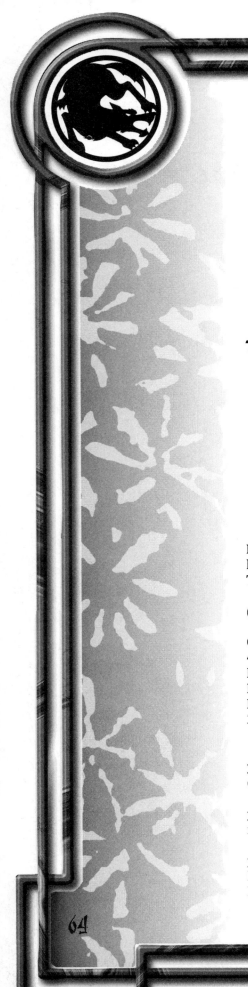

Chapter Four: Who's Who Among the Ronin

TOTURI

Earth: 4
Water: 4
    Perception 5
Fire: 3
    Intelligence 7
Air: 4
    Awareness 5
Void: 5
School/Rank: Akodo Bushi 4
Honor: 3.1
Glory: 9
Advantages: Allies (many), Ear of the Emperor, Great Destiny, Sensei (Suana, Kage), Tactician, Natural Leader
Disadvantages: Obligation (Kage), True Love (Hatsuko)
Skills: Athletics 2, Battle 5, Courtier 5, Defense 3, Etiquette 4, Hand-to-Hand 4, Heraldry 3, History 5, Iaijutsu 2, Kenjutsu 4, Law 3, Lore (many) 3-5, Meditation 4, Oratory 4, Rhetoric 3, Shintao 5, Theology 3

He is a man without a family, yet he carries himself with dignity.

He is a man without a clan, yet bushi follow him with loyal ferocity.

He is a man without a name, yet his name is spoken in hushed whispers across the Empire.

For his actions during the Coup, the courtiers of Otosan Uchi mock him with the same disdainful air with which they refer to Scorpions, tsukai and eta. Yet among ronin, he is a hero.

He is Toturi, and he is a contradiction.

After his banishment from Lion lands, Toturi spent many months traveling. He has seen the gradual deterioration of diplomacy between the Great Clans. He has sensed the growing discontent of the people. He has seen the injustice and tyranny wreaked by the Imperial Legions in the name of Hantei. He does not understand exactly what is happening to the Empire, or how things have fallen so far, but his instincts tell him that it will only worsen. He remembers the moment in which he took up the burden he thought necessary, claiming the throne when he thought the Hantei were no more. He remembers the shame he felt for his own pride when Sotorii entered the throne room, alive and well. If his honor and family name must be the price he pays for wisdom, he will not let the lesson go to waste.

For many months, Toturi waited for someone among the Great Clans to do something, to rise up and unite Rokugan under the new Emperor. He was disappointed. The Lion and Crane war on

each other. The Scorpion are broken, scattered to the winds. The Phoenix are reluctant to become involved. The Unicorn spend their energy fortifying their own position. The Crab, while strong, have their own war. The Dragon are silent, as always. The Minor Clans are wracked with disharmony and infighting. The Imperial Families do nothing, and even the once-peaceful Miya serve the Hantei with earnest loyalty while the seeds of war are sown. Toturi despaired that no one would pull Rokugan from the brink of destroying itself.

That is why Toturi's Army exists.

Make no mistake, Toturi realizes his limitations. He knows that he is only one man, a man with faults and limitations. He knows that the ronin and ashigaru who follow him owe him no loyalty, and the esteem they hold for him could disappear in the heat of battle. He knows that his force is small, unaccustomed to fighting as a unit, and lacks resources. He realizes that any Great Clan army could easily destroy what he has carefully built.

Toturi has not sent out the call to arms because he thinks he will succeed. Toturi has formed his army because he believes that someone must do something. If it will not be the clans, then it will be the ronin. If they fail, so be it, but Toturi will march into Jigoku before he allows Rokugan to be torn apart because he did nothing.

This passion is the reason why the ronin follow Toturi with such ferocity. Toturi cares about every man and woman that serves under the banner of the wolf. He knows every soldier by name, and respects them as equals. He knows that these ronin owe him nothing, and he owes them everything. Toturi is very much like his opposite number, Yugoro, in that he is the linchpin of his army. Without his fire, his compassion, his charisma, the army would be no more. Every day Toturi pledges that he will lead with courage and honor. Every morning he pleads to the ancestors that he will not fail again. Toturi struggles not to

grow too close to any individual under his command, for he knows the day will come when he must lead them to their deaths. Though all who follow the wolf banner know and love him, he has no close friends.

It is a small price to pay to save the Empire. He will carry the burden. He is Toturi.

MIKIO

Earth: 3
Water: 2
Fire: 4
   Agility: 5
Air: 3
   Reflexes: 5
Void: 6
School/Rank: Kakita Bushi 3
Honor: 2.6
Glory: 0
Advantages: Balance, Kakita Blade, Kharmic Tie (Toturi – 5), Quick
Disadvantages: Social Disadvantage (Ronin), Dark Fate, Obligation – Doji Hoturi (2), Antisocial (4)
Skills: Archery 2, Courtier 3, Etiquette 1, Horsemanship 2, Hunting 2, Iaijutsu 5, Instruction

MATSU HIRORU

Matsu Hiroru is a lost soul. He has been stripped of his honor by the terrors he has seen. He has been a pawn in the great games of Akodo Kage. He has seen things he cannot, will not understand. The rest of the Empire considers him dead. He may very well be. Every day, he wears a different name. Every day, he presents a different face to the world as he slips from one false identity to another. He no longer knows who he is, who anyone is. With one exception.

While traveling through Crane lands, he met a young girl. While riding out on her own, a sudden storm had struck and her horse broke a leg in the mud. The girl was a cripple, one foot badly clubbed, and was unlikely to be able to return home on her own. Normally, Hiroru would not have become involved, but something in the girl's demeanor moved him. She was beaten but not defeated, weak yet courageous. And what was a cripple doing trying to ride alone in the first place?

Hiroru helped the girl to the nearest village. He never told her his name, but she told him much of herself. She was an emissary from the Crane Courts, and had taken the horse "to feel the wind in her hair." Her name was Doji Shizue. She was passionate, idealistic, unafraid. Hiroru has not seen her since.

He has not stopped thinking about her.

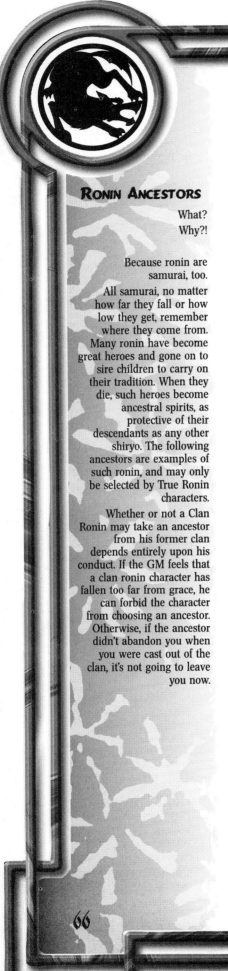

Ronin Ancestors

What?
Why?!

Because ronin are samurai, too.

All samurai, no matter how far they fall or how low they get, remember where they come from. Many ronin have become great heroes and gone on to sire children to carry on their tradition. When they die, such heroes become ancestral spirits, as protective of their descendants as any other shiryo. The following ancestors are examples of such ronin, and may only be selected by True Ronin characters.

Whether or not a Clan Ronin may take an ancestor from his former clan depends entirely upon his conduct. If the GM feels that a clan ronin character has fallen too far from grace, he can forbid the character from choosing an ancestor. Otherwise, if the ancestor didn't abandon you when you were cast out of the clan, it's not going to leave you now.

3, Intimidation 5, Kenjutsu 5, Leadership 4, Sincerity 2

Doji Mikio's path has always been clear. Early in his career, it was obvious that he would become an exceptional duelist. He moved swiftly through every kata, rising among the ranks of Kakita Toshimoko's favored students. For years he was friendly rivals with Doji Hoturi, but the two always confined their competition to the dojo. Unlike Hoturi, Mikio favored the way of the sword over etiquette and social niceties. Mikio's tongue was clumsy and he often stumbled through the court. He had no patience for painting, nor any appreciation for poetry. Hoturi tried his best to help Mikio cast away his awkward nature, but it seemed that he was destined to be a simple warrior.

Mikio accepted his limitations. Since childhood, he had been plagued by nightmares, terrible dreams that he would rise to the cusp of greatness and then fail. He reasoned that the less important he was, the less chance there would be that the nightmare would come true. Thus, Mikio did not mind in the slightest when he was assigned as yojimbo for the Doji ambassador to the Badger.

As the years passed, tensions between the Lion and Crane grew. Doji Hoturi became concerned that he, or another Crane, would one day be forced to battle his childhood friend Akodo Toturi. Though Hoturi could do little to stop the war, and would certainly not betray the Crane, he could not stand by and do nothing to show that he still valued their friendship. Summoning Mikio from the Ichiro provinces, Hoturi sent him to offer his services to Toturi. Mikio was reluctant to abandon his clan and his school, but obeyed.

Toturi accepted Mikio's services gladly, realizing the value of his friend's gift. Mikio was assigned as captain of Toturi's personal guard. Though the act won Toturi few friends among the Matsu, the Akodo family grew to appreciate Mikio's skill. Mikio served Toturi as if he were Lion born, and when the war exploded, Mikio stood always at Toturi's side as his personal champion. On three separate occasions, Mikio stepped forward to duel Crane challengers seeking Toturi's head. The Matsu that fought under Toturi's command were forced to admit that Mikio's loyalty seemed unquestionable.

In truth, Mikio had no more love for the Lion clan than any Crane. His loyalty was purely for Toturi. In Toturi, Mikio saw everything that he was not. Toturi was clever, resourceful, unpredictable. Toturi was a leader. Mikio had no doubt in his mind that the Lion Champion was destined for great things. Mikio would never be great; he would never be remembered. His nightmares told him as much. If he could just share in Akodo Toturi's destiny, however, then perhaps he might have a chance to know greatness.

Even after the Scorpion Coup came to its grisly end and Toturi met his dishonor, Mikio had no doubts. Though Toturi was shattered by the events, Mikio let nothing break his confidence. When Doji Hoturi invited Mikio to return to his service, Mikio refused. "Can I leave him now?" he asked Hoturi in reply. "When he needs me more than ever?"

Mikio and several dishonored Akodo followed Toturi for some time, though Toturi desired no company. One by one, the Akodo acceded to Toturi's wishes and left him to his melancholy, until only Mikio remained. When Toturi ordered Mikio to return to his clan, Mikio refused a final time. Toturi did not ask again, fearing that the fallen Crane would commit seppuku rather than abandon him. In time, Mikio's earnest loyalty and dedication began to pull Toturi out of his depressed stupor, helping to recover some small measure of what he once was.

The day Toturi issued his call to arms to the City of the Rich Frog, Mikio was certain more than ever that he had made the right decision. He knows that Toturi is destined to save the Empire, and when he does, Mikio will be by his side.

He will not fail.

Dairya

Earth: 3
  Stamina: 4
Water: 3
  Strength: 4
Fire: 4
Air: 4
Void: 3
School/Rank: Phoenix Clan Ronin 1
Honor: 3.8
Glory: 4.5
Advantages: Combat Reflexes, Idealistic, Proud, Quick, Strength of the Earth (2 pts.)
Disadvantages: Benten's Curse, Black Sheep, Forgotten, Missing Eye, Sworn Enemy (Kakita Toshimoko)

Skills: Archery 3, Athletics 2, Battle 2, Defense 3, Hand-to-Hand 3, Horsemanship 3, Hunting 3, Iaijutsu 4, Intimidation 3, Kenjutsu 4, Spellcraft 1, Wrestling 2

Perhaps the most famous ronin in the history of Rokugan, Dairya has continued his quest to perfect the style of the blade. His task has become more and more difficult in recent years, for as the tales of his prowess grow there are fewer and fewer who dare to face him. Only the brashest Matsu or most arrogant young Kakita dare to test their skill against him. He longs to face Kakita Toshimoko once more to avenge the loss of his eye, but lies spread about his duel with the Grey Crane's student have resulted in a bounty on his head within the lands of the Crane. Dairya is nothing if not patient, however. The coward Toshimoko will leave the Crane lands eventually, and his life will be forfeit when he finally does. On that day, the whole of Rokugan will finally know that there is no greater master of the blade than Dairya.

The recent coup in Otosan Uchi and subsequent loss of the Akodo family and Scorpion Clan has affected Dairya surprisingly little. He lost his clan long ago, and the thought of others suffering the same fate has no effect whatsoever on him. Either they will be hardy enough to survive the hardships they will experience, or they will not. It matters not to Dairya. What does matter is that the fighting in Otosan Uchi could eventually spark conflicts across the face of Rokugan. Strife, conflict, war…these are the things that make the heart of a wave-man rejoice.

In recent months Dairya was seen among the samurai of the Islands of Silk and Spice. The Mantis lord Yoritomo paid Dairya very well to teach the ways of the blade and bow to the samurai in his service. The Son of Storms' dream that the Mantis will one day stand side by side with the Great Clans of Rokugan struck Dairya as naïve and idealistic, but ambitious. Despite this, Yoritomo commands the ronin's respect, for he is a man of great strength and vision. What's more, the Mantis knew of Dairya's skills and paid him both the respect and price he was due. Though he recognized and respected the Mantis's cause, it was not his.

While with the Mantis, Dairya heard of the fighting between the Crane and the Lion, and of the Crane's campaign against the remnants of the Scorpion Clan. Despite his animosity toward the Cranes, the call of battle and wealth called to Dairya, and he returned to the lands of the Empire to quench the fire in his soul. Knowing of Dairya's near-legendary skill with the blade, the general of the Crane forces overlooked the ronin's history with Kakita Toshimoko and paid him to join the battle. Dairya quickly found himself fighting in the Scorpion lands alongside former Akodo samurai. Their sorrow and grief disgusted him, and he was unable to remain with them for long despite the pay he was receiving from the Crane.

Having heard that Morito Tokei had left his apprenticeship with Naka Kuro to seek the Black Ronin, Dairya traveled through the lands of the Lion in search of his old friend. The sight of the

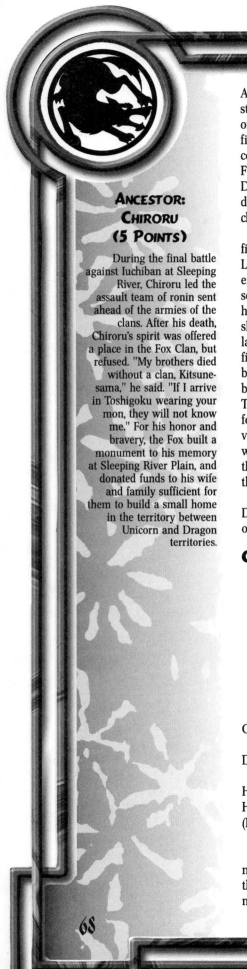

ANCESTOR: CHIRORU (5 POINTS)

During the final battle against Iuchiban at Sleeping River, Chiroru led the assault team of ronin sent ahead of the armies of the clans. After his death, Chiroru's spirit was offered a place in the Fox Clan, but refused. "My brothers died without a clan, Kitsune-sama," he said. "If I arrive in Toshigoku wearing your mon, they will not know me." For his honor and bravery, the Fox built a monument to his memory at Sleeping River Plain, and donated funds to his wife and family sufficient for them to build a small home in the territory between Unicorn and Dragon territories.

Akodo Deathseekers and the struggle of the Matsu to bring order to the beleaguered clan filled Dairya with fresh contempt for the Great Clans. Foul-tempered as he was, Dairya left many brash samurai dead in the road where they challenged him.

Dairya was not successful in finding his friend Tokei in the Lion lands. He did, however, encounter the object of Tokei's search: the Black Ronin, Toturi himself. The two exchanged sharp words on a muddy road late at night in the heart of a fierce storm. What was said between the two is uncertain, but Dairya now rides with Toturi. When asked why he follows Toturi, Dairya responds very simply, "He remembers who and what we are, even though we may have forgotten the truth ourselves."

With the faintest of smiles, Dairya adds "How fortunate for him that he is not our master, eh?"

GINAWA

Earth: 3
Water: 3
Fire: 2
    Agility: 3
Air: 3
Void: 3
School/Rank: Akodo Bushi 2
Honor: 1.1
Glory: 2.3
Advantages: Driven (to find his lord's killer), Great Destiny, Quick Healer
Disadvantages: Compulsion (Sake, TN 20), Dishonored, Insensitive
Skills: Archery 2, Bard 1, Battle 1, Defense 2, Hand-to-Hand 3, History 1, Horsemanship 2, Hunting 2, Investigation 2, Kenjutsu 3, Lore (Bushido) 1, Stealth 2, War Fan 1

Ginawa's long quest to find the assassin who murdered his lord has yet to bear fruit. Each day the disheveled warrior finds his search more and more frustrating, and sake's sweet oblivion more and more appealing. Were it not for the raging lust for revenge that the eponymous bloodsword builds within his breast, Ginawa might have succumbed to failure and self-loathing long ago.

When the armies of the Lion left for Otosan Uchi to crush the Scorpion forces holding the Imperial City, Ginawa watched them with an aching void in his heart. Having denied it for years, he finally accepted that he longed to ride alongside the Akodo once more, serving his lord loyally and with honor. When the Emperor destroyed the Akodo family, the irony did not escape Ginawa: even had he saved his lord's life, he would only have become ronin regardless.

The banishment of the Scorpion Clan further complicated Ginawa's search. Although he could never be certain, he felt sure that the assassin responsible for his lord's death was a Scorpion. With their numbers scattered to the four winds, the likelihood of finding someone who could tell him the killer's name, much less of finding the killer himself, became all but impossible. Nevertheless he continued his search, moving among the ronin of Rokugan with a feverish pace, desperate for results and all the while feeling his opportunities slip through his fingers.

For a while, Ginawa lost himself in a dark haze of intoxication. He finally awakened from his stupor with the familiar sensation of vengeance. If he could not find the assassin who murdered his lord, he could at the very least avenge the injustice done to the Akodo line because of a single man's dishonorable actions: Toturi. The disgraced Lion's blood would quench the raging bloodlust that coursed through Ginawa's being, resonating through his katana, up through his arm and into his heart and mind.

Once again, Ginawa set out among the ronin, this time seeking a new target, and the lands of the Unicorn, Lion, and Phoenix fell under his scrutiny. While visiting Shiba territory, he found a ronin who had heard word of the Black Ronin in the lands of the Dragon. With a red haze obscuring his vision, Ginawa rode west to find his target.

In the lands of the Dragon Ginawa found as many ronin as he had ever seen in one place. The wave-men had come to mock the great Akodo Toturi, reduced to the state of a simple ronin. Upon meeting him, however, many stayed to hear his words and see what course of action he would take. Ginawa vowed to himself that he would make their choice a simple one.

When Ginawa finally found Toturi, the Black Ronin was meditating at a shrine high in the mountainous lands of the Mirumoto. Clenching the hilt of Revenge so tightly that his entire being trembled, Ginawa approached him. Toturi heard the ronin's approach, and looked up to see Ginawa. Their eyes met.

In that moment, the crimson haze bled away from Ginawa's vision. He saw in Toturi the same quiet honor and nobility that his own lord had demonstrated. He saw the horrible sadness that the ronin felt for his family, and yet he still felt that Toturi's first loyalty was to Rokugan.

Over the next few days, their conversations reminded Ginawa of who and what he was, and cleared from his mind the corrupting influence of the Bloodsword he carried. When Ginawa left the lands of the Dragon, he left with a sense of honor he had almost forgotten in his years as a ronin. Although he declined to ride with Toturi for the time being, he has sworn to return when and if Toturi has need of him.

Ginawa now rides throughout Rokugan, renewing his search with a clarity and focus he has been without for many years.

HASAME

Earth: 2
    Stamina: 3
Water: 3
Fire: 3
    Intelligence: 4
Air: 3
    Awareness: 4
Void: 2
School/Rank: Shinjo Bushi 1
Honor: 2.4
Glory: 1.6
Advantages: Driven, Heart of Vengence (Unicorn), Higher Purpose (Knowledge)
Disadvantages: Social Disadvantage (Ronin)

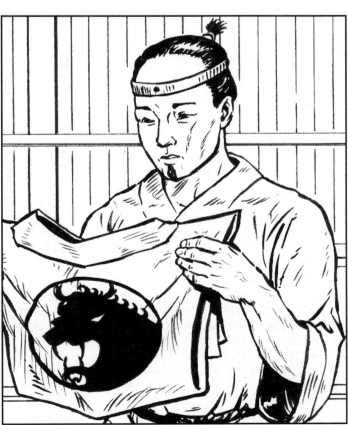

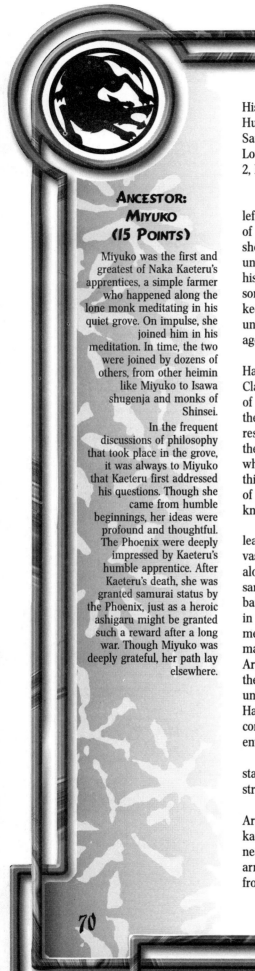

Skills: Craft (Storytelling) 1, Defense 2, History 3, Horse Archery 2, Horsemanship 2, Hunting 2, Iaijutsu 1, Kenjutsu 3, Lore (Burning Sands) 2, Lore (Kolat) 2, Lore (Shadowlands) 2, Lore (Unicorn) 4, Naginata 2, Oratory 1, Research 2, Rhetoric 2, Sincerity 1, Yomanri 2

Hasame is no longer the young man who once left the Unicorn Clan to serve the Lion. The events of the past months have aged him much. The shock and anguish he felt over the events unfolding in Otosan Uchi were compounded by his growing fear that the agents of the Kolat are somehow involved. Certainly, this scheme is in keeping with the knowledge he and his father unearthed in the lands of the Crab so many years ago.

With the destruction of the Akodo line, Hasame has lost his position within the Lion Clan. Although the Matsu who assumed control of the province at which he was stationed shared the general Lion view of ronin as a useful resource, their desire to expunge every aspect of the Akodo's rule led them to dismiss those ronin who had served them. Truly without a home for this first time in his life, and fearful of the threat of Kolat assassination, Hasame left the world he knew behind to travel far to the east.

On the Islands of Silk and Spice, Hasame learned how fortunate he had been to serve as a vassal of the Akodo. The Mantis bushi he worked alongside despised him, regarding him as a fallen samurai of the clans. He endured their slurs and baiting for long months, serving alongside them in silence as the yojimbo for a wealthy Mantis merchant. Among the Mantis there was only one man he would call friend, a young bushi called Arashi. Hasame and Arashi frequently found themselves working alongside one another, and unlike his Mantis brethren Arashi never mocked Hasame. Though the two were not close, Hasame considered Arashi his only ally in an unfriendly environment.

Until the night he awoke to find Arashi standing over him, kama raised for the killing strike.

The fight was brief but bloody. In the end Arashi lay dead, his throat torn out by his own kama. Badly wounded, Hasame spent two weeks near death in the ship's hold. The wound to his arm was a grievous one, and the care he received from the Mantis was mediocre at best.

During his convalescence he had much time to think on what had happened. Had Arashi been a Kolat assassin? Had they finally decided Hasame must die for his knowledge after all these years? He could think of no other solution. The ramifications of this were two-fold: Hasame now knew, without question, that he was going to die. He could not hope to hide from them forever, for their agents were everywhere. But he likewise knew that if they were hunting them, he could hunt them as well. He had just slain one of their assassins, after all. They were men, flesh and blood like himself. No more, no less.

The young man who stood on the docks of Mura Sabishii Toshi as the Mantis vessel departed for the Islands of Silk and Spice was nothing like the Hasame who had left Rokguan over a year earlier. His stride was cautious, yet proud. The depths of his eyes showed resignation, but also determination. He faced an impossible obstacle, yet he was prepared to assault it with every fiber of his being. In short, Hasame had grasped the concept that governed the life of Crab berserkers. Death is inevitable; it is the blow you strike while dying that matters.

Hasame waited in Mura Sabishii Toshi for several weeks to see if another attempt would be made on his life. When none materialized, he left the city for the lands of the Phoenix. Capitalizing on the Phoenix Clan's relatively accepting view of ronin, Hasame hoped to apprentice himself in some way to a member of the Asako inquisitors. He felt sure that from the Asako he could learn ways to perceive the movements of the Kolat. His hopes were dashed when the Asako, suspicious of this eager young ronin, informed him that there was no place for him among them.

Undeterred, Hasame traveled to the lands of the Dragon Clan in hopes of finding a Kitsuki magistrate who would take him on as a yojimbo. Before he could locate a suitable candidate, however, he found a camp of ronin, all apparently following the Black Ronin himself: Toturi.

Torn by conflicting emotions, Hasame observed Toturi from a discreet distance. He desperately wanted to believe that Toturi was the man of honor that the other ronin claimed he was, but he feared that the role the former Lion Champion had played in the recent coup, specifically his rumored claiming of the throne for himself, indicated he was an agent of the Kolat.

ANCESTOR: MIYUKO (15 POINTS)

Miyuko was the first and greatest of Naka Kaeteru's apprentices, a simple farmer who happened along the lone monk meditating in his quiet grove. On impulse, she joined him in his meditation. In time, the two were joined by dozens of others, from other heimin like Miyuko to Isawa shugenja and monks of Shinsei.

In the frequent discussions of philosophy that took place in the grove, it was always to Miyuko that Kaeteru first addressed his questions. Though she came from humble beginnings, her ideas were profound and thoughtful. The Phoenix were deeply impressed by Kaeteru's humble apprentice. After Kaeteru's death, she was granted samurai status by the Phoenix, just as a heroic ashigaru might be granted such a reward after a long war. Though Miyuko was deeply grateful, her path lay elsewhere.

Finally, Hasame chose a course of action. He would ride at Toturi's side, serving him loyally as a retainer. His former allegiance to the Akodo made this easy enough. In time, he would find the truth about the Black Ronin. If he found Toturi to be the man he appeared to be, then he would lay down his life to serve him. If, however, he found that the former Lion was a tool of the Kolat, then Hasame's last action in this world would be to take the life of one last Kolat.

Naka Kuro

Earth: 5
Water: 5
Fire: 5
Air: 5
Void: 6
School/Rank: Isawa Shugenja 5
Honor: 3.9
Glory: 6.8
Advantages: Ancestor (Naka Kaeteru), Ascetic Can't Lie, Chosen by the Oracles, Forbidden Knowledge, Great Destiny, Higher Purpose (Teach the Empire), Kharmic Tie (Naka Kaeteru), Magic Resistance (3 pts.), Precise Memory
Disadvantages: None
Skills: Advanced Medicine 4, Calligraphy 5, Cipher 4, Courtier 3, Etiquette 3, Heraldry 4, History 5, Lore (Many) 3–5, Meditation 5, Oratory 3, Origami 4, Painting 4, Poetry 3, Research 5, Rhetoric 5, Shintao 5, Spellcraft 5, Theology 4

Although incredibly powerful in the ways of the kami, Naka Kuro could no more prevent the tragedy of the coup in Otosan Uchi than he could foresee it. Even this renowned sensei, whom so many see as a paragon of serenity and harmony, has been affected by the grief and horror that permeates the Empire. Naka Kuro cannot see the future with certainty, but he does not need to do so in order to know that war is blossoming on the horizon. The blessing of enlightenment means little when the innocent are dying.

Everywhere he travels, people come to him for answers. He calms them and gives them what reassurance he can, but for the first time in his long life he wonders if his comforting wisdom rings true.

Kuro has been pleased with the progress of his student Morito Tokei, who has proven even more capable than Kuro suspected. Tokei and his brother have joined the cause of Toturi, the so-called Black Ronin and former champion of the Lion Clan. Kuro approves of this as well, for he needs no magic to see that Toturi is a man of honor, and a man with an unknowable destiny. Were Kuro a different man, perhaps he would join Toturi as well; but Toturi is fated to walk his path without the counsel of Naka Kuro.

Unbeknown to any in Rokugan, Naka Kuro has subtly aided many former Scorpions in their efforts to escape the Imperially sanctioned pogrom launched against them by the vindictive Crane Clan. Kuro neither defends the Scorpion nor condemns the Crane, for each have merely obeyed the wishes of their respective lords. He aids the Scorpion merely because he knows their destiny has not yet reached its conclusion. The

Ancestor: Miyuko (15 Points)

The Grand Master of the Elements wished for Miyuko to carry on his teachings, not only to the Phoenix but to all of the Empire. With the blessings of the Isawa, Miyuko became a ronin.

Descendants of Miyuko must be shugenja. These individuals wield their illustrious ancestor's deep understanding of the dance of the Elements. All spell effects which depend upon the shugenja's rank (including Damage Ratings) operate as if the ronin's Rank was that of a Clan shugenja with equal insight.

ANCESTOR: "REZAN" (4 POINTS)

Many critics acclaim Rezan as the greatest poet in history. They are wrong; he was a terrible poet, but a fearsome duelist. While visiting the Doji court, Rezan fell into an argument with a poet over which lady at the court was the most beautiful. The argument ended with Rezan challenging the Doji to a duel. The Doji accepted, but twisted the letter of Rezan's challenge to force him into a duel of poetry.

Each would compose a poem in tribute to their lady. The Doji's choice was a young Crane, and Rezan selected a young woman who hid her face behind a scarlet veil. To the horror of the Crane court, it was discovered that Rezan's choice was none other than the Emperor's daughter, traveling in disguise to maintain her anonymity. The Doji could not win the contest without shaming the Emperor's daughter. The Crane not only intentionally failed, but failed miserably and heralded Rezan's poetry as the finest in the Empire.

future of the Akodo is unclear to him, and he has thus far left them to their own devices.

Kuro has recently spent a great deal of time among the Empire's various brotherhoods of monks. He fears that when the inevitable war comes, the innocent heimin and hinin will suffer a disproportionate amount of the burden. He attempts to allay the fears of the monks, encouraging them to find solace in meditation with the Fortunes and the Tao. "We have been given the answers," he tells them. "We need only to understand them."

The magistrates of the Emerald Champion have also received Kuro's attention. He travels from city to city, each time stopping to speak with the Imperial Magistrates. These august servants of Rokugan have played a key role in the preservation of peace throughout the Empire since the death of the Hantei. Now with the new Emperor lying upon his deathbed, their duty has become even more important. They are men of virtue, and Kuro hopes that he can encourage them toward the path of wisdom. He is certain that they serve as one of the linchpins that keeps Rokugan from spiraling into war, a fate he wishes to prevent as long as possible.

It is Kuro's desire to forestall war so that the peasantry of the Empire will have time to prepare. With every journey he takes, he visits more and more villages, blessing crops and livestock, trying to prevent outbreaks of the plague that rages across portions of the country, and seeking to inspire hope and courage in the common man. It is a difficult task. The death of the Son of Heaven, and the subsequent illness of his son and heir have badly shaken the world view of many heimin. Some believe the Fortunes have abandoned them, while others suspect the Lady Sun is punishing them for the death of her beloved son's descendant. Plagues of the body and crop Kuro can try to heal. Plagues of faith and spirit are harder to defeat.

Recently, Kuro met a ronin in his travels, a mysterious figure who spoke of omens, portents, and destinies. His insight into the future was infallible, and Kuro was filled with wonder at this strange, hooded ronin. Kuro now suspects that the troubles that plague his beloved Rokugan are the symptoms of some great, cataclysmic event that will either give the Empire the shape it will have for the future…or destroy it utterly. As he has so many times in his long life, Kuro has once again placed his confidence in the ways of the kami and

the Great Cycle. What is meant to happen shall happen, and Naka Kuro will play whatever role fate has seen fit to give him.

He hopes that will be enough.

TOKU

Earth: 2
Water: 2
Fire: 2
  Agility 3
Air: 2
  Reflexes 3
Void: 3
School/Rank: None (True Ronin)
Skills: Archery 1, Battle 1, Defense 2, Horsemanship 1, Hunting 2, Iaijutsu 1, Kenjutsu 2, Law 1, Lore (Bushido) 1, Poetry 1, Shintao 1
Honor: 2.6
Glory: 1.1
Advantages: Great Destiny (Monkey Clan Champion), Kharmic Tie (Akodo Toturi), Luck (3 points)
Disadvantages: Driven (Become Samurai), Heimin, Idealistic

Since that long–ago day when he fought side-by-side with an Ikoma ronin against bandits intent on invading his village, Toku has striven to live his life according to the tenets of bushido. He attempted to return to the life of a simple farmer, but his interest in bushido had been fanned into a passion that could not be quenched. Toku left behind his village, the remnants of his family, even his birth name. With the steed of a dead Otaku, the katana of a slain bandit warlord, a copy of Akodo's *Leadership* and a set of armor pieced together from a dozen dead samurai, Toku set out to become samurai.

For nearly a year Toku wandered throughout Rokugan. He took great care to avoid the lands of the Unicorn, for though he respected them greatly, he feared that his beloved steed would be taken from him were he to encounter a member of the Otaku family. In the lands of the Phoenix, Toku was hired to accompany a merchant caravan to the lands of the Dragon Clan. The young man's serious demeanor and obvious devotion to the code of bushido caught the interest of a Mirumoto warrior, who spent some time educating Toku in the basic skills of a bushi. A visiting dignitary from the Crane lands noticed the two men practicing together and, in what he believed would be a jest of monumental

Since that time, poets have invoked Rezan's name in order to draw honor and attention to their work. As a result, hundreds of wonderful poems have been written by "Rezan."

A character with a kharmic tie to Rezan is descended from one of these many poets. He may roll and keep a number of extra dice equal to his Void for all Poetry skill rolls.

proportions convinced the Mirumoto to sponsor Toku's participation in the Topaz Championship.

The arrival of a true ronin at the most prestigious gempukku ceremony in the Empire was met with thinly veiled revulsion. The Crane had no choice but to permit him to participate lest they insult their allies among the Dragon. To everyone's shock, the young man performed admirably. He did not win a single event, but he passed virtually every test and participated in the dueling contest at the conclusion of the tournament. Standing aside while the other participants of the tournament swore their oaths of fealty to their various daimyos, Toku was struck with the realization that though he had been born heimin, his actions and skills had convinced the others that he, too, was born samurai. That any samurai present would execute him without thought for a simple accident of birth if the truth were known was of little concern to him.

He would define himself by his actions, not his heritage.

At the very moment this thought cemented itself into Toku's mind, he glanced up to see the Lion Clan Champion, Akodo Toturi himself, looking at him. With an amused smile on his face, Toturi-sama gave Toku a slow, appreciative nod.

He felt his spirit soar within him as he bowed his head in respect to the great warrior: this was a sign that his quest to truly become samurai would succeed.

For years, Toku wandered Rokugan, learning the ways of the bushi from whatever teacher he could find. Though dismissed by most as another dishonorable ronin, those few samurai who spent time with Toku were amazed to find a young man consumed with devotion to the code of bushido. Toku would ask those he met to read to him from the pages of Akodo's Leadership, smiling at the truth and beauty of the words.

When word of the attempted coup in Otosan Uchi reached Toku, he wept. That those born into the ranks of the samurai could so disregard their responsibilities was unthinkable to him. The news of Toturi's banishment from the Lion Clan was an even greater shock to the young warrior. He immediately set out to find Toturi and see for himself if the great man could truly have fallen so far.

When he finally found Toturi in the lands of the Dragon, he found the same quiet presence he had seen years before at the Topaz Championship. The two spoke for hours in a quiet corner of a teahouse about honor, bushido, and the state of the Empire. When the morning sun appeared in

ANCESTOR: HIRO (3 POINTS)

Hiro considered himself a clever rogue, hero of the peasants, and brave antagonist of samurai everywhere. In reality, Hiro was a cutthroat, notorious bandit lord. He was utterly ruthless. Those who defied him, died. Magistrates who hunted him were hunted in turn by the horde that followed him. Hiro was not loved by the masses; he was hated and feared by everyone, even his own men. Only the fact that he was a tactical genius and brilliant criminal mastermind kept his own followers from rebelling against him. At the height of his power, it is believed that Hiro led over one thousand bandits from a fortress deep in the Spine of the World mountain range. He is said to have been the founder of the Forest-Killers, and the creator of their deadly technique.

the sky above the mountains, Toturi left the lands of the Dragon journeying south into Rokugan. Toku rode at his side.

SHOTAI

Earth: 4
Water: 4
    Strength: 5
Fire: 2
    Agility: 5
Air: 1
    Reflexes: 4
Void: 3
School/Rank: Matsu Bushi 3
Honor: 4.1
Glory: 0 (Outcast)
Advantages: Death Trance, Kharmic Tie – Toturi (5), Strength of the Earth x 2, Irreproachable (5)
Disadvantages: Weakness (Awareness), Frail Mind, Black Sheep (all Disadvantages are result of his injury)
Skills: Athletics 3, Battle 4, Courtier 3*, Defense 2, Diplomacy 3*, Etiquette 4*, History 3, Intimidation 4, Kenjutsu 5, Knife 2, Kyujutsu 3, Shintao 4, Sincerity 4*

* indicates abilities Shotai is no longer capable of consciously using

Shotai was once a great man. In his mind, he still is.

Many years ago, Ikoma Shotai was a great diplomat. So agile was his mind that Akodo Arasou appointed him emissary to the Scorpion. Though most would have considered the assignment a punishment, Shotai prospered for many years. He foiled many Scorpion plots before they began and even enacted a few schemes of his own, all for the glory of the Lion.

A year after Akodo Toturi rose to become Champion of the Lion, Shotai returned with grave news. He had learned that a Scorpion ronin, rumored to be ninja, had gained access to the Winter Court by blackmailing a minor Isawa functionary. Shotai had dealt with the Isawa traitor, but the assassin had eluded his grasp. Shotai was determined to stop the assassin personally, and had only stopped at Akodo Castle to report before he continued north to Kyuden Isawa. To his surprise, Toturi insisted on accompanying him personally. Shotai was reluctant. He had heard rumors that the new Champion was weak and inexperienced, but could not argue with his lord.

During their breakneck journey to Kyuden Isawa, Shotai and Toturi were attacked by a band of the assassin's ronin accomplices. Together, they fought off the larger force and escaped northward to save the Hantei. During the battle and subsequent chase, Shotai developed a grudging respect for Toturi. This man was not the weakling the Matsu made him to be, but a keenly perceptive warrior. The only flaw he noticed in Toturi's character was his tendency to over-analyze a situation, causing him to hesitate at inopportune times.

They arrived at Kyuden Isawa just as the assassin made his move. However, as the two Lion burst into the Hantei's chambers, the ninja turned his poisoned blade toward Toturi instead. Toturi hesitated only for a moment, a moment that would have been his last had Shotai not leapt to his defense. The ninja shattered Shotai's katana and stabbed him deeply in the throat. Toturi quickly dispatched the ninja, then summoned healers to save the life of the valiant Ikoma.

Shotai's life was saved, but not his mind. Since that day, the former diplomat's mind has been fragile. Most of the time, he lingers in a fugue state, staring into the distance and clutching the hilt of his broken sword. He mumbles to himself at times, quoting from the Tao or the proud histories of the Lion.

Only when battle begins does Shotai awaken, returning to the last moments before the ninja's blade struck. Every foe that stands against him is an "accursed Scorpion." Every man that fights at his side is "Toturi-sama." Toturi has become "Hantei" and the broken Ikoma serves his lord with earnest devotion and limitless ferocity.

Toturi blamed himself for Shotai's condition, and had the old bushi sent to a monastery near Shiro Akodo to be properly cared for. Toturi visited Shotai often, spending long hours discussing tales of glory and heroism. Sometimes, the light would return to Shotai's eyes and he would be almost as he once was.

After the Coup, Toturi was banished from Akodo lands. Shotai was left alone. The monks continued to care for Shotai dutifully, but the old ronin paid them no mind. In his world, they did not exist. His condition began to worsen. Sometimes, he would not move or eat for days.

Recently, a monk came to Shotai's room, eagerly bringing him news of Toturi. "I hear," the monk said as he presented the old bushi's meal, "that your friend Toturi-sama has found a new home in Dragon lands. Isn't that nice?"

Shotai's eyes opened for a moment. "The Hantei has returned? Is it time for the new Empire?"

The monk became worried at the strange glint in Shotai's eyes, and quickly changed the subject.

On that night, Shotai escaped from the monastery. He has not been seen since.

TOHAKU

Earth: 3
> Willpower: 4

Water: 4

Fire: 3

Air: 2
> Reflexes: 3

Void: 3

School/Rank: Akodo Bushi 1, Mirumuto Bushi 2

Honor: 3.8

Glory: 0.7

Advantages: Death Trance, Multiple Schools, Heart of Vengeance – Lion, True Friend – Togashi Mitsu (3)

Disadvantages: Nemesis – Kitsu Motso, Dishonored

Skills: Archery 2, Bard 2, Battle 3, Defense 2, Etiquette 3, History 2, Iaijutsu 3, Investigation 3, Jiujutsu 2, Kenjutsu 4, Law 3, Lore (Dragon Clan)

In time, the full weight of the Imperial Legions were leveled against Hiro's fortress. Hiro's men fled or were slain. Hiro died alone, riddled with arrows, but with his yumi in his hand and a smile on his face. Hiro's final shot had slain the Emerald Champion.

Hiro had many liaisons, and left many children to carry on his name. Characters with a kharmic tie to the bandit lord roll and keep an extra die on all rolls to influence others by intimidation or coercion. Descendants of Hiro automatically have their Honor reduced to zero. If their Honor ever rises above one, the benefits of this ancestor depart forever.

ANCESTOR: SUN TAO (11 POINTS)

In every version of Sun Tao's tale, the great general ended his days as a ronin. Ronin who know his tale will be quick to point out this fact, and many ronin claim to be descended from Sun Tao. There are no records of Sun Tao ever having children, but the only surviving records of the general's life are sketchy.

The Kitsu believe that Sun Tao did have children, for his spirit still watches over a select few of those who claim to be his descendants. Descendants of Sun Tao have a remarkable ability to adapt to their environment, learning from their mistakes almost instantaneously. After some time living with the wisdom of Sun Tao, mistakes no longer exist. After any failed skill roll the character may spend one Void Point to add 10 to the result. If this new total would result in a success, then the roll becomes successful. Any Raises that were originally made are negated. This effect may only be used once per day.

2, Lore (Lion Clan) 2, Meditation 2, Mountaineer 3

Akodo Tohaku was once a magistrate. Early in his career, Tohaku led a small band of samurai on a crusade against bandits prowling the mountains near Kyuden Ikoma. Under Tohaku's direction, and with the unexpected assistance of the ise zumi Togashi Mitsu, the magistrates crushed three separate bandit hordes and unveiled evidence revealing a possible link between the juzimai and a courtier at Shiro Daidoji. The evidence meant nothing in the courts of the Empire, but the Lion stepped up their patrols in the area and soon the problem vanished altogether. After his victory, Tohaku's skills won him high regard. He quickly worked his way through the ranks of the clan as daimyo after daimyo sought his service as a retainer. Eventually, he found himself in the service of Kitsu Motso.

Motso was a capable, if sometimes arrogant lord. Tohaku served his master dutifully. When others mocked the Kitsu for his arrogance and temper, Tohaku always defended Motso's name. If Motso noticed Tohaku's loyalty, he said nothing, for such was only to be expected.

In time, Tohaku came to know a samurai-ko named Matsu Yuyiko. Yuyiko was smitten with Motso, and though the young general occasionally returned her affection and spoke highly of her in public, he usually ignored her. The Matsu expected the two to marry eventually, sealing the bond the unofficial bond between the Kitsu and his Matsu allies. Motso never gave any indication for or against the matter.

After some time, Yuyiko began to grow frustrated. When she noticed the skill and prowess of Motso's magistrate, Tohaku, she formulated a plan. Yuyiko turned her attentions to Tohaku in an attempt to make Motso jealous. Tohaku rebuffed Yuyiko as politely as he could. Yuyiko was insulted by Tohaku's refusal. Motso did not seem to care.

Then came the day that Tohaku noticed several items of great value missing from Motso's home, among them several maps and other items of confidential material. Tohaku believed it could be none other than Motso's ronin advisor – no one else had access to such materials. Tohaku went to his master immediately to report his suspicions. When he arrived, he found an angry Motso waiting. Motso accused him of disloyalty, of

treachery, of scheming against him, and of theft. Yuyiko was there, as was the ronin. All three looked upon Tohaku with quiet anger and disapproval.

With that, Tohaku was cast out of Motso's service. Upon the testimony of a spurned samurai-ko and Motso's villainous ronin advisor, Tohaku was dishonored. After the shock faded, it was replaced with anger. Tohaku wanted nothing less than Motso's death, to make him pay for his arrogance and stupidity. In that moment an old friend returned to Tohaku's life, the ise zumi who had helped him in his crusade against the bandits years earlier.

Togashi Mitsu pleaded with Tohaku to set his anger aside, to find enlightenment rather than vengeance. Tohaku agreed, but only for his friend's sake. They journeyed to Togashi Mountain. Under Mitsu's recommendation, the Mirumuto have taught Tohaku the secrets of the daisho technique. The Togashi family have tried to help the angry Lion find his center through meditation.

For all the Dragon's efforts, none of their efforts to rehabilitate Tohaku are helping. All Tohaku can think of is how the Togashi meditation shall help him to focus so much better as his Mirumuto techniques bring two swords down to sever Motso's head. When the Akodo were destroyed, Tohaku became even more enraged, vowing to strike down every Lion that still lived. Mitsu was forced to confine the Lion in a cave until he calmed down.

Tohaku knows that revenge is neither healthy nor honorable. Until he can work his anger out of his system, he plans to stay far from the Lion. He's not sure just yet whether he really believes he can find enlightenment, but he's trying.

HISA

Earth: 2
    Willpower: 3
Water: 2
Fire: 4
Air: 3
    Awareness: 4
Void: 3
School/Rank: Bayushi Bushi 2
Honor: 1.3
Glory: 0.0
Advantages: Bland, Heartless
Disadvantages: Social Disadvantage (Ronin), Haunted (4), Insensitive

Skills: Acting 2, Archery 1, Defense 2, Heraldry 1, Hisomu 2, Iaijutsu 1, Kenjutsu 3, Kuenai 2, Poison 2, Sincerity 3, Stealth 3

Hisa remembers when he could sleep.

Hisa was born to the Bayushi family, cousin of Bayushi Shoju. He was a decent swordsman and an adequate officer; in any other clan, he would have been unremarkable. Among the Scorpion he was appreciated, for Hisa was discreet, following orders without question and guarding his mouth well. Shoju expected great things from Bayushi Hisa, so the young samurai was among the first to be chosen when Shoju made his plans for the siege of Otosan Uchi. Certainly, once Shoju began the new Bayushi Dynasty, there would be a place of honor for Hisa.

When the battle grew thick, Hisa was sent to relieve the troops at the south wall. By the time he arrived, the south wall had fallen. Lion troops had flooded the city, slaughtering Scorpions as they marched. A rain of arrows fell upon Hisa's unit.

Soshi Tomita, Hisa's chui, turned with fear in his eyes. "Bayushi-sama, what will we do?" he screamed.

Hisa opened his mouth to reply, but before he could issue a command, his men died. Tomita fell to his knees, an arrow lodged in one eye, spitting blood. His mask hung crooked to one side, a look of utter surprise frozen upon his face. Hisa glanced about, uncertain. He saw the soldiers of the Lion charge, and recognized the face of Matsu Tsuko. The few remaining defenders were hacked down. Hisa saw Tsuko's unit head directly for his position. He did the only thing he could do.

He crawled under Tomita's corpse and pretended to be dead.

Hisa lay in the blood and filth for hours, praying he would not be found. He prayed to the Fortunes for luck. He prayed for forgiveness, for what he had done had not been an act of subterfuge or strategy. It

had been an act of cowardice, and Hisa knew it. When the sun set, Hisa had no illusions. He knew what was happening in the Palace and had no desire to throw his life away. Sneaking through the darkened streets, he discarded his armor, mask, and banner and leapt into Golden Sun Bay. He swam as far down the coast as he could before his limbs grew tired.

Somehow, he had managed to keep his sword. He wrapped its hilt in thick twine to conceal the Bayushi mon, then made his way to the nearest village. Hisa congratulated himself. Already, he had formulated a plan to vanish into society's underbelly. He would be an outcast, but he would survive.

That night, the dreams came. Every Scorpion who died in the Coup visited Hisa, accusing him, mocking him, threatening damnation for his disloyalty, demanding atonement. The next night, they came again, and every night since. Hisa rarely sleeps, and fears he will soon go completely insane.

The spirits of the fallen demand atonement. Hisa must prove his worth before he can be free. He has traveled extensively in the last two years,

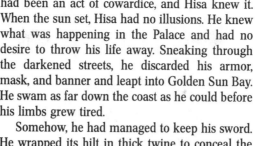

ANCESTOR: SUN TAO (CONTINUED)

The use of this ability is always obvious. The character makes a mistake, but comes back instantly, making another maneuver or correction to negate the results. Often the success seems to be nothing more than dumb luck. For example, an archer missing a moving target may make an improbable ricochet shot off of a nearby tree, striking his foe.

Chapter Four: Who's Who Among the Ronin

working with mercenary bands, gathering information. To Hisa's surprise, ronin know much about clan samurai, and heimin sometimes know even more. He knows which families are strongest, which clans are wracked with internal strife, and where to hire disgruntled, angry bushi cheaply. All of this is information that the Scorpion will value highly, but the ghosts tell him it is not enough. Not yet. He must remain alive and undetected to carry messages between the Scorpion armies. But what Scorpion armies could they mean? The clan is broken, in hiding, scattered.

No time for questions. If Hisa would be sane again, he must obey the demands of the dead.

TZURUI

Earth: 3
Water: 2
    Strength: 4
Fire: 2
Air: 2
    Reflexes: 3
Void: 2
School/Rank: None
Honor: 2.5
Glory: 0.0
Advantages: True Friend – Toku (1/5), Higher Purpose (prove his bravery)
Disadvantages: Social Disadvantage (Ronin), Dependent (daughter), Lost Love (wife)
Skills: Athletics 2, Battle 2, Defense 2, Horsemanship 1, Hunting 1, Iaijutsu 1, Kenjutsu 2, Yarijutsu 3

Tzurui's life has not been glorious, but Tzurui never wished for glory. He was born to the Nanbu, vassals of the Soshi so minor that Bantaro often forgot their existence. Nestled in a small valley near the Spine of the World, the Nanbu lived in peace for generations. Their lands were in view of White Shore Plain, as close to Unicorn territory as Scorpion. Occasional commerce and trade through the valley kept them abreast of events, and helped the village to flourish and grow.

In his youth, Tzurui was betrothed to Iuchi Ochiyo, a shugenja of minor note. She was a sickly girl, sent away by her family as much to relieve themselves of the burden of her existence as to establish contact with the Nanbu. Tzurui did not consider her a burden. He fell deeply in love, and dedicated his time to caring for his "delicate flower." She loved him in return, and they were happy for a time.

Sadly, Ochiyo's health grew worse. During the birth of their first child, Kochohime, Ochiyo died. In Ochiyo's final moments, Tzurui promised that he would always protect their daughter. Tzurui was torn with despair over his loss, but he put his feelings aside for Kochohime. In time, the love he had lost was born again in Kochohime, and the little girl became his entire life.

Then came the Scorpion Coup. Shiro Nanbu was seized and Tzurui was cast out as ronin. During the seizure of the castle, Tzurui did not step forward to defend his master from the Legions, thinking of his daughter first. Though stepping forward would have accomplished nothing, Tzurui blames his cowardice for his current fate. He believes that until he can prove himself worthy, he is cursed. Until he can prove himself a samurai, he will be nothing. His greatest fear is that his daughter will share this curse. He has gone forth seeking battle in which to prove himself, leaving his daughter in the care of the monks who once served the Nanbu.

In his travels, Tzurui has seen little to offer hope. Magistrates treat him like a thief. Peasants dart away as he approaches. In tea houses and way stations clan samurai watch him with grim expectation, as if expecting him to explode into violence at any moment. He is hungry. He is homeless. Life as a ronin is worse than anything he could have imagined. Often, he considers returning to the monastery in shame, but remembers the curse he will leave his daughter and presses on.

Three months ago, Tzurui stumbled into an alley and collapsed among the garbage. His last ounce of hope had drained away after days without food. Weak from hunger and ready to die, he said a final prayer. "Amaterasu," he pleaded, "I beg you to spare Kochohime."

"Who's Kochohime?" asked a bright voice.

Tzurui looked up to see a young ronin standing at the mouth of the alley, a fine horse standing at his side. The boy's armor was awkward and oversized, but he carried himself with pride.

"She is my daughter," Tzurui said. "I'm saying good-bye."

"Why?"

"Because I'm starving to death."

"Oh, why didn't you say so?" the boy replied with a laugh, and tossed Tzurui a rice cake.

Tzurui took the food eagerly, thanking the young ronin for his kindness. The boy called himself "Toku." Gaining strength, Tzurui began to walk. When they came to the crossroads at the edge of the village, Toku glanced both ways then looked at his new friend.

"Which way are you going?" Toku asked.

"This way," Tzurui pointed to the north.

"Where does that road lead?" Toku asked blankly.

"To the Great Climb," Tzurui said. "To battle. To blood. To death. To glory. To a chance to prove myself."

"Oh," Toku said thoughtfully. "I'm going that way, too."

KADO

Earth: 3
Water: 3
    Perception: 4
Fire: 3
Air: 4
Void: 2
School/Rank: Weavers 1
Honor: 1.2
Glory: 3.0
Advantages: Allies (Kolat, Weavers), Clear Thinker, Crafty, Read Lips, Patron – Kitsu Motso, Benten's Blessing,
Disadvantages: Obligation – Kolat, Weavers, Dark Secret (Kolat), Greed (3), Compulsion (Theft – 2), Can't Lie, Social Disadvantage (Ronin)

Skills: Acting 5, Battle 2, Cipher 3, Commerce 1, Courtier 2, Etiquette 4, Forgery 2, Hisomu 5, Hunting 2, Investigation 3, Kenjutsu 3, Knife 2, Kuenai 3, Law 3, Poison 2, Sincerity 3, Stealth 3, Torture 2

Kado is an honest man. He prides himself on it. He believes that honesty is the key to greatness. Without honesty, what else is there? How can a dishonest man remain true to himself? "If you have only one virtue," Kado says, "cling to it tenaciously."

The fact that Kado's entire life is a lie does not jar his morality one bit. He makes a habit of rationalization. He's had a lot of practice.

Raised in the Hidden Temple of the Kolat, Kado was to become an assassin. He was a prized student, though others were much stealthier, quicker, or more ruthless. Everyone who knew him considered him to be a close and trusted friend. Kado made a habit of stealing from his friends, ferreting their possessions away in his own quarters. He didn't really mean any harm; he just saw things he liked and took them. If anyone had ever suspected him, he would have returned the items gladly, but Kado was so friendly that no one suspected him, no one accused him, and Kado never lied.

The Ten Masters knew natural talent when they saw it. Kado's assassin training was terminated and he was immediately enrolled in a different path of study. He was trained in tactics, law, government, everything he would need to become an effective diplomat and military advisor. He was also enrolled in acting classes, and though he did quite well the idea of pretending to be something he was not disturbed Kado's notions of honesty. However, questioning the Masters was outside Kado's character, so he learned dutifully. In time, he was given his mission.

Kado was to join the Lion army.

For a ronin, the Lion army is a deadly place, but Kado was not afraid. He had faith in the Kolat, and knew that they would not wish him harm unless it was for a greater good. He signed on as a lowly soldier. As usual, he made friends.

In a month, he was promoted to nikutai. In a year, he was promoted to gunso. Kado's units were never sent into combat, but their morale was high and they loved their commander. (A few things went missing from the supply tent, but no one thought to blame Kado.)

During a minor battle under the command of Kitsu Motso, Kado took up the fallen Lion banner. (It seemed odd that the standard-bearer was found stabbed, rather than shot, as he was not on the front lines, but Kado was never implicated.) He was invited to Shiro Matsu to be honored for his bravery.

Akodo Kage, revered sensei of the Lion, stepped forward to congratulate Kado personally. "I hope I am not overstepping my bounds," the sensei said with a bow to Motso, "when I say that the Lion would do well to have such a samurai in their service." When Motso nodded, Kage continued. "What say you, Kado? Will you swear your sword to the Lion and forsake all other masters?"

Kado said nothing at first. He could not lie.

"I would turn my sword to your service, Akodo-sama," Kado replied, "but surely the Lion would have little use for a shiftless villain like myself."

Motso laughed out loud. He decided in that instant that he liked Kado's character. He accepted Kado's humble refusal, but appointed him as a personal advisor. Since then, Motso has grown to trust Kado like none other. He considers him nearly a brother. Kado is the first man Motso turns to for advice, and is beloved by both the Lion and ronin troops who serve him.

If a few things have gone missing around Motso's palace, surely Kado can't be to blame. Those who suspected him were dealt with appropriately, and Kado never had to lie. The friends he makes are always willing to do that part for him.

MIKARU

Earth: 3
Water: 2
　　Strength: 3
Fire: 4
　　Agility: 5
Air: 2
　　Reflexes: 4
Void: 2
School/Rank: Forest-Killers 1
Honor: 1.0
Glory: 0 (Outcast)
Advantages: Heart of Vengeance (Naga), Way of the Land: Shinomen Forest, Allies (Forest-Killers), Silent
Disadvantages: Social Disadvantage – Ronin, Bad Reputation (bandit), Driven (to slaughter

Naga), Sworn Enemy – The Balash, Obligation (Forest-Killers)

Skills: Archery 4, Defense 2, Gambling 3, Hunting 4, Jiujutsu 3, Kenjutsu 3, Lore (Naga) 4, Poison 3, Stealth 5, Traps 3

Mikaru is a very angry man.

Born a ronin, Mikaru once had dreams of becoming a hero. One day the clans would notice him, and stand in awe of his unrivaled prowess. The daimyos would fight to gain his fealty. A great destiny waiting, he just had to wait for it to come along.

In time, Mikaru found himself in the lands of the Falcon. The Toritaka weren't as impressed with him as he'd hoped, but young Mikaru was given an assignment nonetheless. He was placed in charge of a watchtower on the edge of the Shinomen, assigned to a contingent of six guards. The fortress was far from any important holdings, so Falcon bushi were not wasted in the duty. Mikaru was in the company of other ronin. Eventually, the others became bored or frustrated and moved on. Other ronin rotated into the vacant positions. After six years of waiting, Mikaru was in command through sheer seniority.

Surely this was the chance he was waiting for. Glory was waiting. He just needed opportunity.

His chance came. One day, a worried scout reported something strange in the forest. Snakes the size of horses! Mikaru was skeptical, but when the first creature emerged from the tree-line, Mikaru became a believer.

The three beasts were small, the size of children. They bore no weapons, and slithered forward calmly with hands outstretched. It seemed to be a gesture of peace.

"It's a trick," Mikaru said. He gave his archers the command to shoot.

The creatures were slaughtered. Mikaru congratulated his men, and dispatched the scout to notify the Toritaka of what they had discovered. Surely, such an accomplishment would win him fealty. Creeping forth to inspect the dead, they found rich necklaces of pearls and bracelets of gold. The lure of riches quickly dispelled all aversion to contact with the dead, and the ronin looted the three corpses.

The next morning Mikaru awoke to find the tower in flames. Glancing outside, he saw flaming arrows raining from the forest. He could hear the screams of his men in the rooms beneath. As each man burst from the tower to escape the smoke and flames, a snake-creature rose from the high grass to butcher him. Mikaru was terrified, but couldn't stand the smoke any longer. He stumbled outside and fell in a heap, begging for his life. When he looked up, he found himself staring into the blazing red eyes of a green-skinned warrior, bow trained upon his heart.

"Is this the bravery of huu-mans?" it said in a roughly accented hiss. "Go now, worthlessssss one. Tell the other cowardsss what you have ssseen. Warn them what happensss to those who sssslaughter the Naga."

Mikaru scrambled away, gibbering thanks for the creature's mercy. He returned to the Falcon as quickly as he could, hoping to stop the scout he

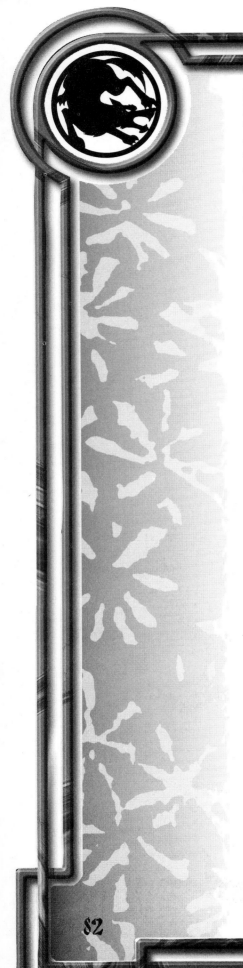

had dispatched and cover his shame. He was too late. When the Yotogi heard of the destruction of the tower, death of the ronin, and diplomatic catastrophe with the Naga, he was beside himself with rage. Mikaru was cast out with the promise that no clan, Great or Minor, would ever accept such a failure.

Mikaru's world was destroyed. His dreams were broken. His hopes were shattered. He would never amount to anything.

It was all the Naga's fault.

Since that day, Mikaru has found a home with the brutal Forest-Killers. The bandits have taught him much about the Shinomen, and Mikaru has used the knowledge well. Already he has killed five Naga. All were alone. Two were children. He has stitched a sash from Naga hides, and wears it proudly though he never explains its origin. He has told no one of his vendetta. This battle is his alone.

When he finds the Naga with red eyes, the war will begin.

YOTSU SEOU AND YOTSU SEIKI

Yotsu Seou
Earth: 3
Water: 3
Fire: 2
Air: 3
      Intelligence: 4
Void: 2
School/Rank: Sword of Yotsu 1
Honor: 2.1
Glory: 1.0
Advantages: True Friend (Yotsu Seiki), Allies (in Otosan Uchi) 2
Disadvantages: Social Disadvantage (Ronin),
Skills: Defense 1, Hunting 1, Kenjutsu 2, Law 3, Lore (Shugenja) 1, Mountaineering 2, Oratory 1, Shuriken 4

Yotsu Seiki
Earth: 2
Water: 2
Fire: 4
Air: 2
Void: 3
School/Rank: Ronin Shugenja 2
Honor: 1.9
Glory: 0.7

Advantages: Clear Thinker, True Friend (Yotsu Seou)
Disadvantages: Social Disadvantage (Ronin)
Skills: Meditation 2, Calligraphy 2, Defense 1, Medicine 2, Law 2, Research 1, Tantojutsu 2
Spells: Amaterasu's Anger, Essence of Fire, The Fires that Cleanse, Arrow's Flight, Call upon the Wind, *Gust of Wind
* Indicates Innate Abilities

The twins, Yotsu Seou and Seiki, are the third and fourth children of the ronin Yotsu. They remember only brief pieces of their childhood in the Mountains of Regret, and although their father maintained land there, they have rarely been sent to visit. Instead, they were raised in the wide streets of Otosan Uchi, reveling in the possibilities and opportunities there.

They do still remember their dead brother, who was given to the Scorpion in the place of the Emperor's son. He had been five years old. The twins were ten.

Since their birth, Seou and Seiki have been inseparable. Even when a traveling ronin offered to teach one of the girls how to be a shugenja, they were not apart. Seou practiced throwing knives at trees while her sister chanted mantra and practiced speaking to the spirits. When the traveling shugenja died in their father's service, he left them two presents. To Seiki he left his spells and traveling case, and to Seou, he left a collection of elaborate shuriken - gathered from the Scorpion lands long ago. On that day, the two girls decided to leave the city of the Emperor and seek their path together.

They have traveled through the lands of the Lion and the Unicorn, passing by the Dragonfly lands without being accepted into the lands of the Dragon, and only recently have they returned home. With their sister's appointment to the position of Governor of the district after their father's death, the twins have begun using their skills to assist her.

While here, however, they have a few agendas of their own to master. First, to find Seou a place within the Seppun guards - her childhood dream - and second, to hunt down traces of the most famous ronin in the Empire.

Toturi.

Seiki saw Toturi when he was still the Lion Champion, and the image of a brave man fighting against terrible odds has burned itself into her mind. Although some would call her feelings 'love', she steadfastly refuses to believe it. Instead, she argues, it is the idolization of someone who has given all that he possessed for the good of the Empire and lived to tell the tale.

Most recently, a traveling ronin has told the sisters of an army gathering in the Dragon lands – an army that may be led by the powerful Toturi. Seiki is obsessed with traveling back to the lands of the Tombo and asking to be admitted once more; Seou resists the idea, wishing to remain in Otosan Uchi and press her current advantage with the Seppun sensei. It is not the first time the sisters have disagreed on the path of their future, but it is the most serious argument they have ever known.

If they cannot resolve it, their lifetime partnership may crumble.

Neither girl wants that, so for now they remain in Otosan Uchi under the command of their sister, Urieko, and serve the district as Magistrates. They are competent, fun-loving and eager to assist with the rise of the Yotsu. Both are sworn to their family with ties of blood and love, though neither one understands the savagery of their brother Shoku or the political finesse of Urieko.

They are a quiet pair, speaking in half-sentences when the mood strikes them, and bowing their dark heads together with whispers over some particularly interesting puzzle. They love to solve riddles and answer conundrums, and they are adept at figuring out even the most difficult crime. While they are in the district, the crime rate has dropped significantly – something that Governor Hida Kosuga appreciates.

Recently, Ureiko has quietly proposed marriages to both girls – one of them, to no less than Kosuga! They have both steadfastly refused all offers, and politely told Ureiko that their marriages will be performed on the day they stop adventuring. Because they are her sisters, Ureiko agreed, but she watches diligently for any sign that the girls might be leaving the city. Ureiko hopes that Seou and Seiki will be happy in the district, and will choose to settle down.

Though their differences of opinion about the future still trouble them, the twins have firmly resolved one thing: the path they will choose to reach their future may be yet unchosen, but they have not left it behind.

Chapter Four: Who's Who Among the Ronin

Chapter Five

Sample Ronin
Characters

Retired Vassal

yourself welcoming the uncertainty, the excitement, the adventure.

You have no regrets.

You have lived your life in service. Now, at long last, you must find your own place. For years, you served your daimyo as a minor functionary, screening visitors and keeping track of your lord's finances. Your master was a warrior, a proud general with little time for such matters. In contrast, you have always had a sharp eye and a keen mind for numbers. It was not a proud or glorious career, but you were skilled at it, and you were content.

Then came the illness. In the night, terrible dreams wake you from sleep and you find blood on your pillow. In times of stress, spasms wrack your body, leaving you weak and helpless. In time, the illness came to interfere with your ability to fulfill your duties. Concerned, your lord summoned the finest healers he could afford, but the men and women who came to tend your illness were bewildered. Your epilepsy was easy enough to diagnose, but your other symptoms bewildered them. It seemed as if your body were slowly wasting away.

You began a regimen of exercises and a strict diet, and your condition began to improve. When you returned to your former duties, the illness returned worse than ever. It seemed almost as if your body was rebelling against the slow and tedious tasks that had occupied so much of your life. The healers agreed. You had spent too much of your life indoors; exercise and travel were needed to make a full recovery. Unfortunately, your daimyo could not afford the expense of another courtier or diplomat. With great regret, you asked permission to step down from your office.

Your request was granted. Your lord thanked you for your years of dutiful service, wished you the best, provided you a small stipend, and wished you all the best.

It is a frightening but exciting time. Though your katana sat for years unused in the family shrine, you carry it always at your side and have learned its use. Rokugan is a far larger and more wondrous land than you ever dreamed while among your books and scrolls. You have seen terrible monsters, mighty warriors, and shugenja capable of working magic straight out of a dream. The life of a ronin is a strange one, but you find

Legend of the Five Rings

Name: Retired Vassal

Clan: True Ronin

Profession: Bushi

Fire
Agility: 2
Intelligence: 3

Air
Reflexes: 3
Awareness: 3

Earth
Stamina: 3
Willpower: 2

Water
Strength: 2
Perception: 3

Void

Void Points Spent:

Insight: 120

Primary Weapon
Poor Katana 2k2

Primary Armor
Light Armor (if any)

TN to be Hit
(Reflexes x 5 + Armor)

15 (20 with armor)

Skills

Calligraphy	1
Courtier	2
Etiquette	2
History	1
Hunting	1
Kenjutsu	1
Lore (Bushido)	1
Poetry	1

Techniques

None

Wounds

4	-0
4	-1
4	-2
4	-3
4	-4
4	Down
4	Out
4	Dead

School: None (True Ronin)   **Rank:** N/A

Advantages/Disadvantages

Precise Memory +3
Clear Thinker +2
Irreproachable +2
Wealth +2
Social Disadvantage –3
Bad Health –3
Epilepsy –4

Glory: 0

☐ ☐ ☐ ☐ ☐ ☐ ☐ ☐ ☐

Honor: 3.5

Experience Points:

Ashigaru Fraud

You always wanted to be a samurai.

When the war began, you were among the first to report for duty. You took up the spear that was handed to you and learned the drills well. In your free time, you secretly learned to use the boken, though the katana was ever denied to one of your rank. You became a fine ashigaru, the finest in your unit. In your first battle, you defeated seven warriors single-handedly and took not a single wound. The lust for war and the glory of combat crept into your blood and soon your home and farm were forgotten. This was what you were born for. The life of the warrior consumed you.

Still, you were not a samurai.

If your gunso had his way, you never would be. Though your exploits on the battlefield matched those of any bushi, he never treated you as anything other than a lowly farmer. After a day of battle, you would be rewarded with back-breaking labor. The day you took the enemy's banner, your gunso snatched it from your hand and absorbed the glory for his own. None of the higher officers ever knew your name, or heard of your heroics. Why should they? What difference did it make? Glory was not yours for the taking. You were nothing but an ashigaru.

You were not a samurai.

And then came the darkest and most wonderful day in your life. The day your incompetent gunso disobeyed orders and attempted to flank the enemy army. The move was foolish, and soon your unit was surrounded. Your gunso attempted to flee, crying out in terror and panic. You watched in anger and disgust as, one by one, your comrades were slaughtered. Only you survived, the berserk fury of the battle driving your spear as samurai after samurai met his doom at the end of your weapon. When it was over, and the enemy had moved on, only you were left standing. You fell to your knees, the earth churned into mud by the blood seeping from countless corpses. Your hand met something hard and cold, buried in the earth. Your eyes opened and fell upon the daisho of your gunso, discarded as he fled. It was then that the idea struck you. No one still lived

who would know. There was no one that would remember you existed, or notice one more ronin wandering Rokugan.

It was so easy.

And now you are a samurai.

Legend of the Five Rings

Name: Ashigaru Fraud

Clan: True Ronin

Profession: Bushi

Fire
Agility: 4
Intelligence: 2

Air
Reflexes: 3
Awareness: 2

(2) (2)

(3) (2)

(2)

Earth
Stamina: 3
Willpower: 3

Water
Strength: 2
Perception: 2

Void
Void Points Spent:

Primary Weapon
Yari 4k2

Primary Armor
Poor Light Armor

TN to be Hit
(Reflexes x 5 + Armor)

15 (18 with armor)

Skills

Athletics	2
Battle	3
Farming	3
Hisomu	2
Hunting	2
Kenjutsu	2
Knife	2
Yarijutsu	3

Insight: 129

Techniques

None

Wounds

	6	-0
	6	-1
	6	-2
	6	-3
	6	-4
	6	Down
	6	Out
	6	Dead

School: None (True Ronin)   **Rank:** N/A

Advantages/ Disadvantages

Crafty	+3
Large	+2
Heimin	–8
Brash	–2
Social Disadvantage	–3

Glory: 0
☐ ☐ ☐ ☐ ☐ ☐ ☐ ☐ ☐

Honor: 1.5

Experience Points:

superior training allowed you to defeat them, and when they lay dead you could not help but feel a sense of triumph.

If someone is trying to kill you, then that someone must know the truth.

Lost Heir

When you were younger, you liked to look at the little silver bird pendant and the katana that rested silently upon its stand, and dream of who your parents might be. One day, you knew, they would return and reveal themselves. They would take you home, and tell you everything was all right. Once you were a true samurai, you would see to it that the gentle monks and ronin who raised you were rewarded.

Unfortunately, that day has not come. All that you know is that you were found on a battlefield, clutched in the arms of a dead samurai-ko. You were found by the monks of Ebisu, who delivered you to the ronin village of Nanashi along with the sword and pendant. When you were old enough, you began training with the noble Eyes of Nanashi, learning the way of the sword and the power of justice. One day, you were granted permission to take the pendant, leave the village, and solve the puzzle of your heritage. You will miss your friends, the only life you have ever known, but you must know the truth.

On dark nights you look at the pendant and wonder what it symbolizes. Is the bird a crane? Phoenix? Falcon? Sparrow? The style is not that of any traditional mon, and you have studied them all. Could it something else? Some samurai's personal symbol? A religious token? Something ancient and forgotten? The monks did not know and you have been able to discover little.

The woman who carried you is a mystery. Was she your mother, or simply a guardian? You have questioned the commanders of both sides of the battle where she died, and neither claim to know of her or the pendant you carry. Perhaps it was only chance that she happened to be carrying you through the battlefield, and a random arrow that took her life. You persevered, though the journey became frustrating. You began to feel as if you would never know the truth.

Seven nights ago, three men dressed in black clothing leapt from the shadows to take your life. They wielded short, straight swords and threw knives tipped with poison. Your luck and

Legend of the Five Rings

Name: Lost Heir

Clan: True Ronin

Profession: Bushi

Fire
Agility: 3
Intelligence: 2

Air
Reflexes: 2
Awareness: 3

Earth
Stamina: 2
Willpower: 2

Water
Strength: 3
Perception: 3

Void
Void Points Spent:

Insight: 125

Techniques
Righteous Fury

Primary Weapon
Katana 3k2

Primary Armor
Light Armor

TN to be Hit
(Reflexes x 5 + Armor)

12 (17 with armor)

Skills

Skill	
Heraldry	3
Hunting	1
Juijutsu	1
Kenjutsu	3
Kuenai	2
Law	2
Seduction	1
Shintao	2

Wounds

4	-0
4	-1
4	-2
4	-3
4	-4
4	Down
4	Out
4	Dead

School: Eyes of Nanashi **Rank:** N/A

Advantages/Disadvantages
Dangerous Beauty +2
Great Destiny +4
Inheritance
  (Silver Bird Crest) +2
Righteous Fury +7
Obligation (Eyes of Nanashi) –0
Social Disadvantage –3
Sworn Enemy –5
Obligation (Lion Clan) –2

Glory: 0

☐ ☐ ☐ ☐ ☐ ☐ ☐ ☐ ☐

Honor: 2.5

Experience Points:

Wandering Duelist

You will prove it to those who spurned you.
You will prove it to your ancestors.
You will prove it to yourself.
To Jigoku with anyone who stands in your way.

You were born to a minor vassal family of a Great Clan. When the time came for your gempukku, you performed the ceremony with poise and honor. At the tournament afterward, none of the other bushi could defeat you. Your skill was incredible. Yet when the visiting emissary saw the milky white eye you were cursed with at birth, you learned that the academy's roster was full that year.

They told you that you were not good enough.

It is time to prove them wrong.

Bitter and angry, you immediately embarked upon a warrior pilgrimage. Now, the roads of Rokugan are your home. You test your prowess against any who will meet your challenge, and with each confrontation, you grow stronger. Often, these duels are with simple boken or shinai, but on the crossroads, away from the prying eyes of the authorities, the katana is your weapon of choice. Kenjutsu, iaijutsu, it makes no difference. You will batter an enemy with your fists, if you must, and you will win.

Your reputation has grown, and your name has begun to carry a weight of its own. Rumor flies quicker than the fastest horse, and you often find that word of your arrival has preceded you by days. Sometimes you are welcomed. Once, you were invited by a local magistrate to serve as her yoriki. Though you appreciated the gesture of respect, the pursuit of justice does not interest you. Only the perfection of your craft will bring satisfaction.

At other times, your fame is double-edged. Other young duelists seek you out to build their reputation by defeating you. Those who are beneath your notice provoke you into fatal duels, wasting your time leaving a trail of incompetent corpses in your wake. At times, it all seems like such a waste, but when you see the gleam in your grandfather's sword, you remember the reason for your quest.

You are worthy.

You are unmatched.

Legend of the Five Rings

Name: Wandering Duelist

Clan: True Ronin

Profession: Bushi

Fire
Agility: 3
Intelligence: 2

Air
Reflexes: 3
Awareness: 2

Earth
Stamina: 3
Willpower: 3

Water
Strength: 2
Perception: 2

Void
Void Points Spent:

Insight: 123

Techniques
None

Primary Weapon
Katana 3k2

Primary Armor
Light Armor (if any)

TN to be Hit
(Reflexes x 5 + Armor)

15 (20 with armor)

Skills

Athletics	1
Battle	1
Gambling	1
Iaijutsu	3
Juijutsu	3
Kenjutsu	3

Wounds

6	-0
6	-1
6	-2
6	-3
6	-4
6	Down
6	Out
6	Dead

School: None (True Ronin)   **Rank:** N/A

Advantages/ Disadvantages

Strength of the Earth +2
Quick +3
Musha Shugyo +4
Balance +4
Combat Reflexes +6
Contrary –3
Antisocial –4
Jealousy (swordsmanship) –2
Bad Fortune (Evil Eye) –1

Glory: 0
☐ ☐ ☐ ☐ ☐ ☐ ☐ ☐ ☐

Honor: 1.5

Experience Points:

For the first time in your life, you begin to feel doubt. You wonder if you can go through with this. Can you sacrifice your honor, your reputation for a daimyo too cowardly to defend himself?

No one can answer this question but yourself.

Wave–Man Assassin

You have been chosen.

You have always known that your life had purpose. Though born to a minor family, and largely ignored by the clan, you have always known. In private, when no one else could hear, your father told you so. He taught you the secret arts of stealth, of poison, of the secret codes of the clan. He told you to share them with no one, and that one day your skills would make you more highly prized than a dozen warriors lucky enough to train at the clan academy.

That day has come.

The news stuck bitterly in the hearts of your fellow samurai. Your daimyo had been bitterly insulted, publicly humiliated in the court, and had done nothing. There were whispers of his cowardice, rumors of blackmail.

Soon, you were visited by one of the daimyo's representatives. He came in the dead of night, with no mon to mark his robes. You would not have believed he was who he claimed to be, had he not spoken in your father's code. The instructions were clear. You were to leave the clan, become ronin, publicly denounce your daimyo, and set out on a secret mission to slay the courtier who had shamed him.

When the mission is complete, you are to commit seppuku to hide the truth of your deed from others. No one in the clan will take responsibility for your actions, yet through them justice will be gained and the daimyo's honor satisfied.

You agreed at once, without a glimmer of doubt. This is what you have waited for. This is what you were trained for. This was why you were created. For weeks, you have researched your enemy, hunted him, learned his ways. The mission is not easy. Life on the road alone is harsh. The weather is terrible. Often, you do not have enough to eat. No one from your clan will acknowledge you, considering you a dangerous renegade. Once, one of your kinsmen became so angry at your presence he nearly drew his sword and struck you down where you stood.

Don't they know? Can't they see what you must do?

94

Legend of the Five Rings

Name: Wave-man Assassin

Clan: True Ronin

Profession: Bushi

Primary Weapon
Yumi 2k2

Primary Armor
Light Armor

TN to be Hit
(Reflexes x 5 + Armor)

20 (25 with armor)

Fire
Agility: 3
Intelligence: 3

Air
Reflexes: 4
Awareness: 3

Earth
Stamina: 2
Willpower: 2

Water
Strength: 2
Perception: 3

Void
Void Points Spent:

Ring values: 3, 3, 2, 2, 2

Skills

Skill	
Archery	3
Cipher	2
Hunting	2
Intimidation	2
Kenjutsu	3
Kuenai	2
Poison	2
Stealth	3

Techniques
None

Insight: 138

School: None (True Ronin)   **Rank:** N/A

Wounds

	4	-0
	4	-1
	4	-2
	4	-3
	4	-4
	4	Down
	4	Out
	4	Dead

Advantages/ Disadvantages

Higher Purpose	
(Kill your Lord's enemy)	+2
Bland	+2
Bad Reputation	–2
Dishonored	–3
Social Disadvantage	–3

Glory: 0

☐ ☐ ☐ ☐ ☐ ☐ ☐ ☐ ☐ ☐

Honor: 1.5

Experience Points:

Wandering Komuso

The life of a bandit is not for everyone. You learned that when the magistrates came, wielding torches and katana to raze your shabby fortress. The leader of your band gave the order to stand and fight. You ran for your life, not caring what happened to your comrades or where you ended up. The last place you expected to find refuge was in a library.

The shugenja were wary, at first. You didn't blame them. You're a suspicious sort of character. However, at the time your urge to repent was very real. Maybe it was spawned more by an urge for self-preservation than a sense of piety, but it was a strong passion nonetheless, and the priests of the Path of the Grand Master helped you to focus it.

In time, you began to believe what the priests taught you. To your surprise, after some time, the wind and rain began to speak to you. The priests told you that you had skill with magic, and that the kami would obey your will. They helped you to perfect the art, and even gave you a satchel of scrolls with which to call upon the spirits.

You were ecstatic in your new life. You not only learned the Tao, but embraced it. Well, most of it. It seems that most of the Tao is just good common sense, and the other parts are mostly guides to treating others kindly. It suited you well. Other parts, especially the parts about eschewing material possessions, don't suit you but you can forgive Shinsei for that.

Now you are a komuso, a wandering priest seeking redemption and spreading the word. You wear a basket hat to conceal your face, so that your past will not interfere with your message. You like that hat. It has saved your life more than once after you discovered that the magistrates are still hunting you. A bounty has been placed on your head. You're quite grateful that the Fortunes found you and saved your soul, but, in a way, you're insulted that your life isn't worth more than a koku.

The life of a komuso suits you. The temptations to return to your old life are few and far between. You don't need to make a living as a bandit. There's so much more money to be made

as a priest! After all, an anonymous priest with the command over the spirits of air makes a most excellent informant. There's nothing in the Tao against espionage, right?

Even a priest has to eat.

Shinsei would approve of what you're doing.

What the priests back home don't know won't hurt them.

Legend of the Five Rings

Name: Wandering Priest

Clan: True Ronin

Profession: Shugenja

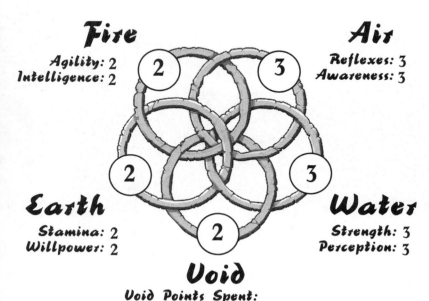

Fire
Agility: 2
Intelligence: 2

2

Air
Reflexes: 3
Awareness: 3

3

2

3

Earth
Stamina: 2
Willpower: 2

2

Water
Strength: 3
Perception: 3

Void
Void Points Spent:

Insight: 143

Primary Weapon
Bo 2k2

Primary Armor
None

TN to be Hit
(Reflexes × 5 + Armor)

15

Skills

Bojutsu	3
Flute	2
Herbalism	2
Hisomu	2
Hunting	2
Investigation	3
Rhetoric	2
Shintao	2
Stealth	3
Theology	1
——————	—
——————	—

Spells
Sense, Commune, Summon, Gift of the Wind (Innate), Whispering Winds, Wind-bourn Slumbers, Path to Inner Peace (Innate), Amaterasu's Blessing, Bo of Water, Cross the Veil of Sleep, Wall of Bamboo

School: None (True Ronin) **Rank:** N/A

Wounds

4	-0
4	-1
4	-2
4	-3
4	-4
4	Down
4	Out
4	Dead

Advantages/ Disadvantages

Voice +2
Read Lips +2
Ascetic –3
Bounty (1 Koku) –2
Social Disadvantage –3

Glory: 0

☐☐☐☐☐☐☐☐☐

Honor: 1.5

Experience Points:

Appendices

Ashigaru PCs

Non-samurai player characters are generally not recommended. A samurai is the Rokugani equivalent of an armored assault vehicle, and an ashigaru is likely to stand little chance against such competition. To put it simply, while ashigaru present an interesting role-playing challenge, they might not be so much fun to play after the first round of combat.

However, heimin are an important part of the ronin world, so addressing them here is entirely appropriate. Some ronin were once heimin, promoted to samurai status for valorous conduct. Some players may wish to take the challenge of creating an ashigaru with hopes of gaining fealty, despite the overwhelming disadvantages (or perhaps because of them!). Ronin characters who choose a career as a village warden have a close connection with heimin, as ashigaru make up the bulk of a village defense force. Ronin wardens will no doubt have a few important ashigaru officers which the GM may wish to give more detail.

Appendix I: Life on the Waves

How to Survive as a Wave-Man

Rokugan is not a land that caters to loners. The Emerald Empire is steeped in tradition. Loyalty and family are one's most important assets. Those who step outside of their place are shunned. Those who forge their own path are disruptive influences.

It's hard to be a ronin.

A ronin is a warrior by trade. Not all wave-men are willing to settle down in a village and become "domesticated." Many are mercenaries. If there's no war, then there's no work. A desperate ronin may turn to banditry, or even foment a rebellion in order to create an environment where employment is available. For this reason, clan samurai see ronin as dangerous.

If a ronin is lucky, he's ignored. If he isn't, he'll end up challenged to a duel with no escape, no second, no daimyo to refuse permission or avenge him if he dies. If he's really unlucky he may end up bludgeoned to death by fearful heimin and buried anonymously in a farmer's paddy. A lone ronin is an rebel, a hair's breadth away from death at every moment.

So how does a lone ronin survive?

By not being alone.

Make friends who will watch your back. If you can't make friends, make tracks. Don't stay in any one place for long, and don't give the authorities any reason to remember your name. The ronin who survive the longest in Rokugan are those who don't leap into the stereotype. Ronin who take every opportunity to laugh at societal niceties, flaunt their freedom, and seed discontent die. It's just that simple. Ronin who make allies, establish connections, find a place to fit in, and get an honest job survive. Nobody makes a living just wandering around looking scruffy and cool. Not in Rokugan.

For example, take Dairya. Dairya seems very much the ronin stereotype, gleefully ignoring all the survival cautions stated here. He starts fights. He's arrogant. He kills people. On the other hand, Dairya is no fool. He has connections, notably a friendship with Morito Tokei, and through Tokei, Naka Kuro. He frequently hires out to the Mantis. He's built a reputation as a dangerous, but dependable bushi. He's always moving. He knows he has enemies, and sees no reason to present himself as a target. Though he despises Kakita Toshimoko, he's careful not to be overzealous seeking revenge. The last thing Dairya wants is an army of Crane magistrates hunting him.

Dairya is certainly dangerous and unpredictable, but he knows how to survive.

So how does a ronin character put this to good use? How does the ronin undo the stereotype that the Great Clans cast upon him?

Don't bother. Let the stereotype be. Samurai don't appreciate being proven wrong, especially by ronin. If a ronin wants to be accepted, he doesn't have to prove that all ronin are honorable, he just needs to prove himself to be the exception. He has to stand out. If a ronin has rare or useful skills, he's likely to be accepted despite his background. Ronin swordsmen are a dime a dozen. Every clan has swordsmen, but a ronin locksmith, spy, or armorer will find his skills in demand. Once a ronin has his foot in the door with the local daimyo, he's got an opportunity to prove that he's the only ronin in Rokugan who isn't a worthless dog.

Many samurai have prejudice against ronin ingrained so deeply that a wave-man will never even get a chance to prove himself. Though there's no tried and true way for a ronin to know where he'll be accepted and where he'll be slapped in the face, each of the Clans have different general policies regarding the treatment of ronin. Awareness of these policies and prejudices could save a ronin's life.

The Crab

The Crab Clan are wary of ronin, but tolerate them so long as they don't cause trouble. Their eternal war with the Shadowlands often leaves the Crab in need of extra warriors, and thus eager to hire mercenaries. The Crab cannot afford to pay much, but such individuals will never find themselves in want of work. Ronin who have not yet proven themselves against the minions of Fu Leng are assigned to a unit led by a Crab samurai, no matter how much experience the ronin have against mundane foes. These newcomers are expected to follow their commander's every command, no matter how strange or harsh. Hesitation can mean death or worse in the Shadowlands, and the Crab have no time for amateurs. Those who cannot follow orders are released from service and ordered to leave Crab territory.

Those who can follow orders earn the Crab's grudging respect. More than any other clan, the Crab is known for granting fealty to ronin, particularly those that prove themselves on the Wall or in the Shadowlands itself. A good number of these heroes are inducted posthumously. This is still a great honor, as a dead ronin's surviving spouse or children become Crab as well.

An odd tradition among the Crab Clan is the practice of "Twenty Goblin Winter." At times, when the war has been particularly brutal and the Crab need new bushi, the Hida daimyo declares a Twenty Goblin Winter. During the five months of winter, any ronin who dares to trudge into the Shadowlands and return with the heads of twenty goblins will be granted fealty in a vassal family, no questions asked.

THE CRANE

The Crane hold the least tolerance for wave-men among the Great Clans. As the architects of Rokugan's culture, the Crane believe that everything has its place and purpose. A ronin's existence defies the Crane aesthetic simply by existing. In the opinion of many Crane, the Empire would just be a better place without ronin.

In Crane territories, ronin are far more likely to be harassed by magistrates or punished on spurious testimony. Ronin are samurai and thus the Crane won't simply slay them at will, but that doesn't mean that they have to be polite, either. Ronin who pass through Crane provinces cannot help but hear the subtle message that the Crane broadcast: "Get out."

Ronin hoping to join the Crane are best advised to seek fealty elsewhere. Crane are notorious for forbidding fealty to wave-men, no matter the circumstances. They take great pride in the purity of their bloodlines, and are loath to sully their line with outsiders. On occasion, Crane Champions have declared granting fealty to ronin illegal.

A few isolated daimyo do not share the Crane hatred for ronin, but even these individuals are loathe to tip the boat by granting fealty indiscriminately. A Crane daimyo who inducts a ronin has far more to lose in respect and cooperation from his superiors than he stands to gain.

THE DRAGON

Every Dragon has a different answer.

The doors of Kyuden Togashi are always open. Any ronin who is prepared to learn the mysteries of the Dragon is welcome. The trick is finding the castle. Those who are unworthy lose their way and are never seen again. Those who find the path and join the Togashi return as ise zumi – more than human, but removed from the humanity that they once knew. The tales of the strange magic and bizarre rituals of the Togashi are enough to scare away most.

The other families are more traditional in their approach to ronin. Most Dragons are reluctant to trust wave-men, but willing to accept those that have proven themselves worthy. If a ronin seeks fealty, the Mirumuto direct him to one of the many heimin villages nestled in the mountains. Though the Mirumuto patrol these villages regularly, many are days away from Dragon outposts and vulnerable to bandits. A ronin who serves well in protecting a village for many years may be granted an opportunity to prove his swordsmanship to the Mirumuto. If he can pass this last grueling test, he is granted fealty and given permission to tend the village as a Mirumuto vassal.

The Agasha and Kitsuki are also selective. As a rule, the only ronin accepted by the Agasha are shugenja who were referred to them by the Togashi. The Kitsuki are a very small family, and selective about those with whom they share their secrets. The Kitsuki only grant fealty to clan ronin who were cast out through no fault of their own, and engage in extensive background checks on all prospective members.

ASHIGARU PCs (CONTINUED)

Both GM and player should be warned in advance – an ashigaru who hopes to become a true samurai has a long road ahead. Ashigaru who win samurai status are extraordinarily rare. Even a particularly bold or heroic ashigaru is unlikely to be rewarded in this fashion, as it sets a nasty precedent. No daimyo can afford to grant every heroic ashigaru samurai status, or there would soon be no farmers left to grow the rice. A ronin is more likely to be offered fealty by every Great Clan than a single ashigaru is to gain samurai status.

Of course, all of that probably still won't dissuade a truly determined player, and role-playing is nothing without nigh-impossible challenges. The following guidelines can be used to create ashigaru characters.

1. The character's Traits and Rings begin at a 1. His Glory begins at 0. The character receives 20 points to spend on Traits, Skills, and Advantages, and may gain up to 10 additional Character Points by taking Disadvantages. Points are spent in the usual manner.

2. The character begins with Farming, Yarijutsu, and two skills of his choice.

3. The character may not learn High Skills, Kenjutsu, Iaijutsu, or Horsemanship.

(Continued on next page.)

ASHIGARU PCs (CONTINUED)

4. The character may not purchase the following Advantages: Ear of the Emperor, Different School, Favors, Imperial Spouse, Kaiu Sword, Kakita Blade, Noble Birth, Sensei, Social Position, Wealthy, Ancestors, any clan or family specific Advantages, or any other Advantages the GM deems inappropriate. The character may not begin as a member of any otokodate or juzimai.

5. The character may not take the following Disadvantages: Adopted Blood, Deathseeker, Dishonored, Forsaken, Social Disadvantage (a farmer's a farmer), any clan or family specific Disadvantages, or any other Disadvantages the GM deems inappropriate.

6. The character receives the Heimin disadvantage, with slight modifications. His status is no secret, he won't be killed if a samurai finds out what he is (unless he starts pretending to be a samurai), and he gains no Character Points for this disadvantage. The character is expected to obey all customs and laws regarding the behavior of heimin. Because of his ashigaru status, samurai will consider him a soldier, and thus a step above the crowd, but he's still just a farmer. Keep your head down.

THE LION

Lion armies make frequent use of ronin mercenaries, offering fealty in lieu of a salary for particularly long and grueling campaigns (such as the Lion-Crane war). Any ronin who survive a campaign of at least three years are sworn to a vassal family, usually the Matsu. This may seem strange, as the Matsu are fiercely proud of their bloodline. Their acceptance of ronin does not change this position. Matsu vassals are treated with more thinly disguised hatred and derision than any other vassal families in Rokugan. After a few hundred years, a family that serves with unquestionable loyalty and bravery may earn some small measure of Matsu respect, but it's not likely.

Gaining fealty is difficult. Lion generals always post ronin troops where combat is most deadly, using them for suicide missions or to cover the withdrawal of more valuable units. Ronin are never given critical assignments and are never entrusted with confidential information. Ronin are outfitted poorly, though a ronin with no sword will always be provided with one. (The cost of the weapon is deducted from his pay). Ronin troops slow the enemy's progress while Lion officers gauge the strength of their opponents. Nine out of ten ronin who hire out to the Lion during wartime desert or die. The Lion find these statistics completely acceptable, and formulate their strategies accordingly. The nine ronin who die or desert need not be paid. The one ronin who survives is obviously the best, and thus worthy of becoming a Lion.

The Kitsu never grant fealty to ronin shugenja, as only those who share the Lion bloodline can be trusted to care for their ancestors.

THE PHOENIX

The Phoenix's general opinion is one of quiet pity. During the Phoenix's campaign against the Snake Clan many centuries ago, many hundreds of ronin were ruthlessly slaughtered. Some were killed by the Snake, but most were killed by the Shiba after the ronin became possessed by Shuten Doji. During the Five Nights of Shame, the Phoenix romanticized the sacrifice of these ronin warriors through poem and legend, tales which have evoked a feeling of compassion toward wave-men.

Sadly, the Phoenix are pacifists, and have little use for mercenaries. Ronin bushi may find work guarding trading vessels or as yoriki, but there is little opportunity for glory. The likelihood of gaining fealty with the Shiba is thus quite small, despite Phoenix sympathy.

Ronin shugenja who hope to gain fealty with the Isawa or Asako will be sorely disappointed. The Isawa are notoriously secretive and extremely distrustful of outsiders. The Asako are worse, as they believe that the Asako name is a great gift that can only be earned through rebirth. If the Asako feel a ronin is worthy to join their ranks, they will come seeking him, not the other way around. At most, the Phoenix may hire a ronin shugenja to catalogue and copy their less important (non-magical) scrolls, perhaps repaying him with a common spell or two after years of diligent service.

Sadly, while most Phoenix are more than willing to share their lands and hearts with honorable ronin, few are willing to share their name.

THE SCORPION

The Scorpion's traditional stance is similar to that of the Crane. They have always considered ronin to be worthless creatures, of no use except as tools. As pawns, however, they are exceptional. Wave-men rarely need any encouragement outside of monetary compensation, don't know much of politics, and are easy to dispose of when they become troublesome. Before the Coup, it was not uncommon for a Scorpion to hire a ronin to do his dirty work, promising fealty for a job well done. When the job was complete, the Scorpion would either find some technicality to invalidate the bargain, frame the ronin for the entire affair, or have the loose end quietly swept under the rug by Shosuro assassins. Occasionally, ronin were granted fealty, but this was usually done for no other reason than to set a precedent or because the individual was simply too useful to liquidate.

Since the Coup, all are ronin. Their opinions of other ronin have not changed much. More information on the Scorpion can be found elsewhere in this appendix.

THE UNICORN

The Unicorn are somewhat confused by the rest of Rokugan's opinion toward ronin. Perhaps it is their gaijin ways, perhaps it may be a result of the hardships they have endured during their eight-hundred-year journey, but the Unicorn tend to be very forgiving of the faults of outsiders. They frequently hire mercenaries as scouts and advanced troops. Those that show themselves to be loyal and honorable may be set a task by which they may earn their fealty, usually involving a quest beyond the borders of Rokugan.

Though the Unicorn are generally accepting of ronin as individuals, they are understandably cautious about giving out their name. Since their return, the Unicorn have met with betrayal after betrayal. They have been used as pawns. They have had their magic stolen. They have been attacked without reason. Even after two centuries, the Unicorn are not certain where they fit. Those that empathize with the Unicorn's quest for identity and can help them in some manner as they adjust to the culture of Rokugan are most likely to find a place among their ranks.

Life on the Road

Along with the lack of respect and constant need for employment that a ronin must endure, many other aspects of samurai life are greatly different. Some of the essential rights and privileges that clan samurai take for granted are gone. Some are present in a largely altered form.

Gempukku

For most ronin, gempukku is a day of little ceremony. For most of the ronin born, gempukku is merely the day that they take up their katana and set out into the world to prove themselves.

The exception to this lies within the otokodate and families such as the Yotsu or Kaeru. For these groups, the induction of a new samurai is very rare, an object of celebration. These gatherings tend to be small, and only members of the family or close friends are invited. Clan samurai rarely attend, as most clans hardly view the creation of another ronin as a thing to celebrate.

Many otokodate brotherhoods have rituals that serve as the young ronin's initiation as well as his gempukku. These groups are very secretive about their initiation rites, though most tend to go a bit easier on those with a father or close relative who has already gained membership.

Seppuku

The seppuku of a ronin is a lonely thing. It is also relatively rare. While those prejudiced against ronin would suggest that this is due to their lack of honor and courage, this is only part of the truth. In many cases, ronin are cast out of

their clan as punishment, and forbidden seppuku. To take one's life against the will of the clan is to risk even greater punishment in the next life. Seppuku is an act intended to cleanse the family's honor, not your own. The seppuku of a man without family or clan accomplishes nothing. In such a case, it is far better to cleanse your name through action than by suicide.

One major difference between the seppuku of a ronin and that of a clan samurai is permission. If a samurai does not gain permission from his lord to take his own life, then he cannot. A ronin has no lord, and thus needs no permission. In some large ronin families and otokodate, permission for seppuku is still necessary. Otherwise, the samurai risks violating his oaths of loyalty or bonds of family. Seppuku is almost entirely unheard of in juzimai, most of whom consider dying for honor impractical. When bandits and assassins take their own lives, it is more often to escape a humiliating execution than out of any sense of true honor.

Weddings

Ronin seldom have the political leverage to arrange a marriage, nor the wealth to attract a bride. Ronin marriages result from love or physical attraction with more frequency than Clan samurai marriages, adding to the tragic-romantic image that grown around the wave-men.

When ronin marry, it is usually to another ronin or a heimin. The children of a ronin and a heimin are also ronin, if they chose to claim their warrior status. Most ronin do not marry beneath their station, as excessive intermarriage between classes would eventually deplete the heimin population.

A ronin who marries into a clan becomes a member of that clan unless the terms of the marriage indicate specifically otherwise. Rarely, daimyo who wish to attract a renowned ronin will offer the hand of a young relative to sweeten the deal. It is very unusual, however, for a ronin to be permitted to marry into one of the Great Clans. See *Winter Court: Kyuden Seppun*, pages 76–80, for more details about Rokugani marriages.

Duels

Legally, a samurai who wishes to challenge another samurai must obtain permission from his daimyo and the daimyo of his opponent to avert potential blood feuds. Ronin are another matter. As they have no lord, a clan samurai needs only

Ashigaru PCs (Continued)

7) The character's Glory can never rise above 0.7 unless he obtains samurai status.

8) The character begins with 1.0 Honor.

9) Ashigaru shugenja do not exist. Heimin with the ability to communicate with kami are recruited by the Brotherhood of Shinsei.

his own lord's permission to issue a challenge. In Crane lands, where there is little tolerance for ronin, many daimyos give their retainers permission to use their own discretion when challenging ronin. Important ronin always announce their arrival well in advance before visiting the Crane in order to avoid any accidents, especially in the vicinity of the Kakita Academy.

A ronin who wishes to challenge a clan samurai is posed with certain difficulties. Legally, ronin are required to obtain permission for a duel. The typical ronin is unlikely to gain any sort of response from a daimyo, much less permission to duel and slay his retainers. Of course, a solitary ronin who illegally challenges a clan samurai and kills him need not worry about a blood feud, as he has no family. The clan's retribution will fall solely upon his own head.

No permission is legally required in a duel between two ronin. However, if one of the ronin is a member of an otokodate, juzimai, or established ronin family his opponent can expect fierce retribution from his dead opponent's allies.

SERVICE

Entering another's service is a duty clan samurai need not worry about. At their gempukku, they are bound to serve their lord. Later, it is possible that their service may be transferred to another daimyo, but this is entirely out of the samurai's hands. A clan samurai need never worry about finding employment; his services will always be needed somewhere.

For a ronin, obtaining work as a mercenary or bandit is usually no problem, but the dangerous nature of these professions can shorten a ronin's life span considerably. Ronin who wish to find positions with greater hope for advancement may have trouble. The overwhelming perception of ronin is that they are warriors without honor. Thus, they cannot be trusted. Many samurai will not give a ronin stranger a chance to prove himself. Most heimin who have the wealth to hire a ronin are likewise wary. If a ronin should break his contract, the heimin has little legal recourse. Only ronin who prove themselves trustworthy are given positions. Only those who have proven themselves trustworthy in important positions can obtain quality employment. Success in a life of service is all about reputation.

Otherwise, the more grueling, thankless, and remote a job or position is, the more likely that a ronin may be trusted not to botch it up. It is for this reason that so many ronin hover on the fringes of society, hoping to find an open door to allow them to prove themselves. Unfortunately, minor duties rarely lead to anything better, and important daimyos can hardly be expected to notice a ronin in the middle of nowhere.

This vicious circle has ended the career of many a noble ronin, driving them into obscurity before they are ever given a chance to prove their honor. A successful ronin is one who recognizes opportunity when he sees it, and seizes upon it. Those who miss their chance for greatness are not likely to receive another.

Equipment

The starting outfit given for ronin in the main rulebook is very generic, a basic idea of what the typical ronin might carry. Of course, no two ronin are alike, so not every ronin will be carrying the same gear. The starting outfit of a clan samurai is provided by his daimyo, free of charge, in order that said samurai might be able to fulfill his duties. The starting equipment of a ronin is either inherited, scavenged, or stolen. Some ronin are wealthier than others, and some are luckier, so results vary. If the GM wishes to introduce this element of chance, he may require True Ronin characters to roll one die to determine their starting outfit.

Clan Ronin characters start with the normal outfit of their school.

Ronin characters with the Luck Advantage may use it to re-roll their results. Likewise, the GM can force characters with Unluck to re-roll a result.

1–2: VERY POOR OUTFIT

All items are Poor Quality

Bushi: Kimono, Traveling Pack, Katana or Light Armor, no koku

Shugenja: Kimono, Scroll Satchel, Wakizashi, no koku

3–4: POOR OUTFIT

All items are Poor Quality, two items of Average quality

Bushi: Kimono, Traveling Pack, Katana, Wakizashi, Light Armor, 1 koku

Shugenja: Kimono, Traveling Pack, Scroll Satchel, Wakizashi, 1 koku

5–8: Average Outfit

Bushi: Kimono, Traveling Pack, Katana, Wakizashi, Yumi, 10 Arrows, Light Armor, 2 koku (All items are Average Quality, two items of Poor Quality)

Shugenja: Kimono, Traveling Pack, Scroll Satchel, Wakizashi, Tanto, 3 koku (All items are considered to be Average Quality)

9: Wealthy Outfit

All items are considered to be Average Quality

Bushi: Katana, Wakizashi, Yumi, 20 Arrows, Light Armor, Helm, Traveling Pack, Kimono, any 1 weapon, 4 koku

Shugenja: Kimono, Traveling Pack, Scroll Satchel, Katana, Wakizashi, Tanto, medical kit, 5 koku

10: Very Wealthy Outfit

All items are considered to be Average Quality, one item of Fine Quality

Bushi: Katana, Wakizashi, Bow, 20 arrows, Light or Heavy armor, Traveling Pack, Kimono, any 1 weapon, steed, 6 koku

Shugenja: Katana, Wakizashi, Traveling Pack, Kimono, Scroll Satchel, Tanto, medical kit, 4 scrolls (blank), Steed, 6 koku

Getting new Equipment

Just as a clan samurai is provided with everything he needs, so is his equipment maintained. A clan samurai whose armor is damaged can have it repaired by visiting the clan armorer. A samurai who loses his katana will have to deal with the shame of misplacing his soul, but replacing the weapon itself will be a simple task. A samurai is a warrior; as such, he is supplied with the weapons he needs to fulfill that role adequately.

A ronin does not have this option. If his equipment is lost, stolen, or damaged he must see to its replacement on his own.

Professional smiths are always found in the employ of a daimyo. Swords and armor are made on commission; a smith never has extras just lying around to sell to wandering ronin. Even if a ronin has sufficient money to pay for a new katana or armor, smiths must see to their lord's requirements first. A ronin may have to wait months or years before he can replace his equipment.

There seem to be only two suitable options to obtain new weapons and armor. The first is for the ronin to learn the skills necessary to repair his own equipment (unlikely, but possible). The second is to enter into the service of a daimyo, and request arms in lieu of payment. Weapons obtained in this way are not likely to be high quality, but they are certainly better than nothing.

Using Ronin in Your Campaign

An important question that many GMs ask regarding ronin is, ironically, the same question many samurai ask regarding ronin.

"Where do these guys fit in?"

They don't. That's the point. Ronin are outcasts from samurai society, and this game is about samurai society. Does that mean that ronin are unusable? Certainly not. While ronin can be extremely challenging, even to an experienced role-player, they are far from useless. Here are a few suggestions on how ronin can fit into your campaign, other than as thugs and punching bags.

1. The Single Ronin – A single ronin character in the midst of a party of clan samurai is the most likely way ronin will be appear in the campaign (usually because one player wanted to be a ronin and nobody else did). The easiest way to explain the ronin's presence is by placing him in the employment of another PC's daimyo. The character is along for the ride, and the other characters have to put up with his presence for the sake of their lord.

At first, the clan PCs are likely to regard the ronin with anything from polite indifference to outright disgust (if they're playing in character). Everyone in Rokugan knows – not thinks, knows – that ronin are honorless dogs that can't be trusted except at the end of your sword. So how does the player of the ronin character deal with this unfair prejudice?

Use it.

Ronin can do things that Clan samurai just can't get away with. They can be seen on the wrong side of town without bringing dishonor to their lord. They can consort with farmers and merchants with little loss of face. Ronin are invisible, anonymous – to a clan samurai, one lone wolf is much like another. Ronin have skills at navigating the underbelly of society that most

THE TWELVE RONIN

The idea of the Twelve Ronin was originally Dairya's, suggested to symbolize the brotherhood of Toturi and his original eleven followers (see "Toturi's Call to Arms"). The Twelve are an elite cavalry unit, designed for hit and run missions and other maneuvers requiring small numbers and surgical precision. So far, the Twelve have been assigned several scouting missions (drawing out the maps Toturi will use on later maneuvers) and have attacked Yugoro's bandits on at least seven missions.

The membership of the Twelve is in a constant state of flux. Each month Toturi selects different ronin to serve in the Twelve. Appointment to the Twelve is a great honor, as this unit not only receives the most critical missions but also serves Toturi in an advisory capacity. An appointment to the Twelve means that Toturi trusts not only your sword, but your mind as well. Ginawa, Hasame, and Mikio have all been consistent members of the Twelve since the foundation Toturi's Army, but the other nine members rotate regularly.

Since he suggested the idea, Dairya has denied any association with the Twelve and refused appointment on three occasions, preferring to work alone.

clan samurai would not lower themselves to participate in. Much like a Scorpion, a ronin can dirty his hands in a way that a normal samurai can't. Unlike a Scorpion, the only person a ronin has to answer to is himself. A clever player will use this to the service of the party. While it might not earn much in the way of respect, at least he might find a useful niche once the other PCs realize what he is capable of.

2. The New Ronin – This is a more severe option, but can be extremely useful for a GM who wishes to educate players in what it means to be a wave-man. Pick one of the PCs, one with a well-developed background, one with highly developed prejudices against ronin. Now, make him ronin. Not off-camera, not between sessions; have the whole grisly affair go down right in front of the party. The PC's lord dies, the PC is blamed for an act of dishonor, or whatever it takes to boot the PC out the back door.

Now, the character has to come to terms with suddenly being on the bottom rung of samurai society. His friends must decide how to deal with the situation. Do they treat him like manure, or do they accept their friend despite his status? The former may seem cruel, but the latter won't make them many allies in the court. Lastly, how will the character treat other ronin? Will he continue despising them, or accept his new lot in life? Will he fight to regain what he has lost or succumb to sorrow?

A kind GM will make this a temporary situation, allowing the character to find some way to redeem himself. A cruel GM will let the character suffer. A truly evil GM will pull this trick on the entire party. Which brings us to...

3. The All Ronin Party – This sort of party can present an entirely new set of challenges. You think you know how to get around in samurai society? Fine. Find your way around from the outside.

Remember, ronin are never magistrates (though they can be yoriki). Ronin are not courtiers. Ronin are lucky if they can find enough to eat. A ronin party will be pestered by the law. (A group of organized ronin is a rebellion waiting to happen.) A ronin probably won't be able to get traveling papers unless he's on a job, bribes a local magistrate, or forges them. When the PCs find employment, they'll be used as scapegoats, cannon fodder, or worse. Ronin can't trust anyone,

because no one wants to trust a ronin. In a party like this, duty, justice, and honor take a back seat to survival. However, a sense of party unity unlike any other is likely to form over time, as the PCs learn to look out for one another, forming a small otokodate of their own.

A large problem with a ronin party is the use of published adventures. Many L5R adventures are designed for parties composed of clan samurai, and therefore rightfully assume a certain level of political authority. Many of the NPCs in these adventures will have no reason to trust a band of ronin. (Though some adventures, like Code of Bushido, would in some ways become much easier.) This is not to say that published adventures cannot be used, but that careful alterations will need to be made on the part of the GM.

For the easiest, quickest fix the GM could simply plan out each published adventure as a "job," choosing one of the NPCs to act as the party's employer. The party will still lack much of the influence and respect of clan samurai, but this simple change can at least get the ball rolling.

Appendix II: Recent Developments

TOTURI'S CALL TO ARMS

The large number of ronin that follow Toturi's banner is as surprising to Toturi as anyone else. At first, he had only three followers: Otomo Yayu, an unknown shugenja; Dairya, a duelist with a reputation for violence; and Mikio, the last of Toturi's loyal retainers. Hoping to gather followers to combat the rampant banditry and lawlessness that had grown in the wake of the Scorpion Clan Coup, Toturi dispatched Yayu to the City of the Rich Frog. Once there, the shugenja posted the following message in the merchant's quarter, where it was likely to be seen by the many ronin who came there seeking employment.

A Call To Arms
For warriors whose duty it is to preserve the
Empire and restrain lawlessness,
What purpose do we serve in fostering chaos?
Let all men and women who have the honor to
call themselves samurai,
Rally beside the Black Lion,
in the shadows of the Great Climb.

The response was incredible. Dozens of ronin arrived within the first week. These were mostly the curious, eager to see if the fallen Lion Champion truly fancied himself a hero, and left soon after. Toturi greeted every bushi that came, treating them as equals and welcoming him to his cause. Many laughed. Some openly mocked him. (After the first incident, this no longer happened in Dairya's presence.) A few, however, believed in his message and remained. Among these first few was Ginawa, also a former Akodo. Ginawa was just a vagabond, floating into the camp because he had nowhere else to go. Toturi refused to judge Ginawa or any of others so long as they carried themselves with honor. At the end of the second week, Toturi's band had grown to twelve.

It was a start.

Their first target was Kyomeru, leader of the Mountain Goblin juzimai. These bandits had terrorized Mountain Goblin's Rest Road since the proscription of the Soshi family, after which time armed patrols had grown scarce. The twelve ronin crushed the juzimai, captured Kyomeru, and delivered him to Shiro Iuchi for punishment. The Unicorn were impressed; their own magistrates had been assigned the task of restoring order to the Scorpion provinces, but the strain of patrolling those territories as well as their own lands had taxed their resources, allowing criminals such as Kyomeru to slip through the cracks.

After their first victory, word of Toturi began to spread. Toturi dispatched Yayu time and again, delivering the call to arms to cities with large ronin populations. Toturi felt that ronin were the key. With no masters, they had no obligations. They would be more likely to answer the call, and free to operate without constraints. Toturi hoped for a band of at least forty capable bushi, and perhaps some shugenja. With that many, he felt he had a good chance against nearly any juzimai or wandering beast from the Shadowlands.

Toturi expected forty. Two months later, he had one hundred, with ten shugenja. The remaining Akodo that had followed Toturi after the Coup returned eagerly, reassured that their lord had regained his courage. Some of the most famous ronin in Rokugan also appeared in answer to Toturi's call. Kamoto. Akiyoshi. Morito Tokei. Even the legendary Naka Kuro has come to offer his magic and wisdom. Ronin have flocked from every corner of Rokugan. Ashigaru have begun to appear in large numbers as well, a fact that Toturi finds disturbing. The simple fact is, he doesn't want an army. He can't afford an army. He certainly can't afford to anger a daimyo by stealing farmers from the fields. He isn't certain what to do as his army continues to grow. The area in the vicinity of the camp is rapidly being stripped of all resources as the soldiers build shelters and forage for food.

Several months ago, a band of Dragon magistrates to arrived in the valley to investigate. Toturi met with them privately for some time. It is unknown what passed during the meeting, but the magistrates proclaimed themselves impressed by Toturi's sincerity and reassured that he does not intend any banditry or encroachment upon Dragon holdings. So long as his camp confines itself to the valley, the Dragon do not seem to mind their presence. Toturi fears for the day that they change their mind; he knows that his rabble are no match for the combined might of any Great Clan.

The rumors that Toturi has met with Togashi Mitsu are true. Mitsu is merely curious. He finds the camp intriguing, and the motley group of men and women who serve under the banner of the wolf are endlessly fascinating. Mitsu is seriously considering joining Toturi's cause, but has not made his intent known. For the moment, he is merely another mysterious Dragon lingering about.

The Mirumuto family, especially acting daimyo Mirumuto Sukune, take offense at Toturi's presence. Daini once worshiped Toturi as the model of a perfect samurai, but he is no longer so certain. Akodo Toturi was a hero. The Black Lion, on the other hand, is a ronin, a failure, a menace who dares to gather an army in Dragon territory! Daini longs for the day that Togashi Yokuni will tire of the camp's offensive presence and send him to deal with them.

Togashi Yokuni's thoughts on the matter are, as usual, unknowable. Yokuni is watching Toturi

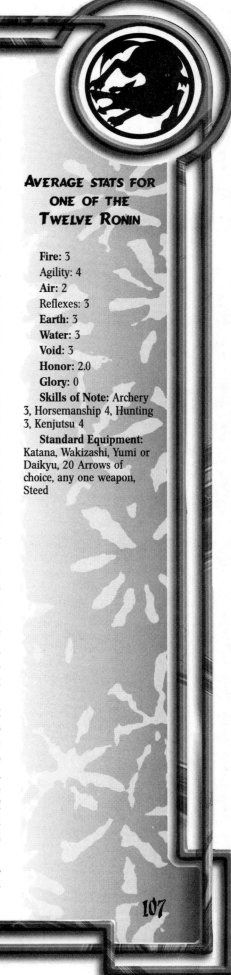

AVERAGE STATS FOR ONE OF THE TWELVE RONIN

Fire: 3
Agility: 4
Air: 2
Reflexes: 3
Earth: 3
Water: 3
Void: 3
Honor: 2.0
Glory: 0
Skills of Note: Archery 3, Horsemanship 4, Hunting 3, Kenjutsu 4
Standard Equipment: Katana, Wakizashi, Yumi or Daikyu, 20 Arrows of choice, any one weapon, Steed

TOHAKU

When news of the Akodo's fate reached the lands of the Lion, most of the Akodo reacted with shame, grief, and despair. One reacted with outrage. Akodo Tohaku expected the Lion Clan to seek the Emperor's mercy, but instead the Matsu seemed all too happy to enforce the Son of Heaven's edict.

Tohaku does not blame the Hantei, for divinity must be a great burden on one so young. He does, however, blame the remaining three families of the Lion Clan for their exuberance in turning on their brothers. He holds a special place in his heart for the Matsu, whom he now considers little more than treacherous, backstabbing zealots with no honor. He is a man divided, for though he longs to serve the Emperor and prove his devotion, so too does he desire for his grandfather's katana to taste the blood of the Matsu line.

(Continued on opposite page.)

closely. In his own inimitable fashion, the Dragon Champion has made certain that the camp does not run short on supplies or resources, though he keeps his interference secret. Yokuni knows that the time will come when Toturi is needed.

THE SCORPION RONIN

All who bear the mon of the Scorpion
or the names of those who serve the Bayushi line have two choices:
Live as ronin or die as traitors.
The Bayushi line ends here.
–Edict of Hantei XXXIX

The Scorpion have lost much in the last two years. Their family names have been stricken from the Imperial records. Their representatives have been cast from the court. Their leaders are in exile and their castles lie in ruins. The pride and joy of the Scorpion, their vaunted loyalty, has been publicly and dramatically disproved. Most of the Scorpion abandoned their names and fled rather than face the Legions. Those who stood proudly by their clan have been crushed. The Scorpion are no more. Even among ronin, they are outcasts.

"When crushing a scorpion, make certain of your kill."
–Shosuro Hametsu

The following message was delivered to these Scorpions shortly before Shoju began the coup: Bayushi Kachiko, Bayushi Aramoro, Bayushi Yojiro, Soshi Bantaro, Shosuro Hametsu, and Yogo Junzo.

I do not intend to fail.
But no man ever triumphed solely by arrogance.
If I should fall, the Empire will be in grave peril. To those Scorpion who survive, let survival continue to become your priority. Only through survival shall we find justice.
Only through survival shall we find revenge.
–Shoju

Like so much about the Scorpion, the clan's surrender to the Imperial edict is a carefully planned illusion. When the Scorpion castles were burned, a large contingent of nonessential personnel were left behind in each to make it seem as though the major families had

committed seppuku. Some Scorpion towns and holdings were ordered to resist the Imperial Legions, insuring their own destruction but making it seem as if all rebellious Scorpion had been slain. Shoju's last command was a difficult one, requiring all Scorpions to turn their back upon the loyalty they treasured so highly and see to their own survival first.

As difficult as it was, the Scorpion obeyed the command without question. That is the way of the Scorpion.

This is not to say that the Scorpion are now ignored as a possible threat to the Empire. Far from it. Imperial Magistrates have specific instructions to place all Scorpion ronin at the top of their lists of suspects for all unsolved murders, thefts, and civic disturbances. Hardly a week goes by in Rokugan that a former Scorpion is not executed for some heinous crime, whether he is truly guilty or not. Scorpion ronin are universally hated. Even those who obeyed the Hantei's edict and surrendered their names are regarded as unreliable scum, and are hunted for what they once were. Former Scorpions may not swear fealty to any clan, and are seldom hired for important duties. Former Scorpions may not legally own property or hold any offices without a direct decree from the Emperor.

All the Scorpions have left is one another.

So not much has changed, really.

It's all in how you look at it.

The following are the most important bastions of Scorpion power remaining in Rokugan. Scorpion influence in each of these locales is kept top secret, naturally.

Otosan Uchi – Yes, you read that correctly. Three known Scorpions live openly in the Imperial Capitol. The first is Kachiko, the only Scorpion allowed to carry the Bayushi name (a not-so-subtle insult from the Emperor). The second is Yojiro, a magistrate who stood against Shoju during the Coup and was allowed to keep his position as a reward for his loyalty. The third is Bayushi Goshiu. Notably absent from Otosan Uchi during the Coup, the courtier was at first forbidden to return to the Imperial City. However, during last year's Winter Court, Goshiu made a surprise appearance and was witnessed openly mocking Kachiko privately and publicly. This amused the Otomo, who encouraged the sickly Emperor to allow the Scorpion to remain, so long as he does not carry his wit too far.

Kyuden Bayushi – The fire that ravaged the upper floors of Kyuden Bayushi left the hidden sub-basements completely intact, as was Soshi Bantaro's intent. From here, Bantaro and a few dozen retainers work toward some private quest. Bantaro and his apprentices have used their magic to create the illusion that the ruined castle is haunted, to frighten away visitors and explain the occasional appearance of ghostly samurai. Those who venture out of the castle always do so at sunset, wearing robes of deathly white and making no efforts to hide themselves. Once they reach Traitor's Grove, these "ghosts" discard their disguise and don armor and weapons hidden among the possessions of past Scorpion betrayers.

Road's End Village – For years the single magistrate assigned to this small and unremarkable village has been on Shosuro Hametsu's secret payroll. Since the Coup, the population of this village has increased dramatically. Over one hundred and fifty Scorpions now live here, including Hametsu, Yogo Asami, and many of the Scorpion's deadliest assassins. Hametsu has begun work on a new herb garden here, transplanting the flora he managed to save from Shiro no Shosuro and supplementing it with local species. The villagers in Road's End have taken these new inhabitants in stride; those that ask too many questions venture into the mountains and do not return.

The Shadowlands – When Junzo departed Shiro Yogo, he led his most loyal retainers directly to the Kaiu Wall. The Wall was only lightly guarded, as most of the Crab army was still in Otosan Uchi, so the Crab did not stand in the way as three hundred Scorpion marched directly into Fu Leng's realm. A day later, the Crab rallied a large scouting party to round up the Scorpions (the last thing the Crab need is three hundred undead Scorpions). They found only a field of mangled corpses. Junzo may have been among them, but the Crab aren't sure. There wasn't much left to identify.

THE FALL OF THE AKODO

Of all the samurai families or Rokugan, there were perhaps none who so exemplified what it means to be samurai as did the Akodo. From the legendary Akodo One-Eye to the most recent champions of the Lion, Akodo Arasou and Akodo Toturi, few in the Empire's history could match the honorable devotion of the Akodo, and none have exceeded it. The passionate Matsu, the introspective Kitsu, the eloquent Ikoma...all looked to the Akodo for guidance and inspiration. No longer.

The family of the Akodo had fallen upon hard times even before the Scorpion's abortive coup in Otosan Uchi. Various disputes with the Matsu family led to a gradual decrease in the size and power of the Akodo family, although there can be no question that they remained firmly in command of the Lion Clan. Many look to the death of Akodo Arasou some years ago in battle with the Crane as the turning point for the Lion. Arasou's marriage to Matsu family daimyo Tsuko could have healed the rift between the families of the Lion, and many believe the zealous warrior would never have failed his family so greatly as the traitor Toturi has. Instead, his death only drove the two great families further apart. If only he had ordered a unit of disposable ronin into the breach instead of charging into the heaviest fighting himself, he would not have been trapped and slain by the Daidoji counterattack; who knows what a Lion Clan united behind Arasou and Tsuko could have accomplished?

Toturi's ascension to daimyo of the Akodo and champion of the Lion caused resentment among the Matsu, who held Arasou in very high regard. For Toturi, there was little but disdain for his relative lack of prowess with the sword and notions of peace.

There is no peace for the Akodo now. Perhaps there never shall be again.

When the Scorpion Clan Champion Bayushi Shoju began his insidious plot to destroy the Hantei and declare himself Emperor, he knew that Toturi and the Lion Clan presented the greatest threat to his success. Their zealous service to the Son of Heaven would demand Shoju's blood for his crimes. With Toturi's brilliant tactical mind leading them, there would be little the Scorpion could do to forestall such a fate. Thus, Toturi must be dealt with before the coup could be staged. With Toturi gone and the passionate bloodlust of the Matsu leading the Lion armies, Shoju could claim an easy victory.

Shoju's wife Kachiko had long since placed a suitable pawn near Toturi in the form of a young geisha. Kachiko had subtler manipulations in mind originally, but this gambit would supersede her ambitions. Toturi was poisoned, the Lion were

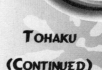

TOHAKU
(CONTINUED)

Tohaku has left the lands of the Lion and resides in the City of the Rich Frog. He is the subject of close scrutiny and whispered concerns wherever he goes, for the seething cauldron of rage that builds within him is visible in his eyes. He awaits the summons of his lord Toturi, knowing without question that the Black Ronin will have need of him sooner or later. Together, they will prove to the Empire that even stripped of their name and honor, the Akodo are men of honor and courage. He hopes it will be soon.

And he desperately hopes the Matsu will attempt to stop them.

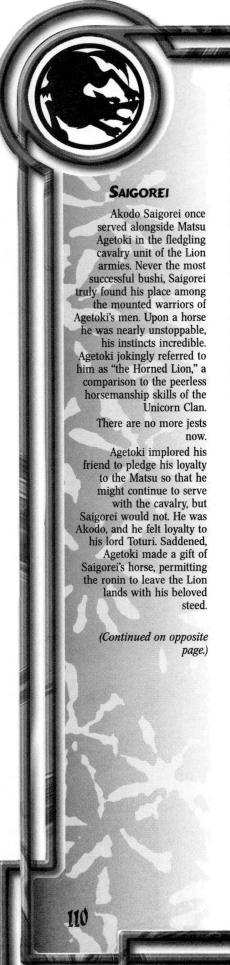

SAIGOREI

Akodo Saigorei once served alongside Matsu Agetoki in the fledgling cavalry unit of the Lion armies. Never the most successful bushi, Saigorei truly found his place among the mounted warriors of Agetoki's men. Upon a horse he was nearly unstoppable, his instincts incredible. Agetoki jokingly referred to him as "the Horned Lion," a comparison to the peerless horsemanship skills of the Unicorn Clan.

There are no more jests now.

Agetoki implored his friend to pledge his loyalty to the Matsu so that he might continue to serve with the cavalry, but Saigorei would not. He was Akodo, and he felt loyalty to his lord Toturi. Saddened, Agetoki made a gift of Saigorei's horse, permitting the ronin to leave the Lion lands with his beloved steed.

(Continued on opposite page.)

rendered ineffective, and the Scorpion were free to make their move.

Unfortunately for the Scorpion, the gambit failed. The poison was not sufficiently virulent, and Toturi survived. Weakened but battle-worthy, he arrived at Otosan Uchi to lead the Lion to victory over the invading Scorpion. A duel took place in the Imperial throne room between Toturi and Shoju. Even with poison coursing through his veins, Toturi settled all doubts regarding his proficiency with the blade when he ended the machinations of Bayushi Shoju by cutting him down in a formal iaijutsu duel.

The events following Shoju's death are subject to debate. It is known that the young Hantei, son of Hantei XXXVIII, had been safely escorted from the city by a band of magistrates who happened to be present within the palace. These heroes managed to get the young Emperor into the hands of the Phoenix Clan, where he would be well protected from danger. There are conflicting claims as to whether or not Toturi was aware that the heir had survived the fighting in the capital. Many malign Toturi's character with accusations that he believed the Hantei line was dead and that he wished to claim the throne for his own. Others closer to Toturi, who knew him prior to the coup, suggest that he merely wished to prevent another from claiming the throne by declaring himself regent until the young Hantei could claim the throne following his gempukku ceremony. Whatever the case, when the Phoenix army escorted the Son of Heaven into the Imperial Palace, he found the pale, weakened Toturi slumped in his father's Emerald Throne.

After taking the throne, Hantei XXXIX condemned the traitor Shoju, denying him the honorable cremation rites of a samurai and ordering his corpse be treated like that of a common eta. Furthermore, he claimed that Bayushi Kachiko would become his wife, ending Shoju's line forever. Having faced Shoju in personal combat, Toturi objected, claiming that Shoju should be given the same consideration as any samurai. He also objected to the marriage of Kachiko to the Hantei, for he knew the depths of manipulation and depravity to which the woman could sink and sought to spare the Emperor her predations.

Having experienced so much insult to his family and person in such a short period of time, the Emperor could tolerate no further challenge to the rule of the Hantei line. With the champions of all six remaining Great Clans bowing before

him for the first time as the new Emperor of Rokugan, the Hantei condemned Toturi and his entire line for his actions.

"Akodo Toturi, I know of your dishonor and your treachery. Now I will speak of your crimes against the Empire, so that all will understand when I show you no mercy. Do not think that a boy Emperor is blind to the truth, or that I have not been watching as my city was destroyed and my throne was claimed – first by Shoju, and now, of all my servants, by the one who claimed most to serve my honor." The new Emperor's words were filled with anger and seethed with menace.

"Hear the deeds of 'glorious' Akodo Toturi," the Hantei proclaimed, settling into his Emerald Throne. "The man who abandoned the Lion Clan in their time of greatest need, allowing himself to be trapped and influenced by a geisha. He chose the embrace of a heimin woman over duty to his Lord and to his Empire.

"He spoke in Shoju's favor after the usurper was killed, and proclaimed that Shoju deserved an honorable burial despite his slaughter of the Hantei family.

"And last, he is to be reviled for his treachery – daring to lay false claim to the Hantei throne. For resting where none but the Hantei have been allowed to remain – upon this, the Emerald Throne.

"For these, the actions of a traitorous man, the samurai known as Akodo Toturi is dishonored. He is to be denied a true samurai's right to an honorable seppuku, and must live on in shame.

"Your shame shall destroy not only your own honor, Toturi," the Emperor snarled, "but your entire traitorous line. It is said that the Akodo live as brothers, and so let them die as brothers. We shall see how the Akodo stand by their oaths to you when they learn of your black and corrupted heart."

With this, his first official proclamation as Emperor, the Hantei destroyed the most virtuous and loyal servants of the throne for the perceived failings of a single man.

Word of the Hantei's declaration spread throughout the Empire with the speed of the wind. The anguish experienced by each member of the Akodo family upon hearing the news was compounded by the agonizing choice they must make: where did their honor lie? There was precious little time to make such a choice, for the sunrise of the next day would see death to all who held the name Akodo.

The great majority of Akodo believed that their honor was to the clan of the Lion and in the service of the Emperor. These valiant samurai pledged their lives to one of the other families of the Lion, the Matsu, Kitsu or Ikoma, abandoning their former name and family so that they might continue to serve the new champion of the Lion.

Another faction of the Akodo refused to believe that their lord could act so dishonorably, and chose to be stripped of their name, clan and lands to join him in exile. These ronin spread throughout the Empire to await the summons of their daimyo. Though he may have lost faith in himself, these samurai believed in Toturi's character and honor, and knew that he would have need of them in time.

A third group of the Akodo felt that their lord's actions had not only dishonored them, but also the memory of every Akodo that had ever drawn breath. Tortured by the thought of their ancestors' shame, many of these samurai committed seppuku to cleanse their honor. Those who chose not to take their own lives became Deathseekers, an elite cadre of nameless warriors who hurled themselves against the enemies of the Lion in an attempt to regain the honor of their family by dying for the glory of the Lion Clan.

By the sunrise of the day following Bayushi Shoju's death, only one Akodo remained in the whole of the Empire: Akodo Kage. Spared the purge by Imperial edict, the renowned sensei remained among the Lion, urging the brash Matsu Tsuko to temper her passion with moderation. The new champion of the Lion largely disregards Kage's words, but there are others among the Lion who listen. Toturi's former pupil Ikoma Tsanuri listens to the wisdom of Kage's teachings and hopes that her clan can recover from this devastating blow.

THE AKODO RONIN

With slightly more than a quarter of the Akodo family having lost their family and clan to join the ranks of the ronin, the population of Rokugan's wave-men has increased dramatically. It is easy to distinguish these new ronin from other wave-men, however. Although their eyes show the loss and shame that their entire family feels, they conduct themselves as if they were courtiers in the presence of the Emperor himself. Every statement is respectful, every courtesy is extended to all whom they encounter. Their compassion and sincerity have not diminished with their loss of station.

They are Lion no more, but bushido fills their soul nonetheless.

Samurai of other clans look upon these ronin with a mixture of pity and disgust. That the descendants of one of the kami could have fallen so far from grace is a horrible reminder that though a divine child of the heavens founded each clan, a samurai bearing their name is all too human. The thought that such a fate could befall any such samurai, even themselves or their family, is too unbearable to contemplate. And so the others look upon the Akodo with disgust, pity, and something that approaches hatred.

The heimin of the Empire, with whom the former Akodo are forced to interact for survival, seem divided in their reaction to these new ronin who fill their villages. The bearing and actions of these wave-men mark them as honorable men who believe in the protection of the peasants of Rokugan. However, the actions of their former daimyo and their banishment by the Son of Heaven instill a fear within the heart of every heimin. If the Akodo were capable of such actions before, then the possibility of further atrocities hovers over them forever. A former Akodo is thus a dangerous and volatile commodity, one that could explode into a violent rage at any moment despite their sincere and serene demeanor.

The lands of the Crab are home to very few former Akodo. Those who chose exile over fealty to another family have the sense that there is a task awaiting them, and few wish to squander their lives in combat with the Dark One before determining what that duty shall be. Nonetheless, there are a few haunted ronin who stand alongside the Crab on the wall. Despite the Crab's more accepting stance on ronin, very few of the former Akodo are treated with more than pained indifference. The Hantei's harsh and swift justice upon both the Akodo and the Scorpion has impressed Hida Kisada, and he does not wish to incur the disfavor of what he hopes will be a strong Emperor by pandering to the exiled Lions.

The samurai of the Crane Clan are strangely divided over the fate of the Akodo. Though they rejoice at the perceived weakening of their ancient foes in the Lion Clan, they are greatly concerned that the passion and lust for battle of the Matsu is now unchecked by the rational conservatism of the Akodo. The Crane Champion Doji Hoturi has been silent, though his well-known friendship with Toturi has likely caused him great pain during the tragic happenings of the past year. The

Unlike his childhood friend Tohaku, Saigorei does not feel animosity towards the remaining Lion families. They did only what they must to ensure that the Lion could survive to protect the Hantei and his Empire.

Saigorei is an unfailing optimist. He feels that his loss of status is not the result of his own actions, and thus his ancestors have not left him. Instead, he believes that even as ronin he must exemplify honor and bushido to prove to them that he is worthy of their name even after it has been taken from him.

Once an opponent of the Unicorn Clan, Saigorei now dwells among them, serving as an escort for a Shinjo caravan master. He knows that war is looming on the horizon, and he waits to see what role he will play in the destiny of Rokugan.

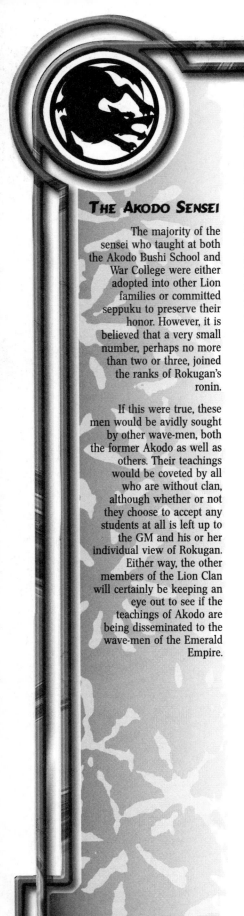

THE AKODO SENSEI

The majority of the sensei who taught at both the Akodo Bushi School and War College were either adopted into other Lion families or committed seppuku to preserve their honor. However, it is believed that a very small number, perhaps no more than two or three, joined the ranks of Rokugan's ronin.

If this were true, these men would be avidly sought by other wave-men, both the former Akodo as well as others. Their teachings would be coveted by all who are without clan, although whether or not they choose to accept any students at all is left up to the GM and his or her individual view of Rokugan. Either way, the other members of the Lion Clan will certainly be keeping an eye out to see if the teachings of Akodo are being disseminated to the wave-men of the Emerald Empire.

Akodo ronin avoid the lands of the Crane, for they expect little welcome there after so many years of hostility between their clans.

A large number of ronin left the Lion lands to settle in the land of the Dragon. There is a sizeable camp of former Akodo situated near the foothills of the Dragon mountains, although it is unknown whether the ronin are waiting for the permission of the Dragonfly Clan to enter the mountains, or if they merely have nowhere else to go. There have been rumors of late that the Black Ronin himself has been seen among these wave-men and has journeyed into the Dragon lands numerous times. Akodo ronin around the Empire watch and wait to see if the time has come for them to stand by the side of their lord once more.

It goes without saying that the Akodo ronin find little welcome within what was once their own land. The other families of the Lion look upon those who chose exile over fealty as little better than brigands or bandits. They are persecuted mercilessly when found within the lands of the Lion, and few choose to remain there. The pain is simply too great.

The Phoenix look upon the fallout from the coup in Otosan Uchi as an unparalleled tragedy. One of the Great Clans destroyed and an ancient family of another clan banished… it is almost too unthinkable for the pacifistic Phoenix to contemplate. They offer what limited aid and hospitality they can to the former Akodo without violating the edict of the Hantei which forbade the Akodo fealty to any family. The families of the Phoenix remember how the cool heads of the Akodo have prevented the brash Matsu from rushing headlong into countless conflicts throughout the history of Rokugan, some against the Phoenix themselves. They look to their southern neighbors now with a mixture of sympathy and concern.

The former Akodo bear the suspicions and malicious intentions of others with the passive stoicism that has been their way for generations. Though they are reviled by many, they take comfort in knowing that at least the former Scorpion among the ronin of the Empire fare far worse. Where ronin formerly of the Scorpion and Akodo meet, there are often harsh words exchanged, and there have been violent incidents throughout the Empire. Even the legendary composure of the Akodo, it seems, has its limits.

The Unicorn Clan has proved to be among the greatest allies of the former Akodo. Even after two centuries in Rokugan, the samurai of the Unicorn cannot grasp the condemnation of an entire family based on the actions of a single man. They silently believe that the Akodo do not deserve the fate they have been given, and many of the ronin have found employment with the Shinjo family.

The minor clans of Rokugan have wisely held their collective tongue about the fallout from the coup in Otosan Uchi. With the hostility that permeates Rokugan now, the leaders of these tiny clans are loath to attract unwanted attention to themselves, fearing that the Great Clans might perceive them as little more than resources to be absorbed before outright war breaks out. Many former Akodo have silently been hired by various minor clans to bolster their ranks and defenses since the coup. The Three Man Alliance in particular has incorporated several dozen ex-Lions into their defenses.

No matter where they are in the Empire, the Akodo ronin are, almost to a man, unfailingly loyal to Toturi. Those who were not either remained with the Lion under another name, became Deathseekers, or cleansed their honor with their wakizashi. They have not gathered in his name, not yet. To do so now would mean certain annihilation for all of them. Instead they scatter throughout the Empire, awaiting what many of them consider to be an inevitable conflict that will spill forth and envelop the nation as a whole. Only then will they flock to Toturi's banner. Only then will Rokugan see that the Akodo have not truly fallen.

The Akodo Deathseekers

Although not technically ronin, the Deathseekers that formerly held the name Akodo are little more than wave-men conscripted into service in the armies of the Lion. Just as the lives of ronin are squandered by the clans on the battlefield to spare the lives of clan samurai, so too are the Deathseekers hurled against the enemies of the Lion with reckless abandon. The former Akodo do so willingly, for only in death may they finally know peace.

The Deathseekers are kept apart from the other soldiers of the Lion forces. They are housed in their own barracks and take their meals separately. Their days consist of little else than training, meditation, and the cleaning and maintenance of their weapons and armor. Their clothing and armor and are bleached white, the color of death. This makes them a visible target among the other troops of the Lion, but they do not care. The enemies of the Lion are eager to eliminate the Deathseekers via archers and spells before the infantries of the two armies meet, for the former Akodo are the most ruthless and bloodthirsty force within the Lion army. Their total disregard for their own safety and morbid desire to utterly destroy all who oppose the Lion have resulted in the greatest number of kills per unit the Lion have ever known, and the highest casualty rate.

Soon, the final Akodo to remain within the Lion will all be dead, perished on the field of battle to purchase the honor of the Akodo ancestors with their lives. Then, no trace of the great legacy of the Akodo will remain anywhere within the lands of the Lion save the sacred Hall of Ancestors.

The Akodo Daggers

Questions have been raised among the former allies of the Akodo as to the whereabouts of the famed Akodo Daggers following the demise of the Akodo line. These inquiries are met with angry silence and malicious stares from the Matsu, followed by a terse insistence that the Daggers are no longer an issue.

In truth, the Akodo Daggers disappeared from the Lion lands with the family's dissolution. Their location now is the subject of a discreet search by the Ikoma historians. Matsu Tsuko has commanded that the Daggers be found and destroyed in the presence of the Emperor, that he might know that his loyal servants in the Lion Clan have eliminated every trace of the treacherous Akodo line.

The five Akodo Daggers were, prior to the destruction of the Akodo, handed down from father to son since the dawn of the Emerald Empire. Each of Akodo One-Eye's children was given one, forged by the students of Kakita in an effort to heal the rift between Kakita and the Lady Matsu. Since that day, each recipient of a Dagger has given it to his or her first-born on the eve of that child's gempukku ceremony. This has ensured a longstanding means of identifying those families among the Akodo with the clearest line of descent from the clan's founder.

Toturi himself still holds one of the Daggers. In the sole confrontation between Toturi and the Lion Clan since his exile, the Black Ronin declined to turn it over to the Ikoma, and none have had the temerity to demand or attempt to take it from him.

There are those who believe that the sole remaining Akodo, the sensei Kage, holds another of the Daggers. Only when Tsuko holds the remaining four will she request that Kage surrender his, and then only for the greater good of the Lion Clan.

Strangely, the Ikoma records lack information regarding the location of the remaining three Akodo Daggers. One was known to be held by the family of Akodo that ended when Akodo Ginawa was cast out from the clan, but that Dagger was not found among the possessions of the household when the distant remnants of that branch were absorbed by the Matsu. Perhaps it is the honor that comes from holding an Akodo Dagger that tempers the bloodlust of the ronin Ginawa's bloodsword.

The Daggers themselves are short, golden blades with intricately carved hilts that include a roaring lion curving about the handle. They are said to confer upon their owners a sense of serenity and stability that stills the emotions and permits a samurai to make decisions based solely upon an Akodo's greatest asset: his honor. Of the myriad heroes who grace the Lion's Hall of Ancestors, the greatest have been holders of one of the Akodo Daggers.

Appendix III: Magic

Spells of Naka Kuro

KURO'S FIRE
Element: Fire
Base TN: 20
Casting Time: 4 Actions
Duration: Instantaneous
Concentration: None
Mastery: 6

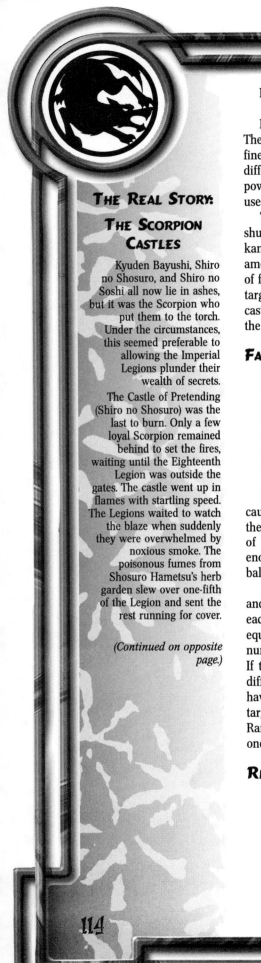

Raises: Casting Time

Effect: This spell is similar in many ways to The Fire From Within. However, Naka Kuro has fine-tuned the invocation in many ways that differ from the original. While this spell is quite powerful, it can be a potentially exhausting and useless endeavor for the unworthy.

This spell draws upon the power of the shugenja's chi as well as the energies of the fire kami. When cast, a shugenja may spend any amount of Void to hurl an equal number of bolts of flame. These can be directed to strike multiple targets, but all targets must be visible during the casting. Each bolts has a Damage Rating equal to the caster's Fire.

FACING YOUR DEVILS
Element: Air
Base TN: 20
Casting Time: 3 Actions
Duration: 3 rounds
Concentration: Focused
Mastery: 5
Raises: Casting Time, Duration

Effect: In casting this spell, the shugenja causes disharmony within the natural rhythms of the target's mind and body. The sudden eruption of chi, strong pitted against weak, can do enormous damage to a soul that is not properly balanced.

In game terms, the shugenja casts the spell and then makes an opposed roll with the target each round. The target rolls a number of dice equal to his lowest Trait and the caster rolls a number of dice equal to the target's highest Trait. If the target fails, he takes Wounds equal to the difference. Alternately, the caster can choose to have the spell do no Wounds but prevent the target from spending Void or voluntarily making Raises for the duration. If the target succeeds on one of these opposed rolls, the effect ceases.

RISE FROM THE ASHES
Element: Void
Base TN: 30
Casting Time: 1 Hour
Duration: Permanent
Concentration: Total
Mastery: 7
Raises: None

Effect: Ritual. This extremely powerful and draining magic can turn back the kharmic wheel itself. The spell must be cast on a single individual or item, and neither the target or the shugenja may move during the casting. When the spell is complete, all corruptive effects and damage inflicted on the target during the last six hours are negated. Wounds, poisons, curses, even the Shadowlands Taint can be retroactively negated. The target and shugenja are both exhausted by this spell, and receive a –2 penalty to all skill rolls until they rest for six hours. In addition, both the Void of both the target and caster is completely spent. This Void loss is more exhausting than normal, and can only be recovered at a rate of one point per day until fully recovered.

For every extra shugenja that participates in the ritual, an extra hour of damage is negated. All shugenja experience the same draining effects as if there were only one caster.

It is important to note the limitations of this spell. This spell cannot resurrect the dead. Though a dead body can be repaired, the soul is carried beyond the reach of this magic and cannot return. Likewise, a broken nemuranai cannot be restored to its former power unless the original spirit can somehow be coaxed back into the item. On the other hand, oni or undead affected by this spell will be restored to full strength, if it is cast quickly enough.

THE PATH NOT TAKEN
Element: Water
Base TN: 20
Casting Time: 10 Actions
Duration: 1 Day
Concentration: None
Mastery: 5
Raises: Casting Time

Effect: This spell is frequently used by Kuro and his students to focus their energies in one particular element. When the spell is cast, the shugenja weakens his link to one element in order to strengthen his bond to another. The spell must be cast while the shugenja's connections to the elements are at their peak, and thus it cannot be cast if the shugenja has cast any other spells since he last rested.

The effect of the spell is quite potent. The maximum number of spells the shugenja may cast in the strengthened element is raised by half the value (round up) of the weakened element. The number of spells he may cast in the weakened element is reduced to zero. Though spells can be recovered naturally by meditation, these maxima remain the same and thus spells of the weakened element cannot be recovered until the duration ends. This spell cannot be voluntarily ended before the duration expires.

CLAY HORSE

Element: Earth
Base TN: 20
Casting Time: 5 actions
Duration: 12 hours plus the caster's Earth in hours
  Concentration: None
Mastery: 4
Raises: Duration, Casting Time, Durability

Effect: A strange magic adapted from Naka Kuro's studies of Crane tsangusuri and Unicorn travel spells, the Clay Horse is both a spell and a minor nemuranai. To cast the spell, the shugenja must have a clay statue of a horse, between 2 inches and a foot in height. (A clay horse can be produced by meeting an Agility + Sculpting TN of 10, or an unskilled Agility roll of 20.) When the spell is cast, the shugenja gives the horse to another and asks them to name it. Only the person who first names a Clay Horse may ever use that particular horse for the effects of this spell.

So long as the spell's effects last and the target carries the horse, he is unaffected by exhaustion and does not sleep. This includes forms of sleep and exhaustion caused by magic or poison – the bearer of the horse is immune. If the target ever loses or breaks the horse, the spell ends. The target begins to feel exhaustion only when the spell expires, any labor or activity performed while under the effects of the horse does not tire him in any way.

Users of this spell should be aware that a Clay Horse can be very fragile. Every time the spell expires, there is a chance that the horse will break and be forever useless. The owner of the horse must roll dice equal to his Earth, and if he cannot meet a TN of 40, his horse shatters. This TN is lowered by 5 for every raise the sculptor made while crafting the horse, or every raise the shugenja made while casting the spell. The TN is lowered by 10 if the clay horse is fired in a kiln.

Nemuranai

FUKUSHU (REVENGE) — THE FOURTH IUCHIBAN BLADE

Fukushu was the first of the four bloodswords forged by Asahina Yajinden. Until the blade found its way into the possession of Lion Champion Akodo Meikuko, she had a reputation as a cool and level-headed general. Only days after she received the gift its curse began to warp her gentle good nature.

Meikuko was visiting the Emperor's court, where she made the acquaintance of an ise zumi named Togashi Moho. Moho's frankness and strange philosophies had made an impression upon the Hantei, and the Emperor appointed Moho as one of his personal advisors. At one particular meeting of the court, the Emperor had posed a hypothetical question.

"Were I to lower taxes to ease the burden of the people, where should I start?"

"Among the Lion," Togashi Moho quipped. "Perhaps emptying their larders would remind them of the hands that fill them."

Meikuko was incensed. "Do you imply that we neglect our duty to the Emperor?"

Moho shook his head. "In fact, I meant to remind you of your duty to the people," he said. "I apologize if your sense of self worth is so fragile that you misunderstand me, Matsu-sama."

Meikuko demanded satisfaction, and turned to the Emperor to request permission to challenge Moho to a duel. The Hantei valued both retainers, but did not wish to show favor. He gave Meikuko her permission three days later, long after he privately advised Moho to return to the mountains. The snows would set in soon, and the Hantei hoped that Meikuko would forget the unintended insult during the long winter months.

Unfortunately, Yajinden's blade had changed Meikuko, and the Hantei's judgment of her character was incorrect. Meikuko declared war on the Dragon in the Emperor's name and led an army of 20,000 Lions to seek justice. Only 2000 survived. At the top of Togashi Mountain, Meikuko took her own life with the Bloodsword. Her name became synonymous with "mistake."

The blade was recovered centuries later by Shiba Kojiro, the last master of Morikage Castle. The events that led to the destruction of Morikage are still not fully known, but Fukushu is believed

THE REAL STORY:
THE SCORPION CASTLES
(CONTINUED)

When Hametsu heard reports, he was disappointed at the low casualty rate, but heartily amused that the plants he had not saved had been put to good use. Oddly, one of the saboteurs, a young bushi named Tangen, survived the fire unscathed. He claims to have been saved from the lethal smoke by a "divine wind."

Of all the major castles of the Scorpion, only Yogo Shiro still stands intact, as Junzo and his retinue abandoned the place long before the Legions arrived. For a time, the soldiers attempted to use the castle as a barracks, but after dozens of serious injuries resulting from lingering Yogo Wards, the Legions simply abandoned it.

to have been somehow involved. Apparently, the blade did not linger within the walls of the haunted castle. Isawa Tadaka of the Phoenix recently saw Fukushu in the hands of the ronin Ginawa. Attempts by Tadaka to obtain the blade met with violent refusal, and it is feared that the erstwhile Akodo has already fallen under the Bloodsword's spell.

Fukushu's powers

Fukushu possesses all of the abilities of a standard Bloodsword (see *L5R RPG*, page 181). Like its sister, Yashin, Fukushu also possesses an additional mixed blessing.

The wielder of Fukushu may spend one point of Honor in order to roll and keep an extra die of damage. Every time the wielder spends Honor in this manner, he must make a Willpower check vs a TN of 20 or fly into a berserker rage. While in such a state, the character will not sheathe Fukushu until every visible enemy is dead.

Not down. Not unconscious. Dead.

The character will not withdraw, will not surrender, and will not use any weapon other than the bloodsword until all enemies have been slain. If the character is disarmed, he may make another Willpower check (this time at a TN of 15) to compose himself. If this check is failed, he will try to retrieve the sword, or, if this is impossible, continue attacking with bare fists. Anyone who attempts to disarm the berserk character will immediately be considered an enemy. After all enemies are killed or escape, the rage fades. The character remembers nothing of the time in which he lost control.

Fukushu can sense those of violent temperaments, and seeks them out. If it has no wielder, Fukushu can attract violent or vengeful individuals that approach within 100 feet. Such individuals must make a Willpower check vs a TN of 15, or they will become curious about the blade and wish to pick it up. Fukushu is quite happy with Ginawa's seething rage, and is not currently seeking another wielder.

THE ARMOR OF SUN TAO

Sun Tao's armor was created in the legendary Kaiu forge, and is a fine example of Crab workmanship, a finely crafted suit with blue silken trim and golden ornamentation. Though Sun Tao only wore the armor for five years, it is believed to carry his spirit. Those who wear the armor say they can hear Sun Tao whispering his lost lessons in their ear.

The armor was held by the Suzume for many generations, as the Sparrow were the first to find the body of Sun Tao's assistant, Terumuto, and bring the bandits who slew him to justice. The armor stood on display in Suzume Shiro until recently. A ronin diplomat who had been influential in the formation of the Three Man Alliance was given the armor as a gift when he left the Sparrow's service. Some years ago, this ronin struck out on his own, headed for the village of Nanashi.

The Armor's Powers

The Armor of Sun Tao's magical qualities increase its wearer's TN to be Hit by his Earth x 5. If leading warriors into combat, the wearer may spend a Void Point to bestow the Blessing of Sun Tao upon a number of his followers equal to his (Water + Battle) x 100. Those affected by the Blessing roll upon the Battle Table as follows: If the army is losing, roll as if it is tied. If the army is tied, roll as if it is winning. If the army is winning, adjust the roll on the battle table by one in either direction. The Blessing's effects last for one Battle Round. Soldiers who are not under the command of the Armor's wearer do not receive the bonus. The armor of Sun Tao is considered Heavy Armor.

THE JADE GOBLETS OF TAIRA

Taira was a legendary ronin shugenja who elegantly combined the fetish magic of the Asahina with the binding magics of the Kuni. When Taira refused an offer to swear fealty to the Asahina and reveal how he had produced his creations, the Crane Champion angrily ordered Taira's execution for stealing their secrets.

Few of Taira's creations remain, but those that survive are extraordinary. The three Jade Goblets of Taira are the most avidly sought. Each goblet is sculpted of gold, with intricate jade inlays covering the entire surface. The goblets' craftsmanship would make them a treasure in itself, but their remarkable powers make these treasures priceless beyond measure.

First, the goblets glow brightly when within 100 feet of any creature Tainted by the Shadowlands. The light the goblet emits is terrible to behold, producing Fear with a Rating of 6 for all Tainted creatures. Second, drinking liquid from the goblet heals all wounds, poisons, and disease that afflict the drinker. Every time the goblet is used in this manner, the GM must roll and keep four dice vs a TN of 15. Every time the goblet is used more than once in one month, the TN goes up by 5. If the goblet is not used for an entire month, the TN goes down by 5, to a minimum of 15. If any roll made while using the goblet fails, the goblet becomes pitch black and loses all of its powers for ten years.

One of the Jade Goblets is currently in the possession of the Kitsu family. A second was in the collection of the Fox, but was stolen by a ronin Scorpion some years ago. The location of the third goblet is unknown.

THE KOEBI JITTE

This extraordinary weapon is carried by Ryhodotsu, the sole remaining member of the Koebi family. Long-time vassals of the Yasuki, the Koebi were wiped out two years ago in an enormous typhoon that blew in from the Tainted regions of the sea. There was no trace of a single living soul; the only item of value left in Shiro Koebi was one of the two jitte given to the ronin Koebi when he first swore fealty to the Crab. The other jitte was lost in the storm, and Ryhodotsu seeks it still.

Both the jitte are crafted of dark black steel and studded with jade. They inflict 2k2 damage, even on invulnerable Shadowlands creatures, and are entirely unbreakable. The weapons have all the normal abilities of a jitte, but give an additional free Raise for disarming attacks. (In effect, the wielder needs to make only a single raise to disarm.) If both jitte are wielded simultaneously, the wielder gains a +5 to his TN to Be Hit and may attack an additional time per round.

FAN OF COMMAND

This gunsen was discovered in the Seikitsu mountain range by a wandering merchant. It is crafted of brilliant red lacquered steel, and has a single kanji painted on one side: "Forever." The fan has passed through many hands, mostly ronin. It has been theorized that the fan may have been a possession of Akodo, but its remarkable condition so many centuries after Akodo's death leads scholars to doubt this notion.

The Fan's abilities depend upon its user. Normally, carrying the fan grants the user the Tactician advantage. If the user already has the Tactician advantage, it grants the Natural Leader advantage. If the user has both Tactician and Natural Leader, it grants the Great Destiny advantage. If the user already has all three of these advantages, it allows him to roll and keep a number of extra dice equal to his Void on all Battle rolls, and add his Void to his Water + Battle when making checks on the Battle Table.

The fan was last seen in Dragon lands, and could be in the possession of the Togashi.

Appendix IV: Miscellaneous

Ronin Villages

A samurai is a social creature. Although notorious for their lack of emotion and formality in interacting with others, it is nonetheless true that the samurai is an individual who longs for the camaraderie of his fellows. The relationship between the shugenja sensei and his apprentice, the bonds of brotherhood between two bushi fighting side by side on the field of battle, the competitive rivalry between courtiers of cooperative clans, and most certainly the ties between a lord and those sworn to serve him all speak to the strong bonds between a samurai and his fellow man. The proud traditions of a samurai's family and clan stem from his close ties to those around him. Alongside them, he is part of something greater than himself. Take that away and he becomes a broken, empty man alone in the world with no heritage to claim as his own.

He becomes a ronin.

The lot of the wave-man is truly one of solitude. Though he longs for the brotherhood that he once felt among the clans, it is forever denied him. While he may respect and admire other samurai, they look down upon him as a disgrace to his family and clan. And though the heimin may look up to him with respect and

Soshi Bantaro's plan is so secret that not even Kachiko has been informed of the details, for Bantaro knows she would interfere. Bantaro failed his master at Otosan Uchi, fleeing in the face of the Elemental Masters, leaving Shoju to die. For that, he is deeply sorry. For that, he will make amends.

After the Coup, Shoju's body was cast upon a heap of Scorpion dead, just another body for the fires. Insane with grief and shame, Bantaro returned to the city, stole Shoju's corpse, and used magic to transport it to Kyuden Bayushi.

He failed Shoju in life, and now he wants a second chance.

Bantaro knows that one of the Black Scrolls has the power to restore his master. He does not know which, only that one of them holds the key. His bushi and shugenja scour the Empire, searching all of the places where Bantaro suspects the scrolls may be hidden. So far, he has had no luck. He is still searching.

The fallen lord *will* return.

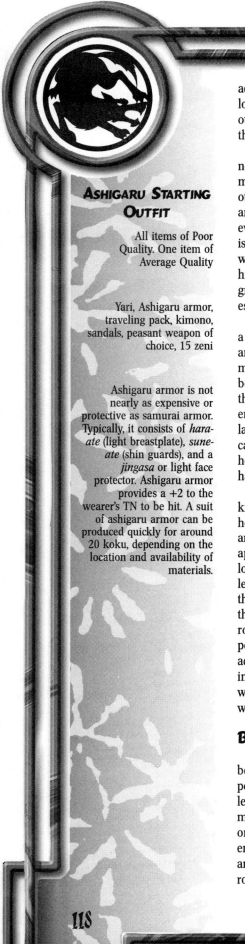

admiration, they can never replace what he has lost, for they are beneath his station. Only among other ronin may he find the sense of belonging that he desires, and even then the odds are slim.

It is not uncommon to find ronin who choose not to associate with one another. For many wave-men with a strong sense of honor, the company of other ronin is too great a burden to bear, for they are only reminded of all that they have lost. For every ronin that chooses isolation, however, there is another who finds the company of his fellow wave-men a welcome relief from the solitude of his existence. These ronin frequently operate in groups, whether as mercenaries, bandits, yojimbo, escorts or some other role.

Although for most the life of a ronin is that of a wandering blade-for-hire, there are those among the wave-men who long for something more permanent: a home. Some find it by becoming a warden for a village that lies outside the boundaries of the clans, while others seek employment in sake houses or geisha houses in large cities throughout the Empire. With the camaraderie of other ronin and a place to call home, some wave-men can find a small degree of happiness in their existence.

On very rare occasions, ronin have been known to band together and create their own home. The results of these labors rarely succeed, and those which succeed rarely last for any appreciable amount of time. The only such locations known to have existed for any real length of time are the village of Nanashi Mura in the southern lands of the Dragon, and the City of the Rich Frog, which although not founded by ronin, is home to a very large wave-man population. The only other ronin village to achieve serious notoriety in recent years was the infamous Village of the Nightingale, around which a scandal blossomed during a recent winter.

Birth of a Ronin Village

The formation of a ronin village most often begins with a single individual, someone who possesses an extraordinary ability to inspire and lead his fellow wave-men. Only the rarest and most charismatic of samurai has the organizational skill and mental fortitude to endure the arduous task of founding a village, and only rarely is such a one found among the ronin of Rokugan.

The notion to create a home village usually only occurs to such ronin late in life. The years of arduous labor and ceaseless combat as a mercenary can weigh heavily upon even the sturdiest of souls. Such a burden is made all the heavier when the bearer has no home to which to return following his travels. The lack of suitable homes for ronin can lead these men to decide to create a home for themselves, a place where ronin can gather and feel a sense of belonging and mutual respect for each other. It is an idealistic, noble idea. Unfortunately, only vanishingly few succeed.

After conceiving of this idea, the ronin must then gather others who share his vision. Although this would seem a simple enough task given the desire for belonging many ronin feel, it is in fact quite difficult. A vast majority of ronin have become jaded and cynical. They view such a notion as naïve, foolish and even time-consuming. Many would prefer to ply their trade in battle rather than spend the time necessary to help establish a home for themselves.

Assuming that the founder has gathered a suitable number of men to initiate the process, finding a suitable location becomes the next task. This is also more difficult than it sounds as most places that meet the requirements for the construction of a successful village already host one. For a population as large as Rokugan's, fertile lands are a valuable commodity indeed.

Once fertile lands and, preferably, access to a river or nearby trade route have been acquired, what will be done with the fertile lands? Ronin, after all, are samurai, and know nothing of working the soil. Farmers must be found to work the land. Most frequently, disgruntled heimin from struggling villages are lured away by the ronin's promises of a unclaimed fertile lands and the security of samurai living within the village, side by side with the farmers themselves. Needless to say, these promises often sound much more appealing than the reality. Those heimin who choose to relocate to the new village will find unworked land all to themselves, but must work twice as hard as they not only have to feed their families but the ronin as well.

Daily Life in a Ronin Village

Assuming that the ronin acquires all the components necessary to found a village, he may find that the life of a mercenary is easier than the first few years in command of a village. These initial years are the anvil against which the village will be tested. All too often, the inhabitants are broken rather than tempered by the experience. Food is scarce due to the number of non-farmers among the village inhabitants. Though ronin may attempt to work the soil alongside the heimin farmers, their inexperience with the craft frequently results in little or no additional yield from the land.

This shortage of food causes complications during the time of taxes. The land upon which the village is founded belongs to the Emperor, as does all the land in Rokugan. Many times, though, few if anyone outside the village even knows that it exists. This makes it an easy proposition to evade Imperial taxes. Unfortunately, this is a temporary fix at best. Imperial representatives eventually will find out the village, and someone will have to answer for the failure to pay taxes.

Even if the ronin within the settlement are particularly honorable and choose to pay the taxes despite the hardships it will bring upon the village, the question of transport remains. With no magistrates or tax collectors arriving, the ronin must transport the goods themselves, which is another drain upon the manpower and resources of the village.

Once these concerns are addressed and resolved, the daily life in villages such as these is still a harsh one, more similar in many respects to the life of the heimin than that of a samurai. The ronin who leads the village is responsible for the well-being of every individual within its borders. He must supervise the crops, see to it that the sick are cared for, attend to matters of defense against bandits and other threats, and deal with any conflicts that arise within the village. Those ronin who dream of founding a village for a quiet, uneventful retirement are in for an unpleasant surprise.

COMPOSITION OF A RONIN VILLAGE

In terms of the structures and population that compose them, ronin villages are similar to other villages of comparable size. Usually there is the ronin who lead the effort to found the village in the first place and his loyal companions, who could number anywhere from five to fifty. Initially the village will also have a comparable number of farmers and their families, all of whom work ceaselessly in large rice paddies to feed the entire population of the village. A very few fortunate villages may also contain a skilled craftsman or two, ideally a carpenter or stone-worker. These individuals lead the way in constructing the village buildings.

Most buildings in a ronin village are homes. Each farming family has a single-room home on the outskirts of the village near the rice paddies. The ronin live in small homes near the center of the village, usually two or three per dwelling. The center of the village contains the largest structure, commonly referred to as a public hall. Meetings of the village populace take place here, and it is from here that the village leader conducts meetings and other administrative functions. This building frequently contains a small, private room where the village leader lives. Villages situated near a waterway may have a very rough pier on which to moor small boats used to ferry rice or other cargo.

Villages that endure the first few years of hardship and begin to increase in size may have a more diverse layout of buildings. As the village grows, craftsmen appear to ply their trade among the villagers. Blacksmiths, carpenters, stonemasons or even brewers can appear in villages that have survived the two-year mark. At this point the village will likely contain at least one sake house, teahouse or inn, with the possibility of a second such facility.

On some occasions, opium has become a problem in these small villages, particularly in the southern portions of Rokugan. The difficult life of a villager can easily lead them to seek comfort and relaxation in the sweet oblivious embrace of opium. This can have two results. If left unchecked, opium use can become rampant throughout the village, causing a considerable decline in the productivity and quality of life of the villagers. Because of this threat, the ronin leading the village generally quash any attempt to bring opium into the village. In addition to the threat posed by the mood the drug evokes in those who take it, ronin wisely fear the possibility of retribution by magistrates for extensive unchecked drug use.

ATTITUDES OF VILLAGERS

As one might expect, the inhabitants of a ronin village are usually none too pleased with outsiders. Although exceptions are made for those who come to the village looking to join its ranks, most strangers are met with equal parts disdain and hostility, particularly if they are samurai from

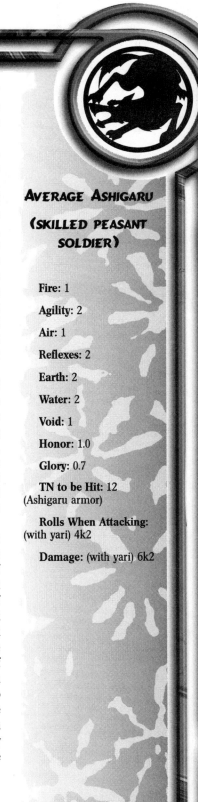

AVERAGE ASHIGARU (SKILLED PEASANT SOLDIER)

Fire: 1

Agility: 2

Air: 1

Reflexes: 2

Earth: 2

Water: 2

Void: 1

Honor: 1.0

Glory: 0.7

TN to be Hit: 12 (Ashigaru armor)

Rolls When Attacking: (with yari) 4k2

Damage: (with yari) 6k2

the clans. The feeling among villagers is that anyone of the clans can only bring discord and unrest to the village. This is their home, created by their hands and hard work. Any attempt to undermine that by the clans will be met with surprising resistance.

These feelings of resentment are particularly noticeable among the ronin who occupy the village. They have spent years as wave-men, feeling the disdain and isolation foisted upon them by the clans. Now that they have a home, a place that they feel they truly belong, they greatly resent the invasion of others who remind them that they are, after all, only ronin. Samurai who find themselves in such a village would do well to act in a courteous manner lest they find themselves facing a hostile and numerically superior force.

This defensiveness on the part of the villagers is understandable given their considerable vulnerability. The nature of these villages dictates that they are small, remotely located, and largely unknown to clan or Imperial authorities, and therefore vulnerable to attacks by brigands and bandits. The only factor preventing such a village's certain destruction within months of its construction is the significant number of ronin within the village who will fight tooth and nail to defend it. Few bands of brigands are bold enough to attempt such a target unless they have vastly superior numbers or are a particularly skilled and seasoned group of warriors.

SPECIFIC VILLAGES

As mentioned, ronin villages are extremely difficult to found and even more difficult to maintain. There are fewer than a dozen at present in Rokugan, and of that number less than half would normally survive to the two-year mark. However, the recent surge in the ronin population following the destruction of the Akodo and Scorpion could greatly affect the fate of these villages. Whether positive or negative, the impact can only be guessed at for now.

SECOND CHANCE VILLAGE

Few gave this village more than two or three months before it was wiped out. Located in the outskirts of the lands that formerly belonged to the Hare Clan, many felt sure that the village would be destroyed by the Scorpion Clan in short order. Unluckily for the Empire, the coup in

Otosan Uchi took precedence over this tiny village in the minds of the Scorpions.

Although many suspect that the surviving samurai of the Hare are hiding among the villagers, thus far none have been found there. Surviving Hare are in fact scattered throughout the Empire, earning funds as mercenaries and yojimbo. They then funnel these funds back to the villagers. It is their fervent hope that when their outcast lord Ozaki finally proves the innocence of the Hare, then they can return to their lands to find a thriving village awaiting them.

THE CITY OF THE RICH FROG

Not truly founded by ronin, the City of the Rich Frog is nonetheless one of the largest ronin gathering points in the Empire. The lack of an appreciable presence of the Great Clans or Imperial forces makes this an ideal spot for ronin to gather and enjoy one another's company. The citizens of the city are happy to have the ronin present as long as they behave themselves, remembering the great sacrifice performed for them decades ago by the ronin Gisei.

More information on the City of the Rich Frog may be found in earlier chapters.

THE VILLAGE OF GOLD

This tiny village sits upon the northern edge of the Spine of the World Mountains, far south of the the City of the Rich Frog. The Village of Gold is on the site of an old mine that was abandoned by the Crab Clan decades ago. Although the site of one of the richest gold veins in the Empire, the mine-shafts here were too unstable, and miners were killed on a daily basis. Eventually, it was decided that the cost of restocking the mining town with workers and supplies over such a long distance was not cost-effective when weighed against the amount of gold that was brought safely from the mine. The village was abandoned, and the mining shafts mostly collapsed by Kaiu engineers.

Enterprising ronin and peasants have made their home next to the mountains and are attempting to make a living scraping gold from the remaining shafts. In the year that the village has been in existence, nearly two dozen men have been killed in the unstable shafts. Still, there is no shortage of peasants willing to try for the gold, and the ronin in charge of the village are certain that the gambit will pay off. With war looming on the horizon, however, there are many clans who may reevaluate the worth of the mine. How long it remains in the hands of the villagers is in question.

THE HOUSE OF THE GREEN KOI

Although not a village per se, the House of the Green Koi is a center for employment for elite ronin mercenaries. Situated in the Eastern Hub Village of Otosan Uchi, the House of the Green Koi caters almost exclusively to the needs of wave-men. The food and drink are fresh and of adequate quantity, but the primary reason most ronin gather here is to locate suitable employment. The founder of the House is a retired ronin who was well known among the clans for his exceptional and confidential service. From time to time, those Clans who require skilled ronin to perform questionable tasks or simply to augment their own forces contact the owner, who in turn passes the information on to those ronin who have proved themselves to be both skilled and discreet.

THE VILLAGE OF THE NIGHTINGALE

This village no longer exists. The ruined remains lie along a small river near Gisu Castle in the lands of the Phoenix. The ronin who founded the village, a veteran named Niban, was responsible for the kidnapping of the Hantei's niece during a recent Winter Court of the Asako. He paid for his crime with his life, and the lives of those who followed him. There are rumored to be survivors of the battle, but no one claims such a dubious honor.

Nanashi Mura

Nanashi Mura is located at the southern edge of Dragon territories, roughly equidistant between The City of the Rich Frog and Kyuden Tonbo. It is currently the largest permanent settlement of ronin in the Emerald Empire, though Toturi's Army is swiftly approaching its size.

Unlike most villages, there are few heimin or eta in Nanashi Mura. Those who live here perform menial duties or act as servants. There are no farms in the area; Nanashi Mura's food supply is entirely imported. This is intentional on the part of the Dragon, who feel there is no particular need for the settlement to grow too independent.

Any ronin who wishes to live in Nanashi may build his own home or occupy one of the many vacant huts that dot the village. The huts closest to the road are never vacant, and are occupied by the most influential and famous ronin in Nanashi. A small monthly donation (1 zeni) is required from all citizens toward the support of the Eyes of Nanashi. Businesses must pay 1 bu per month and obtain a license from the village headman.

The following section describes locations of importance on the map of Nanashi. The town's origins and history are described in Chapter 2.

1. Watchtowers – Each of the outer towers is manned at all times by an Eye of Nanashi. The towers are the only defensive measure the ronin have found it politic to construct. Each tower is equipped with a large bell that can be used to alert the village to danger.

2. The Silent Garden – This inn serves as one of two secret gambling houses in Nanashi, and is the much nicer of the two. The inn has a friendly rivalry with the Wretched Frog (area #10) that might have exploded into violence long ago if not for the Eyes. The Silent Garden features a large, beautifully maintained story garden that the guests are free to wander. The proprietor is Monaka, a former Kakita Artisan. Inhabitants of the Broken Wing (area #3) frequent this establishment.

3. Broken Wing – One of the three major "neighborhoods" of Nanashi, Broken Wing is inhabited mostly by dismissed ronin of the Crane and Phoenix Clans. Some of the huts here are so poorly constructed that they collapse whenever there is rough weather. The most notorious denizen of this neighborhood is a flamboyant samurai-ko named Inoko, a former Shiba who claims she was expelled for pummeling her incompetent gunso unconscious while out on maneuvers.

4. Magistrate's Manor – This small castle is the home to the attendant Dragon magistrate, Mirumoto Taki. Unlike the rest of the village, the magistrate's manor is well fortified, with exterior walls, palisades, and archer slits cut into each wall. Taki has twenty low-ranking Mirumoto bushi guarding the manor at all times, and half a

AVERAGE PEASANT LEVY
(UNSKILLED PEASANT SOLDIER)

Fire: 1
Agility: 2
Air: 1
Earth: 1
Stamina: 2
Water: 1
Void: 1
Honor: 1.0
Glory: 0
TN to be Hit: 5
Rolls When Attacking: (with crude spear) 2k2
(Add +10 to TN for unskilled attack rolls)
Damage: (with crude spear) 3k1

Special: Lacking finesse or training, Peasant Levies use mob tactics to overwhelm opponents. In such a case, make a single attack roll of 7k2 for each six peasant levies that mob a target.

Damage for such an attack is 3k1, plus an additional 3k1 for each 10 by which they exceeded their attack roll, to a maximum of 6 successful attacks.

Bushi characters gain an extra attack against Peasant Levies using mob tactics.

TAKUAN

He began his career protecting the mercantile interests of the Crane, but life as a merchant did not interest Takuan. Setting out on his own, he fought for several years in the service of the Crab, traveled as a caravan guard for the Ide, and served as a diplomat for the reclusive Sparrow. Though he follows bushido fervently, he does not seek fealty. He does not yet believe he is worthy. Not yet.

For the last three years, Takuan has lived in the city of Nanashi. Under his leadership, the city thrives. He knows well that some of the nearby clans, particularly the Lion, consider a successful city of ronin a potential danger, and has been cautious not to upset their prejudices by allowing any disturbances within Nanashi. Even the bitter rivalries between the ronin of Broken Wing and Bushi Row have died down to a low murmur under his charismatic leadership. Crime has died down with Takuan in charge. He has even managed to form a friendship with Mirumoto Taki, the Dragon magistrate.

(Continued on opposite page.)

dozen that attend his person when venturing into the settlement.

5. Sake – The name says it all. This proprietor of this sake house is a man named Razan, a humorless ronin with deep scars on both arms. Razan absolutely refuses, under any circumstances, to discuss his past. The heavy suit of lavender-lacquered armor mounted at the rear of the house seems to indicate that Razan was once a Unicorn, or that he slew one. The sake is unremarkable, but inexpensive.

6. Nanashi Dojo – Without a doubt the most popular establishment in the settlement, the three-story dojo welcomes all citizens to practice the art of the warrior. The field in back is equipped with archery targets, with ample room for practicing horse archery. Over a dozen sparring chambers compose the two bottom floors, which can be hired for private use for a small fee. The top floor is for the permanent exclusive use of the Eyes of Nanashi. Samurai seeking to hire mercenaries are encouraged to do so in the dojo rather than risking themselves in the back alleys of the rougher neighborhoods.

To those with an eye for defense, the dojo is a miniature fortress. The outer walls are quite thick and the stores in the basement could feed every citizen for up to a month. The ample space of the dojo and practice yard could house nearly the entire population, if the need arose. Past magistrates have noted this violation (Nanashi is forbidden any defenses), but have let the matter slide. In the long run, the settlement does need some form of defense against bandits and invaders. If problems arose, a clan army could still shatter the dojo's feeble defenses with ease.

The current sensei of the dojo is Muso, a retired true ronin. He is a clever swordsman and an excellent teacher, but also happens to be stone deaf.

7. Tempered Jade – This tea house is small, serene, tidy, and always empty. Few citizens can afford the exorbitant prices of the fine teas offered here. The only regular customers are Dragons from the magistrate's manor, travelers, and monks (who are always served for free). The owner of the tea house is a pious old woman named Yuasa. She offers nearly every variety of tea in Rokugan, including imported Unicorn teas and spicy, rare herbs from Phoenix territories. As the name subtly

suggests, she does have a small supply of Tea of Jade Petals, and will sell it, discreetly.

She then dispatches her son to Shiro Asako, discreetly. He reports the sale to the Inquisitor who supplies his mother with the tea, discreetly. The Inquisitor's yojimbo can arrive in the village within days to deal with the tea's purchaser, discreetly.

Yuasa has made quite a fortune selling out Tainted ronin, discreetly.

8. Bushi Row – Some of the finest mercenaries in Rokugan dwell in this neighborhood. The majority of the ronin who live here are former Crabs or Lions. Though they obey the laws of Nanashi, the ronin who live here treat former Cranes or Phoenix quite badly. Such individuals are strongly encouraged to move to area #3. The current spokesman for Bushi Row is a grotesquely fat former Crab named Tadachika. Tadachika no longer hires himself out as a soldier, but works as an agent, protecting the interests of the wealthier mercenaries in Nanashi and seeing that they find employment that suits them.

9. Stables – Horses can be stored, rented, or purchased here. Let the buyer beware: the steeds offered tend to be weak and sickly. The animals are fed cheap fodder and cared for poorly. The stable master is a former Otaku named Shosetsu, cast out of the clan for the same incompetence he displays here. The Eyes of Nanashi have attempted to force the stable master to improve his operation on several occasions, with no success. The small building next door is Shosetsu's shabby home.

10. The Wretched Frog – This large restaurant is secretly a gambling house maintained by Kaeru Hayashi, an entrepreneur from the City of the Rich Frog. Sadly, the place seems to be cursed. Compared to the Silent Garden, the Wretched Frog is small, poor, and has an odd stink to the floorboards that won't wash away. It has a small but dedicated patronage, mostly ronin from area #8, that look upon the Silent Garden with a burning jealousy. Hayashi is a ruthless, honorless, cowardly man. He wishes he could do something to ruin his competitor's business, but fears the wrath of the Eyes of Nanashi.

11. Itode Grove – When Nanashi was built, the Dragon declared this stand of ancient oaks sacred, forbidding the ronin to remove them. In actuality, the trees have no special importance, but the command tests the village's loyalty and resolve. The grove is a nuisance, blocking Nanashi Mura's view of the plains to the southeast and hampering Nanashi Mura's ability to defend against threats from that direction.

Recently, the grove has become home to a half dozen Scorpion ronin. These spies simply watch for now, calculating the city's possible worth in the plans of the fallen clan.

12. Sugu's House of Joy – Yasuki Sugu is not a ronin. He is a Crab Clan merchant, and proud of it. Sugu imports items both mundane and extravagant from throughout Rokugan. Most items for sale here are utilitarian and inexpensive (Sugu knows his customer base well). Since Sugu also imports the village's food, the village has an unspoken rule: no one messes with Sugu. If the Yasuki is ever dissatisfied with business here, he could easily pack up and move on, leaving Nanashi to find a new supplier. No one wants that.

The House of Joy also functions as a pawn shop. Sugu occasionally offers swords or scraps of armor under the table, invariably items stolen from battlefields and the like. You can pick up a katana for cheap, if you don't mind carrying the blade of a dead man.

13. Sake – Yet another sake house with an original name. The establishment is owned by a ronin named Ujikira, an ancient, scrawny man with white hair down to his waist. Anyone who dares to ask Ujikira's story will invariably be told a different tale than the person who asked last. The sake is a bit better here than at Razan's place, but the servants are lazy. Cleanliness is not a high priority. "A dirty cup makes the sake taste better," is Ujikira's motto.

14. Meeting Hall – This large building is usually vacant. It is only used for city-wide meetings, which happen rarely.

15. Headman's House – The headman is always the leader of the Eyes of Nanashi, elected by his brothers and keeping the position until death or retirement. The current headman is Takuan, a renowned ronin hero. Takuan had been working as a diplomat in the Suzume Hills when he first heard rumors of Nanashi, and came to see

if the tales were true. He soon found a home, joining the Eyes of Nanashi and quickly rising to their most important office. He is a brilliant leader, who truly cares for the welfare of the city. He puts the survival of Nanashi before all other concerns.

16. Otokodate House – The headquarters and barracks of the Eyes of Nanashi. Only one-third of the membership is actually here most of the time, as the others are out patrolling the city or undertaking missions abroad. Roughly fifty ronin currently serve in the Eyes of Nanashi.

17. Highway's End – This neighborhood is home to the most downtrodden and dejected ronin that Nanashi has to offer, most of whom were cast out of area #3 or area #8. Most are true ronin or Minor Clan ronin with few useful skills. The majority will find a brief future in the front lines of an army, followed by an unmarked grave. This is a somber, melancholy place. Few visitors stop here for long.

18. Fuyari's Shrine – Shinjo Fuyari's ashes are interred here in a small shrine, honoring his noble sacrifice.

19. The Steel Room – This iron shack serves as Nanashi Mura's prison. There are no windows, and the walls are made of light metal reinforced by wooden beams. In the winter, the shack becomes unbearably cold. In the summer, it is filled with unearthly heat. Those who spend the night here and survive think twice before breaking the laws of Nanashi again.

20. Temple of Ebisu – Shortly after the city of Nanashi was founded, this brotherhood of warrior-monks arrived, built this temple, and offered their assistance to the cause. The monks taught the Eyes of Nanashi their secret technique, and patrol the city at their side. The brothers have taken a vow of silence, and do not reply to any questions regarding where they came from or why they are here. All that is known is that they serve Ebisu, the Fortune of Honest Work, who seems to have adopted a certain fondness for Nanashi. The temple is secluded from the rest of the village, surrounded by a tall wooden fence and cherry trees. Those who are not members of the brotherhood or the Eyes are not allowed on the premises.

TAKUAN
(CONTINUED)

Takuan knows that Nanashi cannot last. He knows that one day the warlike Lion's tolerance will be exhausted. With this in mind, Takuan has begun to formulate contingencies for the survival of the citizens of Nanashi. These plans are very sketchy at the present, but he believes that their best and brightest hope may lay, ironically, in an alliance with another Lion.

Toturi.

Others among the Eyes disagree with this plan, but Takuan hopes to convince them before it is too late.

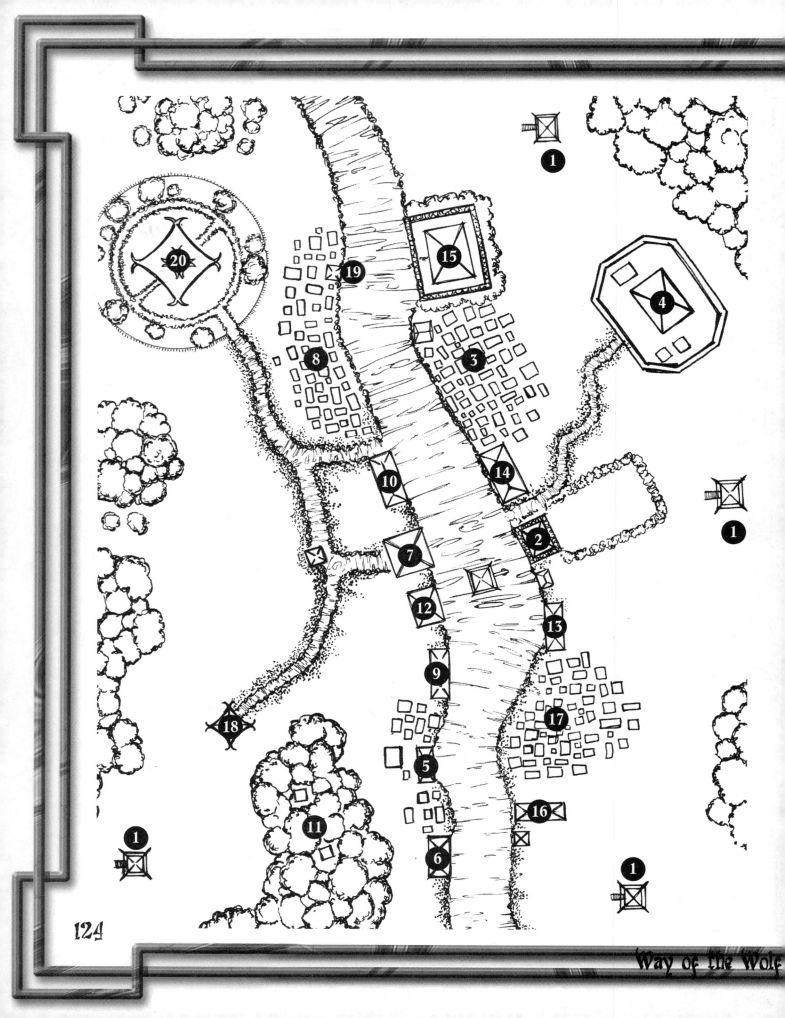

Legend of the Five Rings

Name: **Clan:** **Profession:**

Primary Weapon

Fire
Agility:
Intelligence:

Air
Reflexes:
Awareness:

Primary Armor

TN to be Hit
(Reflexes x 5 + Armor)

Earth
Stamina:
Willpower:

Water
Strength:
Perception:

Skills

Void
Void Points Spent:

Techniques

Insight:

Wounds

☐ -0
☐ -1
☐ -2
☐ -3
☐ -4
☐ Down
☐ Out
☐ Dead

School: **Rank:**

Glory:
☐☐☐☐☐☐☐☐☐

Honor:
☐☐☐☐☐☐☐☐☐

Experience Points:

Legend of the Five Rings

Name: Clan: Home Province:

Allies and Enemies

_____
_____
_____
_____

Weapons & Equipment

_____
_____
_____
_____
_____
_____
_____
_____
_____
_____
_____

Gifts, Bestowments and Recognitions

_____
_____
_____
_____

History and Glorious Deeds

_____
_____
_____
_____
_____
_____
_____
_____
_____
_____
_____
_____
_____
_____
_____
_____
_____
_____
_____
_____
_____
_____
_____

Legend of the Five Rings

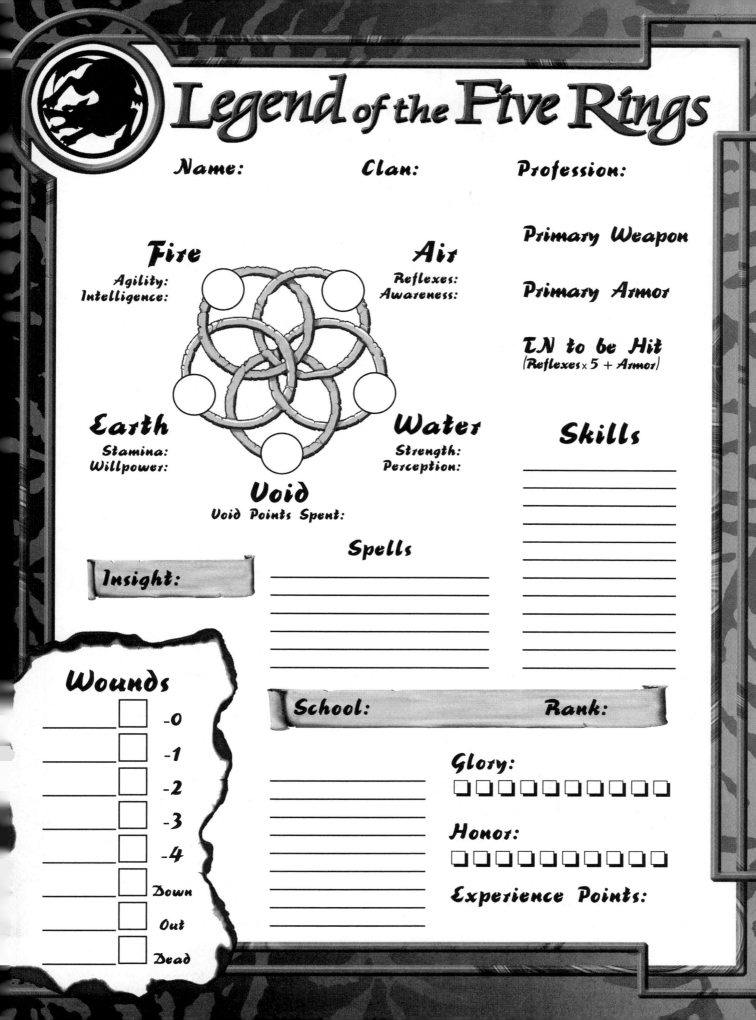

Name: Clan: Profession:

Fire
Agility:
Intelligence:

Air
Reflexes:
Awareness:

Primary Weapon

Primary Armor

TN to be Hit
(Reflexes × 5 + Armor)

Earth
Stamina:
Willpower:

Water
Strength:
Perception:

Skills

_____
_____
_____
_____
_____

Void
Void Points Spent:

Spells

Insight:

_____
_____
_____
_____
_____
_____
_____

Wounds

_____ ☐	-0
_____ ☐	-1
_____ ☐	-2
_____ ☐	-3
_____ ☐	-4
_____ ☐	Down
_____ ☐	Out
_____ ☐	Dead

School: Rank:

_____
_____
_____
_____
_____

Glory:
☐☐☐☐☐☐☐☐☐☐

Honor:
☐☐☐☐☐☐☐☐☐☐

Experience Points:

Legend of the Five Rings

Name: **Clan:**   **Home Province:**

Allies and Enemies

_____

_____

_____

_____

Weapons & Equipment

_____

_____

_____

_____

_____

_____

_____

_____

_____

_____

Gifts, Bestowments and Recognitions

_____

_____

_____

_____

History and Glorious Deeds

_____

_____

_____

_____

_____

_____

_____

_____

_____

_____

_____

_____

_____

_____

_____

_____

_____

_____

_____

_____

_____